The Revolutio ⌐ꓕoes

Chicago Studies in Ethnomusicology

A series edited by Philip V. Bohlman, Ronald Radano, and Timothy Rommen

The Revolution's Echoes

Music, Politics, and Pleasure in Guinea

NOMI DAVE

The University of Chicago Press
Chicago and London

The University of Chicago Press, Chicago 60637
The University of Chicago Press, Ltd., London
© 2019 by The University of Chicago
All rights reserved. No part of this book may be used or reproduced in any manner
whatsoever without written permission, except in the case of brief quotations in
critical articles and reviews. For more information, contact the University of Chicago
Press, 1427 E. 60th St., Chicago, IL 60637.
Published 2019
Printed in the United States of America

28 27 26 25 24 23 22 21 20 19   1 2 3 4 5

ISBN-13: 978-0-226-65446-1 (cloth)
ISBN-13: 978-0-226-65463-8 (paper)
ISBN-13: 978-0-226-65477-5 (e-book)
doi: https://doi.org/10.7208/chicago/9780226654775.001.0001

Library of Congress Cataloging-in-Publication Data

Names: Dave, Nomita, 1973– author.
Title: The revolution's echoes : music, politics, and pleasure in Guinea /
    Nomi Dave.
Other titles: Chicago studies in ethnomusicology.
Description: Chicago ; London : The University of Chicago Press, 2019. |
    Series: Chicago studies in ethnomusicology
Identifiers: LCCN 2019016007 | ISBN 9780226654461 (cloth : alk. paper) |
    ISBN 9780226654638 (pbk. : alk. paper) | ISBN 9780226654775 (e-book)
Subjects: LCSH: Music—Political aspects—Guinea.
Classification: LCC ML3917.G9 D38 2019 | DDC 306.4/842096652—dc23
LC record available at https://lccn.loc.gov/2019016007

Contents

Acknowledgments

Over the past few years, I have had the great fortune to know and work with many wonderful people, without whom this book would have never been possible. Some of the lions of Guinean music, young and old, passed away during this period, and I begin by honoring them: Abdoul Karim "Chuck Berry" Camara, Mohamed "Branco" Camara, Lansana Condé, Mory Sidibé, Talibé Traoré, and the great M'Bady Kouyaté.

M'Bady and Diaryatou Kouyaté—N na Diaryou—were my first family in Guinea, and I am grateful beyond words to them and the other members of the extended family, in particular to Cheick, Demba, Diamadi, Fallaye, Hadja, Na Mama, the late Na Naitoo, Na Oumou, Séfoudi, and Soundjoulou. My other musical family in Guinea is at La Paillote, where I have spent countless hours in the company of great musicians and friends, including Mamadou "Le Maître" Barry, Youssouf Condé, Mamadi "Monyoko" Diabaté, Sékou "Bembeya" Diabaté, Laye Dioubaté, Papa Kouyaté, and Jeanne Makolé.

Elsewhere in Conakry I owe great debts of thanks and friendship to Moussa Yéro Bah; Alya Bangoura; my dear friend Alya Camara—*I booré nu kobiri fen ma, i tan xa saabui fen*—and his family; Boubacar Diallo; Telivel Diallo; Amara Keita; Fifi Tamsir Niane; Aly Sanso Sylla; and Takana Zion. And most particularly, my deepest thanks to my friend Pépé Séverin Théa, to my savior (on many occasions) Ivana Jelic, and to the wonderful Mamadi Koba Camara. To all of you, *Barika Barika, Alu ni ke! Albarka, wo nu wali ki fan nyi!*

I have had the inordinate luck of being mentored by two of the most brilliant and generous scholars there could be. In Oxford, Martin Stokes showed me what it means to explore the world with clarity and humility. He is a constant source of inspiration, and a model of gracious intellect, integrity, and warmth—from tea-fueled tutorials to (unpaid) babysitting in the pub. I am forever grateful to you. During a postdoc year at Duke University, I had the pleasure of working with Louise Meintjes, who is always full of good humor, who lent me a car for the year and didn't blink when it got bashed in, and whose insight, rigor, and unfailing consideration I cannot thank enough. My thanks also to dear friends from the Oxford years, Neil Carrier, Tom Hodgson, Hélène Neveu Kringelbach, Hayley Lofink, Ioannis Polychronakis, Jonathan Roberts, Pete Smith, and Anna Stirr. And to those at Duke, including Paul Berliner, Jonathan Dueck, David Font-Navarette, and Charlie Piot. Many thanks as well to all who participated in the Dictatorial Aesthetics workshop at Duke; they helped me immeasurably in thinking through and reforming ideas. I am deeply indebted to those friends and guides who have closely shaped this work, some by reading chapters, others through conversation and comments on earlier versions of the arguments: Adrienne Cohen, Lucy Duràn, Mathieu Fribault, Angela Impey, Aly Kaba, Sinkoun Kaba, Mike McGovern, Amanda Villepastour, and Bob White. And to Graeme Counsel, for friendship since we first met in Conakry in 2009, for your dedication to Guinean music and musicians, and for all your tremendous work.

At the University of Virginia, I have had the joy of finding myself in an exciting and open-minded department, populated by great human beings. I am grateful to my colleagues in the Department of Music and across the university for all their support and friendship. A huge thank-you to Michelle Kisliuk, Bonnie Gordon, Richard Will, Karl Hagstrom Miller, Ted Coffey, Fred Maus, Michael Puri, Luke Dahl, A. D. Carson, Scott DeVeaux, Matthew Burtner, Joel Rubin, Judith Shatin, and Jim Igoe. My thanks also to my students, particularly those in the "Arts and Human Rights" course I taught at Duke, for reintroducing me to idealism and challenging my cynicism; and to the students in my "Music and Authoritarianism" and "What Good Is Music?" graduate seminars at UVA, for sharp thinking and stimulating conversation on many of the issues in this book. I also thank the institutions who have generously funded this work: the National Endowment for the Humanities, the Mellon Humanities Fellowship from the Institute of the Humanities and Global Culture at UVA, the Bucker W. Clay Dean for Arts & Sciences and the Vice President for Research at UVA, the Society for Music Education and Music Psychology Research, the Chiang Ching-kuo Foundation, and the Zaharoff Fund at Oxford University. My thanks also to the Scholars Lab at UVA for their help with maps.

My sincere thanks to the two anonymous readers at the University of Chicago Press for their detailed and extremely useful comments and criticisms.

I am deeply grateful to Elizabeth Branch Dyson for all her support, patience, and guidance. Thanks also to Dylan Joseph Montanari and Mollie McFee for all their assistance, to Barbara Norton for superlative copyediting, and to the series editors for all of their work and input. Thank you to the journal *Ethnomusicology* for permission to reprint in chapter 4 of this book parts of my article "The Politics of Silence: Music, Violence, and Protest in Guinea" (2014).

I have a big, close-knit family spanning across three continents, from Kenya to the UK and the United States, and my love and thanks to them all, with special mention to Heather and Bob Boon and Heidi and Paul Bichener, for so much laughter and support. To my brother and best friend Apurva Dave and my amazing sister-in-law, Sejal Dave, for everything. And of course, my life would be devoid of all joy without my miraculous husband, Noel Lobley—the DJ is my husband—and our two lovely, crazy boys, Zakir and Kieran.

Lastly, there are three people who deserve my most special thanks.

Years ago in Conakry, I met through a chance encounter by a broken-down taxi a dynamic young music promoter, Mohamed Sita Camara. Sita was a model of kindness and decency, and he quickly became my closest friend in Guinea. His life was brimming with promise and was tragically cut short by illness last year. I miss him dearly.

And finally, my greatest thanks to my golden parents, Nutan and Chandu Dave, for your enduring sense of adventure, your devotion to music, your endless support, your wisdom, and your love. I dedicate this book to you.

Abbreviations

A U : African Union (see also OAU [Organization of African Unity] and OUA
[Organisation de l'Unité Africaine]

C C F G : Centre Cultural Franco-Guinean (Franco-Guinean Cultural Center)

C N D D : Conseil National pour la Démocratie et le Développement (National
Council for Democracy and Development)

O A U : Organization of African Unity (*see also* AU [African Union] *and* OUA
[Organisation de l'Unité Africaine])

O U A : Organisation de l'Unité Africaine (*see also* OAU [Organization of African
Unity] *and* AU [African Union])

P D G : Parti Démocratique de Guinée (Democratic Party of Guinea)

R P G : Rassemblement du Peuple de Guinée (Guinean People's Assembly)

R T G : Radio Télévision de Guinée

U F D G : Union des Forces Démocratiques de Guinée (Union of Democratic Forces
of Guinea)

Introduction

Bob's Bar was a tiny seaside venue in Conakry, Guinea. Before it closed, shortly after the turn of the millennium, it featured an open-front room with a wooden bar propped up on beer crates. Outside were a handful of white plastic chairs on the sidewalk and, hoisted overhead, a tarpaulin salvaged from a refugee camp. The proprietor, Bob, a.k.a. Bob City, was a young man who loved old Guinean music. When the electricity worked (not very often) or there was enough gas for the generator (more likely), Bob would play old cassettes of songs from the 1960s and 1970s. Cascading guitar riffs, bubbling rhythms, blaring trumpets, sweet melodies sung in raspy voices. Sometimes a particular song would cause Bob and his customers to reminisce about the moment that had made this music. There had been a revolution in Guinea. Sitting in the semi-darkness, with the sounds of ocean waves crashing in the background, the patrons would remember its glories and terrors, until the song finished and the talk turned to other things.

In 1968 the Republic of Guinea launched a Socialist Cultural Revolution. "The Revolution" became synonymous over time with the entire rule of Guinea's first president, Sékou Touré (1958–84). Following independence from France, Guinea sought to assert itself both locally and globally as a leader of African and socialist liberation. For the new state, cultural decolonization was as important as political sovereignty, and it foregrounded artistic production and ideologies in its struggle. Today, few people in Guinea dispute the fact that Touré was an authoritarian leader, or that his revolution involved brutal violence and repression. But for many this period also stands as a moment that articulated postcolonial possibilities, new feelings of collectivity, and new sounds of change. While popular memory recalls terror alongside freedom in Touré's Guinea, songs from the era single out joy, modernity, and the leader himself. Touré was a dictator who loved music, and in turn, many musicians loved him.

In this book I examine the aesthetics of authoritarianism through a study of music and performance in Guinea. The practices that linked music to state authority under the revolution did not end with the death of Sékou Touré. Subsequent regimes, artists, styles, and songs reveal the ongoing legacies of the musical and political past. Today, two generations after Touré's death, many musicians in Guinea continue deep-rooted practices of avoiding dissent and engaging in praise for the powerful. Across genres and generations, they often adopt cautious, conservative, and strategic positions toward the state, ranging from carefully constrained social commentary to lavish praise. Moreover, it is musicians and audiences, rather than government officials, who maintain the relevance and popularity of these forms. *The Revolution's Echoes* examines the choices and subjectivities of musicians who sing for an authoritarian state, and the experiences and desires of audiences who derive great pleasure from this music.

Public Pleasure

Pleasure matters. As I show in the pages and stories that follow, pleasure works beyond the individual and individual experience to create shared meaning and feeling within and across groups. Shared experiences and ideas of pleasure shape the ways in which people interpret and invest in social life, generating alliances and allegiances, influencing collective memories, and crafting collective aspirations. In other words, pleasure operates not just at a private but also at a public level. Throughout this book I thus develop the notion of public pleasure not as a by-product or incidental outcome, but rather as a constitutive force in sociopolitical relations in Guinea.

In Euro-American aesthetics, social theory, and psychoanalysis, pleasure has often been pathologized, held in suspicion as unreliable, un-real, even dangerous.[1] Prominent twentieth-century thinkers famously called for pleasure in art to be "destroyed" (Mulvey 1975) or for art to be released from the "bloated pleasure apparatus" of mass culture (Horkheimer and Adorno 1969: 139).[2] These views configured pleasure as outside of and antithetical to serious thought and engagement, a hazardous distraction from social realities. Avant-garde artists in Africa as well as in Europe and North America thus rejected the "culture of the beautiful" (Harney 2004: 108–9), producing instead art that was intentionally disturbing and unpleasurable.

Yet, others have noted that pleasure cannot be so summarily dismissed (Sontag 1961; Steiner 1995; Kelley 1997). Theorists and commentators increasingly explore the playful and affective dimensions of public life. At the same time, artistic practice from the late twentieth and twenty-first centuries reveals that art today *can* be beautiful—or not—and still be taken seriously as art (Danto 2013).[3]

My aim in this discussion is not to articulate a total theory of pleasure. As Johan Huizinga argues, "The *fun* of playing resists all analysis, all logical interpretation" (1949: 3). Instead, I explore the ways in which pleasure is "bound up with . . . ethical and political commitments," the ways in which a musical-political aesthetics is not "already there" but is "something to be discovered and engaged" over time through feeling and experience (Stokes 2015: 101–2).

In music, pleasure is often the most palpable and immediate aspect of the experience, even if we do not always talk about it.[4] Achille Mbembe argues in a study of Congolese popular music that its value and meaning are found in the "intimate force" that it exerts upon the bodies of its listeners (2006: 63). While Mbembe writes primarily about Congolese selves and bodies, the force he describes is also collectively felt, collectively evocative. Although Mbembe does not address the cultural intimacy of this experience directly, that is what is of particular interest to me: pleasure as a shared set of feelings that creates community among people.

This is not to say, however, that pleasure is a panacea. Affective solidarity at one moment may easily give way to debate and division at the next. In this book I explore both the beautiful and the ugly (Nuttall 2006), the ways in which the two are interconnected and shape each other. At certain times pleasure accommodates moments of violence, disruption, and the abuse of rights, and at other times it works against them. Experiences of beauty and ugliness can and often do coincide, and human beings are adept at apprehending both. My discussion in this regard examines the relationship between pleasure and political power more broadly.

Pleasure's relationship to power and the political is often thought of as purely instrumental or perhaps incidental, particularly when considered in terms of state power and politics. Much work on art and state authority has focused on the ways in which regimes mobilize artistic resources, rather than on the experiences and pleasures of citizens themselves. A common view in such work is that if pleasure plays any role at all, surely it is in the thrill of subversion and resistance. Yet the underlying idea there—that if pleasure is not resisting power, it is nothing more than a form of false consciousness—is one of the ways in which pleasure is reduced as a concept and a phenomenon. The philosopher and cultural theorist Tim Dean notes that in Euro-American thought, we are always looking for a pleasure that is "uncontaminated" by power, pleasure that is unsullied by politics (2012: 481). But theorists such as Dean, and Foucault before him, help us take a different view.

In volume 1 of the *History of Sexuality*, Michel Foucault famously describes pleasure and power as working together in "perpetual spirals," continually amplifying each other (1976: 45). In examining how we understand and approach sex in contemporary Euro-American society, Foucault argues that it is not simply a question of domination and resistance, or of "yes or no"—in other words, of being told that you are not allowed to talk about sex and then getting a thrill from violating that taboo (ibid.: 11). Rather, over the past two centuries pleasure and power have operated alongside and through each other by construing sex as a medical issue and a scientific problem, but also by continually finding loopholes and points of evasion in this approach. For instance, nineteenth-century doctors, psychiatrists, and parents continually worked to classify, monitor, and analyze sexual disorders, thus serving to naturalize such conditions and making them much more discussed, rather than less. In this way "power . . . lets itself be invaded by the pleasure it is pursuing" (ibid.: 45). It is pleasure that stands against and alongside power, that is its coconspirator and counterpoint.

How, then, do public pleasure and relations of power shape each other in Guinea? Political scientists are increasingly interested in the role of emotion in political life, the ways in which emotion renders politics meaningful: Wendy Brown considers how love can shape both loyal patriotism and critical political dissent (2005); Martha Nussbaum asks how emotion can foster political stability and create just and decent societies (2013). While such work focuses on political emotion in liberal democracies, here I consider instead the role of pleasure as emotion and feeling in shaping authoritarianism. My study builds on work in political anthropology that examines the structures of feeling underpinning public life in authoritarian states (Wedeen 1999; Navaro-Yashin 2002; Abu-Lughod 2005). Anthropological approaches to authoritarian regimes such as these again borrow from Foucault by looking beyond the state and its institutions to see power and the political more broadly, as asymmetrical social relations of power found in everyday life. As this book is an ethnography of music and authoritarianism, the state is very much central to my analysis. But as important as state institutions and technologies and ideologies of rule are the structures of feeling, everyday experiences, subjectivities, and flows of people and ideas that create Guinean public life and its ideas of the political.

As Emily Lynn Osborn notes, the very notion of the "political" in West Africa extends beyond formal institutions and Great Men to encompass the household, the domestic sphere, and everyday relations (2011: 6). A number of important studies have shown how states in Africa have mobilized performance as a means of nation building (Turino 2000; Fair 2001; Askew 2002; White 2008), as well as how ordinary "men and women [bring] the nation into being" through their emotional investments in music, dance, fashion, and sports (Moorman 2008: 8). Building on these ideas, I show how pleasure and power in Guinea work together to create and make meaning in this particular public.

Making Music Political

In the summer of 2003 the renowned Malian singer Salif Keita gave a concert in the neighboring country of Guinea. The concert was held in the great hall of Guinea's Palais du Peuple (People's Palace), in the capital city of Conakry. I vividly recall sitting in the audience that night and listening out for tracks from Keita's recent album, *Moffou*. As the evening drew to a close, I was certain that the last song he played that night would be the biggest hit from the album, which at the time was constantly playing in every taxi and nightclub in town. Instead, to my surprise, the strains of an unfamiliar melody began to fill the space, and in an instant the great hall was palpably electrified. There were no cheers or roars; instead, regally dressed women throughout the hall silently stood up and with great dignity and poise began to sway forward in a snaking line toward the stage, slowly waving white handkerchiefs over their heads while pulling out folded Guinean francs to tip the singer. Others sat still and riveted, focused intently on something I could neither see nor hear. What had seemed until that moment a recognizable Afropop gig had suddenly transformed into something else. The audience was rapt, fixed on the words and on an unseen, inner reference point. There was an unmistakable silence and stillness present as audience members engaged in a collective act of listening and feeling that took my breath away.

The song we were listening to was "Mandjou," one that Keita had written in the 1970s in praise of Guinea's first president, Sékou Touré. Adhering to traditions of singing praise (*ka fasa fo*) in this part of the world, the song in part traces back Touré's family lineage, connecting him to great figures in the region's history. Keita had in fact famously performed the song for President Touré in 1977, in the very same hall in which I was hearing it almost thirty years later. For this act Touré had awarded Keita numerous spectacular gifts, including a presidential medal.[5]

On the night of the 2003 concert, however, I knew none of this. At the time I was a young humanitarian worker, based in Guinea but working primarily with Liberian and Sierra Leonean refugees. Guineans were the seemingly closed, often inscrutable people among whom I lived but of whom I knew very little. I was therefore astonished to be confronted with such a powerful wave of sentiment, and with the rather obvious realization that they had such pride in their history and culture.

The fact that "Mandjou" also honored a brutal, bloody dictator added a further twist. Keita has faced some criticism in Mali and in the international press for singing in praise of the tyrannical Touré, but within Guinea the song is largely celebrated.[6] As one friend told me years later, "The greatest song about Guinea was not written by a Guinean. It is 'Mandjou,' by Salif Keita."[7] In the months and years following that concert in 2003, as I learned more about Guinea's history and music, I wondered why anyone would want to acclaim the dictator Sékou Touré in such a way, let alone how they could stomach such music today. I assumed that "Mandjou" must be an outlier, that fundamentally Guinean music was really about dissent and political opposition, that it was about resisting power rather than celebrating tyrants.

My own dealings with the Guinean state often left me infuriated at local politics. In those early years I worked as a refugee protection officer for the United Nations in Guinea, counseling and representing people who had fled civil wars in neighboring Liberia, Sierra Leone, and Côte d'Ivoire. The Guinean state and its rituals of power often proved maddeningly obstructive as my colleagues and I attempted to gain the release of people who had been arbitrarily detained, or to ensure that women and children fleeing conflict were not abused or exploited. Yet despite the vagaries and constant visibility of state authority, my Guinean colleagues and friends seemed remarkably restrained and reticent in addressing politics. While I noisily fumed at military roadblocks or officials asking for bribes—all the while aware that I could easily hop on a plane and leave—my colleagues and friends exercised forbearance. And when I tried to speak to Guineans about their government, they were often highly guarded, at times even hostile and abrasive, to my questions.

The subject of music offered other possibilities, however. Everyone was happy to speak to me about music, as I became captivated with those old recordings at Bob's Bar. But I was disappointed to learn that those songs, much like "Mandjou," were wrapped up in the regime of Sékou Touré. I very much wanted Guinean music to be progressive and for musicians and fans to reject the links with state power. Notwithstanding the many truly humanitarian individuals I met through my work, I became disillusioned with its top-down approach, and felt that perhaps music and art offered a grass-roots solution. As a result, a few years later when I returned to Guinea as a doctoral student, I continually looked for protest music, believing it to be the "real" music of today. Guinea was at the time under a military junta whose tactics of rule became increasingly violent and unpopular, and I was determined to map its musical undoing. Yet as I continually sought out the few songs of dissent, time and time again I found myself surrounded by acts of dictatorial praise and accommodation, from subtle to direct, from youths and from elders, and by almost every musician I knew.

My own search, even longing, for musical and cultural resistance was not an isolated phenomenon. Since the 1980s, anthropological studies of resistance have abounded, describing ways in which the weak evade the powerful through practices as varied as jokes, gossip, stealing, and foot-dragging. Such studies celebrate the vitality and determination of subordinate groups and find heroic struggles in their everyday actions. Resistance becomes a marker of authenticity, seeming to reveal the true voices and "hidden transcripts" of the oppressed (Scott 1990). Onlookers often romanticize resistance as a sign of human agency and resilience while glossing over the systems of power and domination within which it operates (Abu-Lughod 1990). This approach has resulted in something of an overcompensation, searching out endless proof of resistance in everyday acts.

These desires seem to coalesce with some intensity around music. Popular commentators and fans often imagine music to be a particularly truthful and free art form, unencumbered by hegemonic thinking or even material realities. Musicians are hailed for their "incisive relevance to human rights discourse" and their refusal to compromise their artistic and political integrity by selling out (Fischlin 2003: 16). The conductor José Antonio Abreu even argues that music can end poverty.[8] Central to such ideas is an enduring assumption that music is inherently a benevolent and progressive force – a "universal language" of freedom pioneered by fearless champions of the people who, through their musicianship, are able to effect real change (see Dave 2015).

In contrast to such celebration, in his essay "Commitment," Adorno makes an interesting case *against* overtly political music and art, arguing that it ultimately trivializes political reality by rendering it aesthetic and translating it into feelings and stories that can be understood and therefore rationalized by audiences (Adorno, Benjamin, Bloch, Brecht, and Lukács 2007). He is concerned with art as a way to "make men think" (ibid.: 188) and is highly critical of any attempt to simplify, soften, or aestheticize social reality or betray real suffering. For Adorno, the answer lies in emphasizing form over political meanings: truly radical, autonomous art has a "terrifying power" because it does not succumb to the attempt to make meaning out of horror and chaos (ibid.: 188–89).

Although I disagree with Adorno's emphasis on form and autonomy,[9] as well as his argument that pleasure and enjoyment preclude thought and engagement, I find his realism compelling in thinking about art's relationship with politics and violence. This precision often seems to get lost in discussions of political music, giving way instead to many uncritical, idealized assumptions about music inherently being and doing good in the world. I interrogate these assumptions and examine the ways in which music is imagined and represented—by musicians themselves, by audiences, by state bureaucrats, and by journalists and cultural commentators. While there are certainly innumerable examples of music's vital role in social and political movements, a desire for "musical heroes" (Turino 2000: 339) has created an imbalanced representation. Endless books, essays, websites, and liner notes are devoted to protest musicians, yet less has been said about the political ambivalence or indifference of the vast majority of musicians, the contradictory actions of many protest musicians, or the perspectives and experiences of artists who actively support rather than resist existing structures of power. Yet, as Yael Navaro-Yashin notes, rituals of state veneration exist and often have great meaning for people. We need to study "public *participation* in the *perpetuation* of, rather than resistance to, state power" (2002: 129; emphasis in original).

Moreover, it is often assumed that political music and art must be oppositional in order to have artistic merit. Nussbaum writes that "when art is not mediocre, it is in fact all the more unlikely that it will impose a snoozy conformity and homogeneity. When we think of totalitarian regimes that attempted to impose their vision through art, we always find bad art: Soviet realism and its many soporific cousins. Real artists are dissenters" (2013: 390).

Nussbaum's point touches on a central question in aesthetics and ethics, on the relationship between aesthetic value and moral content. In other words, can a song be good if its message is bad?[10] But the question is not so readily addressed as Nussbaum assumes. In order to understand what makes an artwork "good" or "bad," we must understand the historical and aesthetic conditions in which it is produced and interpreted. Revolutionary Guinea provides an example of totalitarianism that mobilized music and performance in its support, while successive authoritarian regimes in Guinea have similarly turned to music to "impose their vision." Yet local listeners do not reject this music as bad art. On the contrary, it moves people, physically and emotionally. It exerts intimate force and creates intimate collectivity. It produces power and pleasure. This is not to say, however, that music in support of dictators is politically inconsequential. Pleasure does not preclude bad politics, as musicians and audiences are well aware. But these songs produce multiple and ever-changing meanings and feelings, and to dismiss them as bad art because they are linked with state authority is to miss their local values.

In a study of Soviet art, Boris Groys (1992) notes that, much like Nussbaum, art historians often celebrate the Russian avant-garde of the 1920s and deride its successor, socialist realism, because of the two movements' relationships with the state: the former seen as independent from state authority, whereas the latter is mere propaganda. But Groys argues that both the October revolution and the artistic avant-garde shared the same fundamental project of aiming to transform the world. Soviet avant-garde artists actively sought and cultivated their political power in the Bolshevik state because it promoted their artistic agenda. Groys thus describes an "aesthetic dictatorship" in which the goals of artists and the state were very much the same: the will to power and, with it, the total transformation of the world.[11]

Groys's analysis helps us counter Nussbaum's wish to distinguish between "real" and (presumably) fake artists. In reality, as Groys so effectively shows, the relationship between artistic value and state power is often less heroic; in fact, "art that is universally regarded as good has frequently served to embellish and glorify power" (1992: 7). Following this account, I reject categorization of artists and musicians as good versus bad, real versus fake, and instead explore various conflicting practices and stances involving music, power, and state authority. Musicians in Guinea are constantly strategizing and playing with categories as they seek to sing, perform, make some money, build their careers, and get by. Allowing for their contradictions and various motivations gives us a much better understanding of what they do and why—and of how they are seen and heard in particular moments and by particular historiographies. My approach in this regard is greatly informed by work in African studies that emphasizes contradiction and polyvalence by highlighting the ways in which African people both accommodate and attempt to transcend the political and material realities of their lives (Barber 1987; Larkin 2008; Gilman 2009; Makhulu, Buggenhagen, and Jackson 2010; Piot 2010; Newell 2012; Shipley 2013). This work counters the "ethnographic thinning" of many studies of resistance (Ortner 2006) by paying close attention to everyday lives, work, hardships, pleasures, and fantasies. I also owe an important debt to studies that challenge romanticized ideas of music and musicians. Maurice Bloch, for instance, argued that song can serve as a powerful means of social control, a position that "seems to go against a generally accepted view of art as a kind of super-communication, a supreme occasion for creativity" (1974: 72). More recently, critical studies on music and politics have foregrounded ambivalence, ambiguity, and disunity in protest (McDonald

2013; Manabe 2016; Novak 2017), presented musicians in their inconsistencies and three-dimensionality (Veal 2000; Guilbault 2007; Stokes 2010; Stirr 2017), and interrogated what music can and cannot do (Sorce Keller 2007; Baker 2014; Daughtry 2015).

Naming Guinea

The Republic of Guinea (fig. 1) travels in a sweeping arc from its capital on the Atlantic coast to cross regions of highlands, savannahs, and dense forests in a corner of southern West Africa (fig. 2). It is home to 12.6 million people, two dozen ethnic groups, and over forty languages. Guinea is predominantly Muslim, with 85 percent of the country practicing Islam, alongside Christian and polytheistic minorities. My ethnography is set in the country's capital, Conakry. As in most West African nation-states, whose maps were carved out by the colonial powers, the capital was strategically placed as a point of maximum extraction from the rest of the country. The engineered movement of people, goods, money, and resources from the "interior" to the coast continued after independence, and as I show in chapter 1, Conakry served as the site for the construction of national culture. Urban life in Conakry does not reflect the everyday experiences of all Guinean people throughout the

FIGURE 1. Map of Guinea

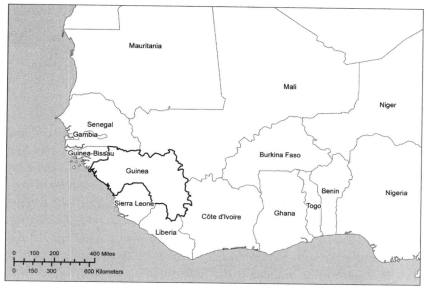

FIGURE 2. Map of West Africa

country, but it does offer a particularly rich site for examining how aesthetics and authority have long interacted in postcolonial Guinea.

Conakry is a multilingual, multiethnic city made up of people and cultures from throughout the country. Soso (alternatively, Susu or Soussou) people constitute its main ethnic group, while large numbers of Fulbe and Maninka people, the two largest ethnicities in Guinea, also live in the city. Other ethnic groups in Guinea, although less well represented in Conakry, include Baga people of the upper coastal area; as well as numerous ethnicities in the southwestern forest region, including Kpelle, Loma, and Kissi people, who often are all grouped together with some other peoples under the catch-all term *forestiers*. Of all these groups, Maninka people have historically dominated the Guinean nation-state because of their ties to the former Mande empire and to the former president Sékou Touré.

The term *Mande* refers to both a precolonial West African empire and its modern-day descendants, reaching from Mali in the north to Burkina Faso and Côte d'Ivoire in the east, through Guinea, and up to Guinea-Bissau, Senegal, and the Gambia in the west. This region includes the northern Mande group of languages such as Maninka (northeastern Guinea and western Mali), Mandinka (eastern Senegal and Gambia, and northwestern Guinea), Bamana (central Mali), and Soso (southwestern Guinea, including Conakry).

The Mande empire existed from the thirteenth to seventeenth centuries, when it was broken up into a number of smaller kingdoms. Yet, as a Guinean musician said to me once, "history continues," and the Mande empire retains meaning and shapes identities into the present day. As Eric Charry notes, the ongoing influence and relevance of its epic history to Mande people, told in the story and song complex of its founder, Sunjata Keita, cannot be over-estimated (2000: 41). Despite Guinea's vast linguistic and cultural diversity, Mande culture and music have long occupied a central role in the national consciousness and therefore occupy an important space in public life. As a result, my ethnography foregrounds Mande culture because of its outsize in-fluence on the nexus between music and politics in Guinea.[12] My discussions focus primarily on Maninka and Soso people, whereas the views and expe-riences of Fulbe people and members of other groups are significantly less represented here. A number of excellent studies of *forestier* and Baga cultures exist (Lamp 1996; Sarró 2009; Straker 2009; McGovern 2013, 2017) and have been invaluable in providing a better understanding of these perspectives. Comparably few studies exist on Fulbe art and performance in Guinea, al-though there are a number of fascinating accounts of Fulbe political experi-ence in the postcolonial state.[13]

When I first arrived in Conakry in 2002 armed with my *Rough Guide to West Africa*, I was sorely disappointed that it contained only one picture of Guinea. While there were pages and pages of vivid photographs from neigh-boring countries, the only image from Guinea was a distant aerial shot of Mount Nimba in the southeastern forest region—green trees on beautiful green hills, but not quite the information I was hoping for at the time. Guinea seemed distant and unknowable. Years later a friend in Conakry observed to me with some frustration that "when I go to France, people have heard of Mali, Senegal, Côte d'Ivoire, but nobody knows about Guinea." In part, the fact that Guinea is less well-known than other countries in the region is due to its political history under the revolution. In 1958 Guinea became the first French colony in Africa to gain its independence, and the new state was her-alded as a leader in the continent's decolonization movement. A few months later a smiling Sékou Touré appeared on the front cover of *Time* magazine with the caption "Black Africa: The Dawn of Self Rule." Guinea and Touré had captured the world's attention. Yet Touré became increasingly paranoid and xenophobic over the course of his twenty-six-year rule, and as a result, the country became increasingly isolated and insular. Over time Guineans became aware of their perceived marginality despite having been raised with the story of their exceptionalism. This tension is at the heart of debates about the revolution's continuing legacies today. There is a sense that Guinea, with its history in the Mande empire and the fight for African liberation, mattered beyond its borders and had a place in the world. What is that place today? Where has Guinea come from, and where is it going?

These questions point to a central theme in this book: naming, both as a musical practice and as a way of understanding the relationship between pleasure, power, and the political in Guinea. Naming is at the heart of local traditions of praise singing in the Mande world. A musician may sing the family name (Mn. [Maninka] *jamu*) of his or her patron and the patron's ancestors, referencing their heroism or noble traits or connections with great historical moments or people; or they may sing an individual name (Mn. *to*) that distinguishes a particular person within a clan or lineage. In the song "Mandjou," Salif Keita sang the *jamu* of Sékou Touré and linked the president back to his ancestors and to holy men in the region's history (Charry 2000: 38, 274). This act of naming creates great pleasure or joy (Mn. *sewa*), as the person whose name is sung feels immense pride in self-recognition and the fact of knowing him- or herself (Mn. *yere lon*). Through song, the person's name is publicly honored and memorialized. As Sory Camara writes, "The name is considered not only as marking the identity of a person, but also and especially, as an honorific attribute that fills the bearer with pride" (1992: 29; my translation). But this pleasure also extends to the collectivity who are present, evoking their shared heritage and history. Listeners feel pleasure at hearing the name of others, or hearing songs naming and recounting the exploits of great figures in epic history. This naming creates a link from past to present and is a marker of cultural strength and survival. As the Maninka proverb states, "I faa tɔ li mɔɔ di faa, i tɔɔ tɛ faa" (You will die, people will die; your name will not die).

The act and aesthetics of naming represent a moment of recognition. As theorists of recognition argue, recognition is about mutuality, about acknowledging the other's existence and human dignity. A key aspect of recognition is affirmation: not only does the subject assert his or her identity, but that identity is affirmed by another. For Frantz Fanon, such recognition, and the freedom that it entails, cannot just be given but instead must be fought for. As he describes, man is "yes and no": "*Yes* to life. *Yes* to love. *Yes* to generosity. But . . . *No* to scorn of man. *No* to degradation of man. *No* to exploitation of man. *No* to the butchery of what is most human in man: freedom" (1952: 173). These positions, both the yes and the no, must be affirmatively claimed and accepted in order for the subject to be recognized as human and equal.

In postcolonial Guinea musical naming adds an aesthetic and affective dimension to this struggle for recognition by demanding that others not only hear and recognize one's existence, but also celebrate it and share in the feeling that it evokes. Such recognition does not, however, necessarily translate into the freedom that Fanon references. For one, as theorists have argued, recognition by itself does not automatically counter material or social inequality but instead must be accompanied by a commitment to redistribution (Fraser 1995). In Guinea, acts of musical naming and recognition occur within a context of staggering poverty and inequality whose real impact on the lives of ordinary people should not be minimized. Moreover, as Charles Taylor notes, the "politics of recognition" that plays out in contemporary Euro-American political debates is rooted in eighteenth-century ideas about the individual and "*individualized* identity" (1994: 28; emphasis in original). In Guinea, on the other hand, the recognition that praise singing creates is a direct appeal to the collective while it also attests to the power of particular individuals. As I will show, anyone can be named through song, but in practice this act is most often directed toward the powerful, and so its outcomes are not evenly distributed. Others experience pleasure from the collective aspect of the act, and through these feelings pleasure and power perpetuate each other. Guinean praise singing, naming, and recognition create meaning and feeling that in turn feed into existing structures of power. Yet, naming is also very much an evolving rather than a fixed practice in Guinea, and new forms are emerging today that make new demands for recognition.

In considering these various dynamics, my analysis pays particular attention to the human voice, in song and speech. Although voice is often used as a metaphor for political participation, I am interested in the material qualities of the voice in Guinea and the meanings that these qualities carry. My ideas here build on important insights in the anthropology of voice, which considers the sound and materiality of the voice to hear how ideas about personhood and social difference take form (Feld, Fox, Porcello, and Samuels 2004; Samuels, Meintjes, Ochoa, and Porcello 2010; Weidman 2014). In ethnomusicology, scholars have explored aesthetics, politics, class, and gender ideologies through close attention to voice and talk about voice (Fox 2004; Weidman 2006; Meintjes 2017).

Vocal aesthetics in Guinea are tied to ideas about power, authority, truthfulness, and social responsibility. Paying attention to the sounds of the human voice enables us to hear much more than words and literal meanings and gives us a much richer understanding of how songs and speech are received and interpreted. Related to these concerns, I also examine strategic silence and quietness, considering the circumstances and practices in which musicians and other people in Guinea choose *not* to use their voices. While some commentators on rights often frame silence in terms of coercion and lack of participation (Spivak 1988; Slaughter 1997), others have explored the meanings that silence can convey (Basso 1970; Herzfeld 1991; Neveu Kringelbach 2007). Much of this work focuses in particular on women's silence. In his essays on the "problem of women" (1975a, 1975b), for instance, Edwin Ardener argues that dominant groups define the appropriate language and means of expression, setting the expressive rules by which others find themselves bound and thus "muted" or "inarticulate."[14] As I show in Guinea, quietness and "mutedness" do not simply represent the absence of words, but rather represent particular strategies of communication and being in an authoritarian state.

Ethics and Methods

In a study on dance music in Mobutu's Zaire, Bob White raises questions about his responsibilities in writing about art and authoritarianism in central Africa: "How can we write about the relationship between politics and popular culture without reproducing a narrative that ends up blaming the victim? How can we ensure that the stories we tell reflect the complexity and dignity of a nation of people who never asked to be governed by a dictator?" (2008: 228). White grapples with the ethics of representing a set of real people who are multiple and varied, who live in political circumstances that they sometimes criticize and sometimes do not. And he notes the danger of suggesting that such abuses of power can only happen *over there* but not over here (ibid.: 227–28).

To these I add some questions of my own. How do we study pleasure in a context of violence, poverty, and dictatorship? How do we represent the beautiful and the ugly without minimizing or overdetermining either? Sarah Nuttall observes that scholars in African studies have often treated beauty as a frivolous subject "in relation to the sublime power of economics or politics" (2006: 13). According to this view, music, art, pleasure, and beauty are seen as superficial points of inquiry in light of endemic social and structural problems. At the same time, outside commentators on African music and pop culture have long celebrated its exuberance as well as the agency and integrity of its practitioners. These representations often insist that African music is political and progressive—that all music matters, but "somehow in Africa it has even more potency."[15]

Chimamanda Ngozi Adichie, in her well-known 2009 TED talk, warns against the "danger of a single story" of Africa and its people. As Adichie notes, African people have long been subject to hardened stereotypes and misrepresentations that do not easily give way. This single story is often one of Afro-pessimism, of poverty and a continent in crisis and violence, far from modernity and the rest of the world. Music, art, and performance provide us important ways to move beyond such narratives by showcasing local creativity and vitality. But in seeking to counter this story, representations of African music and art can create their own problems. Such representations are often mired in their own stubborn stereotypes of primitivism and happy, dancing folk, on the one hand, and of African musical and/or political heroism and agency on the other. These types of celebratory depictions often ignore the ways in which African art forms become commodified and extracted, whether through the unauthorized use of field recordings (Feld 1996) or the gentrification of modern art.[16] But they also insist on a particular way in which African music and musicians must operate politically in order to be validated by others.

In this book I show that musicians in one corner of Africa do not always act in ways that we may perceive as heroic or politically progressive or even "good." Indeed, I argue, we do them a disservice by insisting on one-dimensional caricatures and categories. Instead, we should allow for contradiction, complexity, polyvalence, and practices and beliefs that at times run counter to our own political sensibilities and desires. This is not to say that we relinquish our own values, but rather that we attempt to understand why people might think and act as they do. Ethnography is one way in which we can do this. Katherine Verdery writes that, as an ethnographer, she is "committed to resisting condemnation that would wall off possibilities for understanding" (2018: 190). As Michael Carrithers suggests, ethnography requires from the outset a "sympathetic forbearance, the ability to enter into another person's situation imaginatively without necessarily sharing the other's values or cosmology" (2005: 438). Throughout the present ethnography I represent local musicians, events, behavior, and ideologies in Guinea without rushing to save or condemn them. As Chérie Rivers Ndaliko (2016) notes, the best way to counter stereotypes of African people is to allow them to represent themselves, and in this regard, a written ethnography still presents gatekeepers and constructs particular voices of authority. But by focusing on individual people and their stories in the following chapters, I hope that they will be recognized as three-dimensional, fully human, and self-aware. In their complexity and depth, their lives and experiences stand as testament against a "single story" of the continent.

This study is based on fifteen months of fieldwork between 2009 and 2016, as well as a short follow-up trip in 2017. It also builds on the three years during which I lived in Guinea, from 2002 to 2005, as a lawyer and humanitarian worker for the United Nations High Commissioner for Refugees (UNHCR).

My work during those years involved close interactions with Guinean state officials, security forces, prison wardens, and police officers; civilians facing threats, problems, and sometimes help from these same actors; and local rights advocates and activists who debated and pursued political reforms. The insights I gained through this work have greatly informed my understandings of state authority and political culture in Guinea. Musically, it was during those years that I first became entranced by the sounds of Bembeya Jazz, Espoirs de Coronthie, Sékouba "Bambino" Diabaté, and other musicians whom I discuss here. Upon later returning to Guinea, I had the great fortune to study Mande vocal music with Diaryatou Kouyaté, a singer from a well-known musical lineage. I also learned instrumental accompaniments on *kora* (lute-harp) with her grandson, Demba Diallo. With a few exceptions, including the close relationship I developed with Diaryatou Kouyaté, much of my time during fieldwork was spent with male musicians. This imbalance is due largely to the fact that the professional music scene in Conakry is male dominated, both historically and today. I have begun elsewhere to examine issues of gender and women's roles in Guinean public life (Dave 2019), but the present ethnography addresses these issues only tangentially. Women were often absent from many of the venues and scenes I describe here, but even when they were present, language also created obstacles to my building relationships with them.

I originally began to learn Guinean Maninka, in London and later in Conakry, owing to my interest in Touré-era music. In Conakry, however, I ended up studying music and living for a time with a family of Mandinka-speakers, a language more commonly spoken in Gambia and parts of Senegal and Guinea-Bissau. I also came to spend increasing amounts of time with speakers of Soso, the lingua franca of Conakry, to which I eventually switched my own language study. As a result of attempting to work across these various languages, I had varying levels of competency and relied on speakers' ability to switch to and from French. Most of the translations from Guinean languages here were done in long sessions in Conakry with my friend Mohamed "Sita" Camara, although all mistakes are my own.

This book begins by introducing the foundational moment of the Guinean cultural revolution. In chapter 1 I examine the development of popular nationalist music during the 1960s and '70s and introduce President Sékou Touré, as well as the state-sponsored musicians who promoted his vision. My narrative focuses in particular on the national dance band Bembeya Jazz and its participation in the 1969 Pan-African Cultural Festival in Algiers. The chapter also introduces ideas about public pleasure and naming in Guinea, considering how the regime as well as audiences and musicians mobilized these resources.

In the remaining chapters I explore the legacies of the revolution today, starting in the immediate aftermath of a military coup d'état in December 2008 and tracing the rise and fall of the junta it put in place. In chapter 2 I revisit Bembeya Jazz in 2009, encountering the once-revolutionary musicians as older men, and examine the attempts of the new military regime to appropriate their earlier music. The narrative centers on Bembeya Jazz's role in the "new" cultural policy and on the recirculation of their 1968 song "Armée guinéenne."

Chapter 3 examines more directly the role of pleasure in praise performance, focusing particularly on the voice and vocal aesthetics. The narrative focuses on the flood of praise songs that greeted the new military regime in 2009, with particular emphasis on how local interpretations of vocal timbre shape the ways in which a song is heard. In contrast, chapter 4 foregrounds the notion of quietness and ambiguity—and of when not to name—in Guinean musical and political culture today. I focus on a relatively new genre of youth-oriented urban traditional music known as Soso music. The narrative focuses on the increasing volatility of the military regime in 2009, which culminated in an act of large-scale political violence. I examine the build-up of popular anger against the military regime in 2009 and the corresponding silence of musicians, both young and old.

Chapter 5 continues the story after the implosion of the military junta and the shifting landscape since the country's first-ever democratic elections in 2010. I analyze new types of naming that are emerging through the recent rise in public political participation and debate in Guinea, as well as the emergence of a number of explicit protest songs. I consider both official and popular reactions to these changes and the ways in which older musical pleasures are being lost while newer ones are sought out. The narrative focuses on the strategic, shifting allegiances of a popular reggae star who released an incendiary attack against the president in 2013.

Today, in 2019, as Guinea charts an uneasy transition to democratic rule, spectacles of public pleasure are becoming increasingly unstable as new forms of protest and political voice challenge older aesthetic and political practices. Examining this shifting dynamic allows us to understand the lingering legacies of authoritarianism and the ways in which intimate publics renegotiate the past, present, and future. At its heart, this book thus explores the paradoxes and poetics of everyday authoritarian and postauthoritarian experience.

1

Agents of the Revolution

Touré was a passionate lover of his people's culture, but could also be a paranoid tyrant. Guinea was a beautiful and terrifying place.
HUGH MASEKELA AND D. MICHAEL CHEERS, *Still Grazing* (2004)

In January 1959 the Republic of Guinea appointed a national dance band. The country had declared its independence from France just four months earlier, becoming the first sovereign state in francophone Africa. While other colonies weighed the benefits of continued ties through membership in a Franco-African Community, Guinea opted for a swift break from French rule. This decisive move made waves through West Africa and far beyond, as Guinea plunged forward into a revolutionary future. Its leader, Sékou Touré, emerged as a fiery nationalist and anti-imperialist, determined to create a new African model for the postcolonial era. And by naming the Syli National Orchestra, Touré announced that music would play a role in the struggle ahead.

What did it mean to be "revolutionary" in Sékou Touré's Guinea? What constituted revolutionary practice, and revolutionary music? In the twenty-six years of his rule, from 1958 till his death in 1984, Touré sought to instill new sensibilities and practices in Guinea to engineer a break from past values and older structures of authority. He continually emphasized the narrative of Guinea's radical decolonization in order to underline the revolutionary nature of his regime—and his key role in it. This process nominally saw its peak in 1968 with the launch of the Socialist Cultural Revolution. Yet Touré saw his revolution as a permanent one, predating independence and leading onward into an African nationalist future.

The example of Touré's Guinea shows us that, despite their doctrines and dogma, revolutions are replete with contradictions, as are the lived experiences of citizens living within them. Ideology seeks to present a unified vision of a utopian future, yet it is always contradictory and cosmopolitan. In the case of Guinea, Sékou Touré wished to unify Guineans, and to alienate them from each other; to make Guinea global, and to isolate it from an ever-growing list of countries; to march resolutely into the future, and look continually back to the past; to uplift his subjects with hope, and to instill in them constant fear. The revolution was never a coherent or consistent project, but rather an ever-shifting set of strategies, whims, practices, and meanings that Touré pursued in his quest for influence and domination. Like all ideologues, Touré espoused a worldview that evolved historically in response to its own circumstances, and tried continually to bridge its internal contradictions. In this context, revolutionary music and performance registered and negotiated these inconsistencies and unintended effects, sometimes pushing past the regime and at other times falling closely in step. Popular musicians, both those sponsored by the state and those aspiring to be, actively supported rather than resisted Touré's rule. But their practices also exceeded official directives and ideology, shaping and channeling forms of public pleasure that, as later chapters show, continue to reverberate in Guinea today.

New Sounds for a New Nation

There was a time, as older inhabitants of the city remember, that Conakry hosted a great festival. "*La Quinzaine!*" recalls Linké Condé, a guitarist active on the scene since the 1950s. "Everyone was together and there weren't any thugs or crooks then. The city was alive! There was *ambiance!*"[1]

Condé and many others from his generation fondly recollect the Quinzaine Artistique (Artistic Fortnight), an annual festival of music, dance, theater, poetry, and speeches that enthralled the capital through the 1960s. Reconfigured in 1970 as a biennial National Cultural Festival, the Quinzaine and its successor festivals were the summit of an elaborate national arts competition in Sékou Touré's Guinea. Throughout the 1960s and 1970s this competition amalgamated and appropriated practices from across a vast topography of two dozen ethnic groups. Teams of bureaucrats from Touré's Parti Démocratique de Guinée (PDG) were sent to recruit the most promising artists. Local and regional competitions culminated in the national festival in Conakry, where artists would compete for recognition as the nation's representatives and stars.

Each night of the festival, performances would be held in Guinea's most prestigious cultural and political venue, the Palais du Peuple. The audience would be composed of visiting dignitaries, local VIPs, and members of the public. No concert at the Palais could begin, however, before Sékou Touré had arrived. Seated in the front row, Touré would take notes during each performance and mark each group, distilling his critiques and indicating which groups deserved to advance.[2] Touré aimed to position himself as the ultimate arbiter in the construction of national culture.

Performance in the Touré era was divided into various categories: *ensembles* (traditional choral and instrumental groups), *ballets* (dance and percussion groups), *théâtre militant* (nationalist theater groups), and *orchestres* (modern electric dance bands). All of these groups were tasked with compiling and re-presenting local melodies, rhythms, dances, stories, ritual objects, and poetic texts for the national and international stage. At the top of the system were national groups. In addition to the Syli National Orchestra and a National Theatre Troupe, the National Instrumental Ensemble was created in November 1960, incorporating traditional instruments from throughout the country.[3] The state also appointed two national ballets that still exist to this day, the Ballets Africains and the Ballet Djoliba.

The Ballets Africains originated as the Théâtre Africain, a performance group founded in Paris in the 1940s by two Guinean students, Fodéba Keita and Facélli Kanté. The group later switched from theater to dance and percussion and was renamed the Ballets Africains de Fodéba Keita. Keita, a poet, writer, and choreographer, adapted dances and rhythms from West African ritual performance to stage-friendly- and shortened formats for European audiences. One of his central aims was to promote African culture as sophisticated and modern, embracing the idea of both African tradition and an African modernity "marked by Western civilization" (1957: 206). Upon independence, Fodéba Keita returned to Guinea and was named Minister of the Interior and of Information, a position from which he oversaw cultural production in the new nation.[4] In 1960 his troupe was renamed the Ballets Africains de Guinée.[5] In contrast, the Ballet Djoliba was created in 1964 as a state-controlled national troupe. The group is named after the Niger River, whose source is in Guinea. Djoliba was founded with some initial support from Harry Belafonte, who was Touré's guest in the early 1960s.[6] The new ballet recruited performers from across the country, including the percussionist Mamady Keita, who debuted for Djoliba as a teenager.[7]

Popular music in Touré's Guinea was similarly patterned on earlier, existing models. Electric dance bands such as La Joviale Symphonie, La Douce Parisette, and Le Tropical Jazz had proliferated in Conakry since the late colonial era, playing tangos, foxtrots, and waltzes for European and Guinean audiences. Upon independence, one of the regime's first acts was to ban European music from the radio and live performance, insisting that the country relieve itself of its imperial burden.[8] "Each People has its own Culture," Touré would often declare over his rule. He called for the existing dance bands to cease playing and in their place appointed the Syli National Orchestra. *Syli,* the Soso word for elephant, became a common prefix for cultural nationalist projects in Guinea, including the subsequently formed Syli-Cinéma, the Syli-Photo bureau, the Syliphone record label, and the now-defunct Syli national currency. The term was also linked to Touré himself, with the elephant standing as a metaphor for Touré's strength.

Despite the regime's moves against colonial-era bands, it retained much of their basic style and format. Many of their musicians were recruited into the Syli Orchestra, including Linké Condé and the saxophonists Momo "Wandel" Soumah and Kélétigui Traoré. Moreover, the Syli Orchestra's instrumentation borrowed directly from its predecessors, centering on electric guitar, bass, trumpet, saxophone, drum kit, claves, and conga drums. Percussion instruments were largely borrowed from Cuban rhythms, which had been introduced through imported rumba recordings since the 1930s and were hugely popular throughout West and Central Africa. As Condé describes, the Syli Orchestra was "a school of music" for these musicians, who had to relearn local melodies after years of playing European dance tunes.[9] The Orchestra's mission was to rework the dance-band formula to incorporate and foreground elements of Guinean folk traditions. Other musicians were also recruited, included pioneering guitarists from hereditary musician families, such as Sékou "Le docteur" and Kerfala "Papa" Diabaté, as well as musicians from non-hereditary backgrounds, such as the trumpeter Balla Onivogui and the Martiniquean clarinetist Honoré Coppet.

As more musicians began performing local songs on imported instruments, the Syli Orchestra strained to incorporate the talent swelling its ranks. In response, the government decided in 1963 to divide it into two national dance bands: the Orchestre de la Paillote and Orchestre du Jardin de Guinée (later renamed, respectively, Kélétigui et ses Tambourinis and Balla et ses Balladins). Three years later a regional band from the town of Beyla in southeastern Guinea was accorded the same status after amassing victories at successive Quinzaines and thus became Bembeya Jazz National. Although at one time there were at least seven official national dance bands, these three groups in particular—Kélétigui, Balla, and Bembeya—defined the sound of Guinean pop music through the 1960s and 1970s.

In addition to influences from Cuban *son* and jazz big bands, the dance-band sound borrowed from West and Central African styles: the finger-picking guitar of palm-wine, the trumpet and saxophone of high-life, the Latin rhythms of Congolese rumba. But the songs themselves were distinctly Guinean, often derived from the repertoire of Mande *jeliya*, the art of hereditary musicians known as *jelilu* (Mn. *jeli*, sing.). Touré self-identified as

Maninka and foregrounded Mande music in his construction of Guinean national music.[10] Dance-band songs often adapted melodies from jeli pieces, substituting electric instruments such as the guitar for local ones.[11]

Dance-band songs also borrowed from poetic texts and stories from jeliya, often recounting the heroism of legendary figures from the Mande empire and its descendants. The traditional jeli piece "Kèmè Bourema," for example, narrates a story about Kèmè Bourema Touré, a nineteenth-century warrior who miraculously escaped death. Under Touré, pieces such as these were reworked to render homage to the president and his rule. The band Kebendo Jazz was one of many who adapted "Kèmè Bourema" into a dance song, transposing the *bala* (xylophone) melody to guitar but also repurposing the lyrics in praise of and thanks to Sékou Touré, who claimed Kèmè Bouréma Touré as an ancestor. Throughout the 1960s and 1970s, dance bands from across the country similarly released hundreds of songs praising the president and his various instruments of power, including his party, his revolution, his army, his slogans, and even his wife.[12] In some cases these songs were newly composed or used non-jeli melodies; in others they borrowed directly from earlier melodic and poetic references. Either way, by rendering homage to Touré they built on jeli traditions of singing in praise of the king and nobility. Here, of course, the king was Sékou Touré.

Jeli songs provided a prestigious and culturally familiar template for praise that could now be redirected to the Guinean state and its leader. By foregrounding jeliya, the dance bands not only centered their practice on Mande music, but also sought to evoke affective ties among Mande peoples. For the descendants of the Mande empire, these songs create a powerful sense of pride, evoking shared epic histories and memories. Central to the aesthetics of jeliya is naming—declaiming the names of living people and long-deceased ancestors. By calling on all within earshot to hear and recognize an individual's name, the singer affirms the place of that person in history and the present. Naming generates great social value. The practice also extends beyond the individual to recognize the larger collectivity of which he or she is a part. Songs to ancestors and legendary historical figures evoke the kingdoms and empire of the past, while songs to the living evoke their membership in a glorious community of memory and endurance. Under Touré, these pleasures of self-recognition were rendered double by repurposing these songs as revolutionary national culture. Not only was Guinea claiming a glorious legendary history, but it was using popular music to claim recognition in the modern world. The Bembeya Jazz song "La Guinée" illustrates the work done in this regard:

La Guinée diyara mɔɔ ye	If a person loves Guinea
La Guinée diyananko tɛ sa	What pleases Guinea will be
La Guinée gboyara mɔɔ ye	If a person disagrees with Guinea
La Guinée diyananko tɛ sa	What pleases Guinea will be
Ala nɔ le, mɔɔ nɔ tɛ	God has the authority, not people

As shown here, the song uses repeated phrases to create rhythmic structures in the text, as well as sacred phrases and formal evocations of God to call to a higher authority. Such forms are key features commonly used in jeliya to move listeners (Hoffman 2000: 64). Here the musicians deploy these powerful tropes within a pop idiom to sing of patriotism to the new nation. Beyond facile propaganda, post-independence pop songs singing of the country, of the "PDG," "President Sékou Touré," or his "Révolution Culturelle" served as deeply rooted, culturally resonant vehicles to proclaim the existence and honor of these institutions.

These songs thus made heroes of all who descended from the Mande empire (Diawara 1998: 98). Such knowing emphasis on Mande was key. Touré's regime greatly privileged Mande culture in its construction of Guinean national culture. As the musicologist Graeme Counsel (2015) notes, music from this period is dominated by songs and groups from Touré's Maninka ethnicity. Praise singing to a president created excesses of pleasure and pride that could be shared by all who felt recognized by the song's references—but this recognition was particularly strong for Mande people.

From this model the 1960s and 1970s saw an explosion of creative musical output in Guinea as bands proliferated throughout the country and competed to release new songs. The best of their songs were recorded and broadcast on La Voix de la Révolution radio, and later on the national broadcasting company Radio Télévision Guinée (RTG), as well as on the state-run Syliphone record label.[13] As a series of recordings from the early 1960s announced, these were *Sons nouveaux d'une nation nouvelle* (New Sounds for a New Nation).[14] The optimism of this title is reflected in the sound of revolutionary pop music. Through much of the 1960s, dance-band songs were characterized by punchy brass-instrument arrangements and bright guitar tones. Lively 6/8 rhythms were popular, reflecting both commonly used local time signatures and the contemporary craze for Afro-Cuban rhythms. Musicians claimed modernity alongside pride in the past. The Touré regime wanted in particular to energize young people, and its party youth wing organized festivities to this soundtrack in Conakry's neighborhoods during the annual Quinzaine. Women and young cadres were also instructed to celebrate publicly throughout the year, such as by dressing in white and lining the streets to cheer arriving dignitaries and guests, or by thronging the national stadium for official ceremonies.

Collective effervescence was a feeling to be actively cultivated and strategically deployed in Touré's Guinea. But parallel to the formalized system of the festivals, the dance bands also gave urban youth space to socialize and celebrate in a more intimate, yet nonetheless state-ordained, setting. Beginning in the early 1960s these bands were each assigned a local venue in Conakry—a *bar-dancing*—where they regularly performed. Kélétigui et ses Tambourinis could be found at La Paillote, and Balla et ses Balladins played at the Jardin de Guinée, while Bembeya Jazz was assigned to Club Bembeya.

In Touré's Guinea, night life was a nationalist cause. A 1961 article in the party newspaper *Horoya* (the Maninka word for freedom, often also translated as dignity) describes a dance party in Conakry not just as a night out, but as a necessary step toward modernity:[15] "It was a Saturday night, the moment where the morning breeze starts to appear. The room was packed with dancers, mostly minors. . . . We danced, we danced for the human pleasure of dancing . . . and as I looked around, I contemplated with an indefinable sense of love all these people climbing the hill of civilization."[16]

Music, dancing, and public displays of pleasure were all patriotic acts, to be strategically dispensed by the regime and energetically consumed by its young people. This exuberance was tightly regulated, channeled through the arts system into Conakry and contained within state-sanctioned spaces where Touré's surrogate eyes and ears were always present. In her autobiography the South African singer Miriam Makeba recalls in vivid detail her experiences in Guinea in the late 1960s and 1970s. Exiled from apartheid-era South Africa, Makeba first visited Guinea as Touré's guest in 1967 and moved there a year later, eventually staying for seventeen years. She developed a close relationship with Touré, including singing his praises in the song "Touré Barika" (Blessings to Touré). Her memoir portrays the president in a largely flattering light as her sponsor and mentor. Yet she occasionally includes the frank observations of an outsider. As she observes, "Every club in Conakry has what is called a co-director. This is a man who works directly for the Ministry of the Interior. Anyone who causes trouble knows who they will have to answer to" (1987: 215).

The regime also sought to control music by framing it as a collective endeavor and actively discouraged individual stardom to avoid any rivals. In the early years of independence, dance bands clearly designated their stars and bandleaders in their names, but this style of naming quickly lost its currency. By the mid-1960s band names never referenced individual musicians and instead drew their names from local places or cultural references, such as Camayenne Sofa (referencing nineteenth-century Mande warriors) and the 22 Band (commemorating a failed coup attempt by the Portuguese on 22 November 1970). In this way it was not individual musicians who were celebrated, but rather the symbols of nationhood, implicitly referencing the Father of the Nation himself. As Touré stated in a 1968 speech, "Artists do not create Art. It is created by the people."[17] Even Bembeya Jazz, the period's most celebrated band, did not escape this dogma. In a 1969 concert review, for example, *Horoya* accused Bembeya's lead guitarist, Sékou Diabaté, of "always showing too much individuality in this great band that includes five other instrumentalists."[18]

In his speeches and writing, Touré explicitly framed "African music" as nonhierarchical, communal, and improvisational, stressing that it followed no fixed compositions and continually changed to adapt to the "psycho-social reality of the moment."[19] Musicians' accounts, however, reveal that they did not internalize these interpretations. The dance bands not only composed and arranged their songs, often having to perform them for Touré before wider release, but they were also highly hierarchical and individualistic. Each had its own bandleader, who chose songs, led arrangements, and directed rehearsals, and each had its biggest stars. The bands also competed energetically with each other for status and fans. Bembeya lead guitarist Sékou Diabaté (affectionately known in Guinea as Sékou Bembeya, or by the nickname Diamond Fingers) earned a huge following for his theatrical guitar solos and still remembers fans shouting their approval when he would cavort like a rock star on stage.[20] Such moments were sources of intense personal pride for these musicians as they experimented with new forms of showmanship in order to outdo each other in public.

Artists were a problematic category for Touré. On the one hand, he championed art as a revolutionary agent, capable of affecting social and psychological transformation. His regime feted the nation's top artists and depended on them to create the affective conditions for revolution and solidarity. On the other hand, this agency meant that artists represented a threat to his authority and quest for total control. In Touré's Guinea, there was room for only one hero, and that title was already claimed.

The Revolution and Its Hero

In *The Origins of Totalitarianism*, Hannah Arendt writes of the "perpetual-motion mania" of totalitarian movements, which retain their power "only so long as they keep moving and set everything around them in motion" (1951: 408). The idea of movement(s) is central to her analysis. Arendt argues that totalitarians do not seek simply to gain control over the state, but rather to control individuals through psychological as well as other means. Citing the examples of National Socialism and Bolshevism, she argues that "their idea of domination was something that no state and no mere apparatus of violence can ever achieve, but only a movement that is constantly kept in motion: namely, the permanent domination of each single individual in each and every sphere of life" (ibid.: 432).

In Guinea, over the course of his rule Sékou Touré was increasingly preoccupied with establishing and maintaining total domination over the state and its subjects. Touré continually sought out new forms of control that were, as Arendt suggests, both political and psychological. His key strategy related precisely to motion—framing liberation as on ongoing movement forward. As he wrote in his book *L'Afrique en marche* (Africa on the Move, or Africa Marching Forward), "Unity for its own sake will never be an end in itself, but rather a method of acceleration" toward a progressive future (1967: 89). Progress meant the total emancipation of each individual from any vestige of colonialism and other "backward" ideas. In pursuit of this goal, Guineans were told that they could not afford to rest or become complacent with respect to the many dangers around them.

Despite post-independence accounts of Guinea as a "lively and interesting place,"[21] signs of autocracy were evident early on. Touré was keenly aware of the need to guard against disillusionment as the initial glow of independence faded, particularly since the French had ransacked the country after its independence vote and left its administration and economy in chaos (Barry 2010: 40) Touré quickly mobilized the narrative of Guinean exceptionalism, with public celebrations organized around this theme on the first anniversary of independence in 1959 (Pauthier 2010: 64). Economic decline and disillusionment progressed through the early 1960s, however, opening increasing spaces for political opposition. As early as 1961 the government cracked down on calls for reform by the teachers' union and imprisoned some of its members.[22]

In countering such dissent, from early on Touré called for ongoing vigilance against shadowy enemies and threats (1961). His government fueled the narrative through reports of countless attempted coups d'état from 1960 onward, which became known among the population as the "permanent plot." A 1960 plot involved "counter-revolutionary pro-French" elements, for instance, while 1965 saw the "Petit Touré Plot," in which a rich businessman was accused of conspiring against the government (Kaké 1987: 96, 127). Other "plots" involved students, shopkeepers, state officials, and members of the Fulbe ethnicity, a group that Touré saw as a constant political threat because of its wealth and numbers. The announcement of yet another attempted coup was a renewable resource for the state, justifying a crackdown on critics and tightened control over everybody else.

The regime also mobilized more formal mechanisms. In 1964 it passed the Loi Cadre, primarily an economic move to ban private enterprise and end cross-border smuggling, but also marking a new imposition of centralized political control (Camara 2005: 64–65). The Loi Cadre imposed heavy taxes and strict limits on trade goods, resulting in confusion and disarray as businesses closed and many basic goods became unaffordable. In response to criticisms, Touré called on Guineans to forgo imported products, arguing that "before the Whites came . . . no one knew about sugar" (quoted in Kaké 1987: 123; my translation). Some of the law's provisions were more explicitly political, such as those relating to the organization of PDG party cells throughout the country or threatening members with expulsion for failing to follow the party line. The legal text itself ends with the words, "Vive la Révolution!"

By 1963 Touré was already referring to his regime as a "national revolution" that extended endlessly into the future.[23] The revolution was instituted and formalized within a few years. At the Eighth Congress of the PDG, in late July and early August 1968, the president announced the start of a "Socialist Cultural Revolution." Touré also asserted that the revolution had actually begun before independence, with a preparatory "methodological phase" from 1947 to 1957, a "political phase" during the subsequent decade as Guinea secured its independence, and a "cultural phase" launched in 1968.[24] He used this historiographic revision to frame the revolution as both permanent and continually renewed.

Understanding the need for both timelessness and "perpetual motion," Touré described the revolution as "simultaneously a continuous and dynamic process of transformation of the old order into a new order consciously determined by and for the People."[25] His aim was radical social transformation, with older structures of authority replaced by the authority of the party-state. These ideas were modeled closely on Mao's Great Proletarian Cultural Revolution, reflecting Guinea's close ties with China since the late 1950s. In 1959 Guinea became the first sub-Saharan African country to establish diplomatic ties with the PRC, opening the door to cultural and political exchange and economic assistance over the next two decades. But Touré also borrowed revolutionary language and ideas more broadly from Marxist-Leninism, Nkrumah's African nationalism, and classical political philosophy.[26] Not wishing to be overly indebted to others, his greater aim was that the revolution be synonymous with Sékou Touré.

To rid the alleged threat of backwardness, the regime banned political, religious, and social associations that existed outside the state's power, denouncing them as "subversive" tools wielded by imperialist enemies (Touré 1972: 99). It established local party cells, or *pouvoirs révolutionnaires locaux*, in towns throughout the country, and re-imagined schools as *centres d'education révolutionnaire*. Art and culture were particularly in danger of elitism, Touré argued, and needed to be brought back into the revolutionary mandate. Like Mao, he called for a "mass" society, one in which culture belonged to the people.

In practice, of course, the idea of a mass society was meant to eradicate rivals and uplift Touré as the national hero. The hero (*ngana*) occupies an important role in Mande culture, as the figure that bridges the tension between tradition and innovation—breaking from society to pursue his exploits before returning triumphantly home and to glorious praise.[27] For instance, in the epic *Sunjata*, about the founding of the Mande empire in the thirteenth century, Sunjata Keita is the heroic figure who is driven into exile but through battle becomes the leader (*mansa*) of the new empire. Moreover, the figure of the hero as the courageous worker who leads the fight into a utopian future was deployed frequently in socialist art and ideology. In Guinea, Touré mobilized these narratives of the hero—through Mande music and Maoist ideology—to reinforce his personality cult and eliminate his enemies.

It is estimated that Touré's government executed tens of thousands of his compatriots during his regime, while hundreds of thousands fled the country. The regime persecuted anyone perceived as a threat, including writers, intellectuals, students, teachers, businessmen, Fulbe people, members of various other ethnic groups, government officials, and anyone else with any wealth or power. The launch of the revolution provided further cover for this violence as Touré purged the country of "counterrevolutionaries." Thus, in 1969 he arrested his former friend Fodéba Keita, the founder of the Ballets Africains. While Keita had held various ministerial posts in Guinea, Touré increasingly saw him as a rival and a voice outside his control. Keita was accused of instigating the "Kaman-Fodéba Plot"—disseminating subversive material, denigrating the president, and planning a coup d'état against him.[28] Keita was detained for two years and executed in 1971. Ironically, as Minister of Defense and Security, Keita had zealously implemented Touré's program. One of his ministerial acts was to commission Camp Boiro, a notorious prison synonymous with the regime's brutality, and where Keita himself was ultimately imprisoned and killed.

It may seem strange that Keita, a poet and choreographer, was involved in state security and defense, but Touré's concern was always with his ministers' loyalty rather than their qualifications. Touré also shuffled his cabinet frequently to avoid any one individual's accumulating too much power. Between 1958 and his arrest in 1969 Keita thus served as Minister of the Interior and Information, Minister of Defense and Security, and Secretary of State for the Rural Economy.

Moreover, revolutionary music and performance had long been implicated in violence in Touré's Guinea. A key example is the government's demystification program, which from 1961 to 1963 aimed to stamp out traditional and esoteric religious and social practices. The program's particular targets were the country's northwestern coast and southeastern forest region. In a piercing analysis, Mike McGovern argues that these peripheral regions became the "designated national space of Otherness" in Touré's Guinea, serving as examples of backward and primitive cultures against which Guinean modernity could be defined (2013: 43). While the highland and savannah regions of Guinea were dominated by Fulbe and Maninka people, both converts to Islam, the upper coast and the forest region were inhabited by polytheistic groups that had largely retained their spiritual lives, which predated colonialism and Islamic reform movements of the nineteenth and early twentieth centuries. McGovern notes that, by identifying their practices and beliefs as barbaric and antimodern, the state was able to tap into a long-standing image within Guinea of these groups as "savages," offering a mirror against which dominant groups could imagine themselves. Nonetheless, although government bureaucrats conducting demystification missions arrested and tortured spiritual leaders and burned ritual objects, they also recruited the best performers and appropriated the most spectacular dances and objects from these regions into national cultural troupes and representations (ibid.: 441). These dances and objects represented much of the core of the ballets' repertoire. The process of demystification was one of selective violence through which powerful local forces were neutralized, appropriated, and contained within a state-controlled "national" culture.

Jay Straker has provided critical insight into the impact of revolutionary theater on communities in the southeastern forest region. Young people from the region were often taken from their families and home villages and exposed to grueling training and hardships in the name of militant performance. As Straker notes, families at times fled across the border into Liberia to keep their children from being forcibly recruited (2009: 183). Straker also details the sexual exploitation of girls in the system. Young girls and teenagers were taken in the belief that their virginity made them better dancers, and were beaten if they resisted (ibid.). Once recruited, they were made to dance bare-chested for state officials and often forced to have sex with them.

Militant theater tore apart the lives of these young people as well as the social fabric of their home communities.

Through programs such as these, the regime sought social transformation by alienating people from their past loyalties and groups and orienting them toward a future dictated by Touré himself. As Arendt writes, total loyalty to the leader "can be expected only from the completely isolated human being who, without any other social ties to family, friends, comrades, or even mere acquaintances, derives his sense of having a place in the world only from his belonging to a movement, his membership in the party" (1951: 429). Loyalty also has deep roots in Mande cultural ideologies. The paired concepts of *badenya* (mother-childness) and *fadenya* (father-childness) are direct references to relationships in polygamous households, in which children share the same father but not the same mother. More generally, they reference solidarity and loyalty to the group (*badenya*) versus rivalry and competition (*fadenya*) (Hoffman 2000: 33; see also Bird and Kendall 1980; McNaughton 1988; Skinner 2015). Osborn notes that notions of treachery, trust, and rivalry between siblings often appear in Mande narratives (2011: 28). Such cautionary tales warn of the perils of malevolent social relations within a group when fadenya is pushed too far and unity is lost. These dangers of treachery (Mn. *yanfa*) took on new meaning under the revolution, as citizens were warned to be loyal to the state.

While revolutionary music and performance sought to create affective solidarity with the regime, these forms also operated as part of a system in which human beings were systematically isolated from one another. As Straker (2009) notes, the national arts system meant that young people, as well as powerful forms of local knowledge, were continually redirected away from their home areas to the capital, Conakry. Touré also cultivated social isolation and fear by warning citizens to be constantly vigilant to traitors and threats, eroding relations of trust and encouraging spying and informing. By supplanting older associations and networks, the revolution sought an internal reworking of the self, as a movement that "conditions all our way of life, our behavior, our social relations, our relations with nature and penetrates to the very depths of our private life."[29]

Alongside these various technologies of violence and control, the revolution also introduced new and repurposed practices of language, voicing, and naming in Guinea. Touré's personality cult evolved to such a degree that it became obligatory to replicate his very behavior. The use of the color white is a prime example. While Touré initially wore dark European-style business suits, by the mid-1960s he always wore an all-white *duruki-ba* (long, flowing robe, or *grand boubou*) and held a white handkerchief in public. White is associated with purity in Islam, but the color became inextricable from Sékou Touré, with rumors linking his white clothing and accessory with his spiritual powers (Kaké 1987: 177–78).[30] Citizens were expected to dress similarly in homage to the president, a practice that reflects long-standing links between fashion and politics across the continent (Fair 2001: 84–85; Allman 2004: 5; Gilman 2009: 54). The waving of white handkerchiefs also became a revolutionary gesture of loyalty in Guinea that still evokes Touré today.[31]

Such mirroring behavior also extended to speech. As Lansiné Kaba observed, "To make a public speech without quoting the President . . . will impair the speaker's promotion, if not his life" (1976: 212). School children were made to memorize key parts and passages of Touré's writing, which was often reprinted at length in *Horoya*. Kaba notes that it even became obligatory to answer the telephone with the phrase "Prêt pour la révolution"—"Ready for the revolution" (1976: 212). This "enforced ventriloquism" (Thomas 2002: 37) meant that Touré's words filled public life through the mouths of his subjects.

Touré also sought to fill public life with the very sound of his voice. He is still remembered today for giving endless speeches, often lasting hours at a time, while audience members were expected to stand and listen in rapt attention throughout. The historian Ibrahima Baba Kaké writes that Touré's record was an eight- to ten-hour speech to party members in September 1959 (1987: 101). Popular rumor attributed this oratorical ability to supernatural forces and saw it as greater proof of his power (Diawara 1998: 81). The national recording and broadcasting services further enabled his voice to be amplified and heard in recordings that were transmitted throughout the country and beyond. Radio broadcasts filled the air in Conakry, with loudspeakers sometimes set up on the city streets.[32] The president would take to the radio to denounce the latest plot attempt, for instance, such as in the hours after the attempted invasion of 22 November 1970.[33] Television broadcasts frequently showed Touré addressing his party congress in "lengthy 'magisterial' speeches and their translation and commentaries in the three major native languages" (Camara 2005: 110), or, in one famous recording, holding an extended press conference in Paris in 1982. A DVD of his speech in front of François Mitterand during that same visit can still be found for sale in Guinean street markets today. And despite his militant anti-imperialism, his public speech was always in French, a language that could be understood well beyond the boundaries of Maninka ethnicity.

In speeches, Touré used his voice to create tension through rising and falling pitch contours and hard, staccato emphases on syllables. His vocal patterns were also characterized by audible exclamation marks and dramatic pauses, his dynamics often shifting quickly from a low whisper to a torrent of angry shouting. In her work on Mande jeliya, Barbara G. Hoffman notes that local conventions hold that nobles and leaders should not use loud voices (2000: 93). Rather, it is the jeli's role to broadcast the leader's words. As a non-jeli, Touré was subject to these norms, yet technology provided him a means to get around them. The microphone became his mediator, allowing the president to speak directly—and loudly—for himself.[34] His own, distinct voice—his "grave and melodramatic tone of voice" (Camara 2005: 122)—became a familiar feature of the revolutionary soundscape. As Fanon (1965) writes, audio technology materializes revolution through the specter of voice itself.

Political aesthetics in Guinea prize the ability to project one's voice over space and time, building on jeli performance skills of combining "volume with the appropriate content" (Hoffman 2000: 16). Through jeliya, Mande kings and nobles had spokespersons whose role was to relay the leader's name and heroic exploits far and wide. By projecting their voices, jelilu would demand that all within earshot recognize the object of their praise, thus claiming and extending the leader's power. These stories and songs would then be spread by others and across generations, ensuring that the leader would not be forgotten. The leader needs to be spoken and sung about in order for his power to resound and his name to endure. Touré adapted these traditions of naming through revolutionary music and performance, as well as the constant evocation of his name in public life. In addition, he mobilized various technologies of rule to have his voice projected, amplified, broadcast, and reproduced—from the revolutionary exigencies of reproducing his words to the forced attendance at his speeches and their transmission over radio and television.[35] He insisted that his own voice be heard—not just metaphorically but physically—so that it could cover and conquer ground in its wake.

Look to the Past

In August 1968, a few weeks after the launch of the Cultural Revolution, the members of the national dance bands were summoned for a meeting at the headquarters of Touré's party, the PDG. The meeting, chaired by leaders of the PDG's youth wing, was officially described in the party newspaper as a working session to elaborate a new direction for Guinean music.[36] The youth-wing leaders presented the musicians with a three-point proposal. First, the dance-band musicians were told that they must create new pieces based on the directives of the revolution. Secondly, the musicians were required to compose a repertoire of "concert music" for a series of galas in honor of Sékou Touré and his guests. And thirdly, the dance bands were from then on required to perform weekly before party leaders, who would oversee the bands' music. Upon receiving these instructions, the newspaper account reports, the musicians adopted the proposal unanimously.

The state's directives about revolutionary performance were often inconsistent, unclear, and loosely implemented. At times the state attempted to establish objective guidelines for performance, setting out criteria to judge popular music, such as "theme treated, presentation, melody, harmony and execution."[37] Touré claimed that African music was improvisational and adapted continually to the "psycho-social moment." Yet he also wished for music to be "rational" and "scientific" and periodically announced measures to formalize musical practice.[38]

Beginning in the late 1960s the Guinean government mandated that popular music, along with other art forms, demonstrate "revolutionary realism." The term was taken directly from Chinese cultural ideology. Maoist artistic and literary theory had initially borrowed the Soviet notion of socialist realism, but by the late 1950s Mao had adopted the term *revolutionary realism* to suggest a distinct new realism in art that emphasized a march into the future (Meserve and Meserve 1992: 33–34). While Chinese officials defined and elaborated the new term as an artistic and literary method (ibid.: 24–26), such a discussion never took place in Guinea, and the term's meaning was never clearly articulated. Rather, in practice revolutionary realism served as an amorphous catchall phrase to describe total adherence to party ideology and control, a policy of "no objection" (Camara 2005: 64). In music, this directive primarily meant lyrical praise of Touré and the PDG. At the August 1968 meeting, for instance, the national dance bands were told that at the next Quinzaine they "will surely sing about our national agricultural and literacy campaigns." Indeed, songs on these very subjects soon followed.

Musicians did not simply follow these directives blindly, however. Rather, they understood that there was a particular formula of success, which would bring them significant benefits. As the late Mory Sidibé, the trumpeter with Bembeya Jazz and the 22 Band, acknowledged to me, "The revolution only wanted us to sing certain types of pieces. But if we did, the revolution was happy with us." Members of the national dance bands also recall that so long as lyrics followed the party line, they had some leeway to do as they liked.[39] As Marissa Moorman notes in her work on music and politics in Angola, music can still thrive in periods of political violence and repression; indeed, such historical moments may even be remembered for their effervescence and "fun" (2008: 83–84). In Guinea, the revolution represented a moment of explosive creativity and even freedom for many local musicians. They were able to continue using imported electric guitars, brass instruments, and drum kits even while Touré condemned capitalism and the "cultural sabotage" of the West.[40] By 1968 the party had declared that "one fact is definitely settled in Guinea, that music fans only have ears for African hymns, chants, ballads, work and celebration songs and instrumental arrangements drawn from their own national repertoire."[41] Yet musicians with the national dance bands experimented enthusiastically with American popular genres such as jazz and funk. Through the 1970s newer local bands such as Kaloum Star and Camayenne Sofa featured electric organs and guitar wah-wah pedals in their sound, while syncopated funk drumbeats became increasingly common. Although jazz and funk are African American genres whose popularity in Guinea suggests ties across the Black Atlantic, it should be noted that African American music was also expressly used as a tool of soft power by the U.S. government. During the Cold War the United States sent jazz bands and blues musicians to perform in Guinea.[42] As Gayatri Spivak argues, "American expansion would use African-Americans to conquer the African market and the extension of American civilization" (1988: 376). Yet, despite these implications, sounds such as these were sanctioned by the state and promoted through the festivals.

Of course, the "perpetual motion mania" of Touré's Guinea meant that musicians needed to be periodically reminded of their revolutionary duties. At the 1968 PDG meeting a new emphasis was placed on referencing musical traditions: the national dance bands were told to adapt "the great African hymns" for contemporary audiences.[43] The reference here was to jeliya, which evoked the glorious past but also served as a resonant vehicle for presidential praise. Thus, a review in *Horoya* commended the army dance band, the Orchestre de la Garde Republicaine, for its adaptations of the Mande epic "Janjon" and the hunter's song "Kulanjon," reworked in praise of Touré and the PDG. *Horoya* noted that the musicians had successfully "understood that the African concert must depict great African figures and moments of African history alongside the present concerns and the future of our people."[44]

Similarly, the band Kélétigui et ses Tambourinis scored a big hit with its 1968 song "Soundiata," an adaptation of a praise song to the Mande emperor Sunjata Keita. Kélétigui's rival band, Bembeya Jazz, were keenly aware of this success. As the national dance bands jockeyed for popularity and recognition from the regime, Bembeya determined that they were not to be outdone.

Around this time it was announced that the remains of two nineteenth-century Guinean resistance heroes, Samory Touré and Alpha Yaya Diallo, were to be repatriated from Gabon and Mauritania respectively to Guinea.[45] The regime launched a competition for a song to celebrate this event, with the theme of "a dedication to heroes in their resistance struggle against the colonial invader." Bembeya rehearsed assiduously in response and by early October presented a new composition.[46] Touré is reported to have approved the song with the words that it was "not bad," and the song was released to great fanfare (Morel and Keita 2011: 72).

The song in question was "Regard sur le passé" (Look to the Past), released by the national label Syliphone later that year. "Regard sur le passé" signaled a stylistic and textural shift for the dance bands. For one, the orchestration prominently features bala (xylophone) alongside electric guitar and brass instruments. The song begins with a trumpet fanfare played by Achken Kaba and leading into a descending melody on bala that is then elaborated on guitar by Sékou Diabaté. The bala, played by Djeli Sory Kouyaté, then re-enters toward the end of the instrumental introduction and settles into a slow tempo cycle that underpins most of the piece. As Charry observes, the use of bala represents a move away from the Cuban rhythms that until that time had characterized Guinean popular music (2000: 263). Cuban rhythms had been popular in West and Central Africa since the 1930s and were a consistent feature of electric dance music. For many West African musicians Cuban music represented an "alternative modernity" to the Euro-American model, a cosmopolitan reference with roots in Africa (Shain 2002: 84). Guinea maintained close relations with Cuba, while Cuban and Guinean dance bands crossed the Atlantic to perform in each other's country. But, as Mory Sidibé said to me, if you wanted to win in the national festival or even to be well considered, you did not play Cuban music.[47] Although Cuban music remained popular, there was a perceptible shift away from it in the 1960s and 1970s—a shift signaled by "Regard sur le passé" and met with party approval.

"Regard sur le passé" (see fig. 3) is a thirty-four-minute praise piece to a nineteenth-century Guinean resistance hero, the Almamy Samory Touré. Samory, as he is often referred to in Guinea, was the ruler of the Wassoulou empire, which occupied a region in present-day northeastern Guinea and southwestern Mali. The empire existed from 1878 until Samory's defeat and arrest by France in 1898. The song's lyrics detail the life of the Almamy (a West African title for an Islamic leader), extolling his virtues as a ruler and his place in the pantheon of great African figures. By presenting this story, Bembeya depicts a glorious and uniquely Guinean story.

Yet while much of the lyrics sing about the Almany and his *sofa* warriors, the song is also a direct homage to Sékou Touré, who claimed the Almamy as an ancestor. Although the veracity of the claim has been questioned,[48] the song's lyrics take this lineage as a fact, as the last recitative passage illustrates:

FIGURE 3. Bembeya Jazz, "Regard sur le passé," SLP 10a, with a picture of the Almamy Samory Touré on the cover. © Editions Syliphone Conakry

Ils ne sont mort, ces héros	They are not dead, these heroes
Et ils ne mourront pas	And they will not die
Après eux, d'audacieux pionniers reprirent	After them, bold pioneers took up
la lutte de libération nationale qui	the struggle for national liberation that
finalement triompha sous la direction	eventually triumphed under the
	leadership
d'Ahmed Sékou Touré,	of Ahmed Sékou Touré,
petit-fils de ce même Almamy	grandson of that same Almamy
Samory.	Samory.
Le 29 septembre 1958,	On 29 September 1958,
la Révolution triompha,	the Revolution triumphed,
nous vengeant définitivement de	avenging us definitively of
cet autre 29 septembre 1898,	that other 29 September 1898,

date de l'arrestation de l'Empereur	date of the arrest of the Emperor
du Wassoulou,	of Wassoulou,
l'Almamy Samory Touré.	the Almamy Samory Touré.

Following jeli traditions, "Regard sur le passé" glorifies Sékou Touré's genealogy by linking him to an illustrious ancestor, in this case his alleged grandfather. In reinforcing the consanguinity of the president and a legendary warrior, the song reinforces the narrative of Touré as national hero. The link is made not just through bloodlines, but also through a coincidence of dates—Samory Touré's arrest on 29 September 1898 and the revolution's "triumph" on 29 September 1958. This second date refers to Guinea's vote for full independence from France, which actually occurred a day earlier, on 28 September 1958, but is slightly fudged here to reinforce the connection. These links position Touré as the obvious and irreplaceable leader of the new nation, a figure who has rightfully inherited the mantle of leadership. "Regard sur le passé" testifies not just to Guinean exceptionalism, but more specifically to that of Touré himself. To emphasize this connection, Bembeya's singer would kneel with a hand outstretched before Touré during the performance of this passage (Lewin 2011: 11).

Lyrically, the song is divided between sections in Maninka sung by Abubakar Demba Camara and spoken sections recited in French by Sékou "Le Growl" Camara recounting the story of the Almamy. The sung and melodic passages are based on various jeli pieces, including "Kèmè Bourema," a praise song to the Almamy's brother, and "Duga," a song lauding the courage of warriors. This mix of *donkili* (song) and *kuma* (speech) is a common feature in jeli music. What is particularly striking here is that the recitation is in French, despite Touré's stated opposition to European languages. Moreover, the delivery of kuma is typically considered a highly specialized jeli art, as this type of speech is historically authoritative and rests on a high degree of knowledge of genealogy and the past. The speaker in this case, however, is not a jeli and instead was chosen for his command of French (Lee 1988: 68).

In this way, "Regard sur le passé" skillfully interprets revolutionary ideology through music. As the PDG youth leaders told the dance bands the previous summer, the regime wanted "concert music," music intended for listening rather than dancing. "Regard sur le passé" thus replaces Cuban dance rhythms with a slow-tempo beat articulated on the locally distinctive bala. By referencing jeli pieces such as "Kèmè Bourema" and "Duga" within a modernized format, the song represents an innovative reworking of the "great African hymns" of the past. Tradition and modernity are integrated into a piece of epic grandeur and length. Additionally, the song's lyrics conform to the demands of revolutionary realism by elevating Guinea—and Touré—to heroic status. That this occurs here in French as well as Maninka reconciles the conflict between the regime's cosmopolitan and cultural nationalist objectives.

"Regard sur le passé" was hailed by the PDG, reportedly receiving a six-minute standing ovation at its debut performance at the Palais du Peuple (Lee 1988: 68).[49] The song represents a paradigmatic moment of revolutionary music in post-independence Guinea. The regime wanted above all music that promoted the party-state and president and that referenced African and Guinean identity by offering a deeply rooted platform for praise. Yet while many aspects of the song were emulated in its immediate wake, to a great degree it remains a one-off. Even after its success, the national dance bands, including Bembeya Jazz, continued to play primarily dance music in shorter pop formats, although now occasionally with local instruments. The song did presage a shift away from Cuban rhythms in the revolutionary repertoire, but such elements were largely replaced by Congolese *soukous* and influences from Ivorian pop music, as well as by funk rhythms, which by the late 1960s were becoming a new signifier of global black modernity. The major impact of "Regard sur le passé" was its elevation of praise to new heights in popular music.

"Regard sur le passé" is rather seldom spoken of in Guinea today, and even its abbreviated form is rarely played on Guinean radio. It never arose spontaneously during my conversations with Touré-era musicians or music fans. Moreover, Bembeya did not feature it in the band's most famous album, the ten-year anniversary recording *Dix ans de succès*. In large part this omission is because "Regard sur le passé" represents revolutionary realist art meant for political events, rather than the popular *ambiance* music for which Bembeya is most beloved and on which the band continued to focus even after 1968. As a result, the song generates more excitement today among world music fans and academic commentators (including this one) than it does in the Guinean music scene.

Yet the regime's aim in part was precisely to rouse international interest. With its central recitative passages in French, "Regard sur le passé" was intended to spread Touré's praise to listeners overseas. For this reason, the song featured prominently in Guinea's contribution to the 1969 Pan-African Cultural Festival, an event that came to greatly define official narratives of the revolution and its global reach.

Algiers, 1969

The regime developed two key concerns through its rule: ensuring absolute control in Guinea and exporting its ideology beyond its borders. The president sought to establish himself as a pan-African, pan-socialist leader throughout West Africa and well beyond, even as his paranoia rendered the country increasingly isolated. Touré tried unsuccessfully to have the Organization of African Unity (OAU) relocated to Conakry in the 1970s.[50] He also hosted numerous notable African and Afro-diasporic figures, including Miriam Makeba, Stokely Carmichael, Hugh Masekela, and Harry Belafonte. Makeba became a special advisor to him and on his invitation even delivered Guinea's address to the United Nations General Assembly in 1976. Touré actively courted such relationships to cultivate his reputation as a pan-African leader. Indeed, in the 1960s and 1970s he was well-known in African American communities as a face of black liberation. Figure 4 shows a flyer for a Touré tribute event held in 1972 at Harlem's Rockland Palace, here renamed Rockland Palace of the People and showing Touré as Syli, the elephant. The event's name takes one of Touré's favorite slogans: "Prêt pour la révolution!"

Yet his pan-African leadership was not uncontested. In the mid-twentieth century, two strains of cosmopolitan thought shaped the black Francophone world. On the one hand was the political and cultural philosophy of *négritude*, a movement started in 1930s Paris by a group of intellectuals, writers, and students from the French Black Atlantic. Négritude sought to foreground and embrace "blackness" in the face of European racism, colonialism, and domination (Irele 1965: 322). The movement's founders included the Martiniquean poet Aimé Césaire and the poet and future Senegalese president Léopold Senghor. Their aim was to accept and examine the black condition as a means of redressing the colonial project of cultural assimilation and erasure. While Césaire and some of his fellow writers from the Caribbean were more explicitly political in their aims, Senghor and others from Senegal focused more particularly on exploring and defining the parameters of relations between Africa and Europe (Harney 2004: 32−33).

In contrast to négritude, a more militant ideology emerged by the 1960s, championed by African leaders such as the Guinea-Bissauan nationalist Amílcar Cabral, the Beninese writer and politician Stanislas Spero Adotevi, and Guinea's Sékou Touré. These and other figures promoted African and third-world liberation in revolutionary terms, calling for the total overthrow of colonial political and cultural domination. While Senegal's Senghor maintained close relations with France and emphasized the fraternity of a "Universal Civilization," militant African nationalists denounced these ideas as

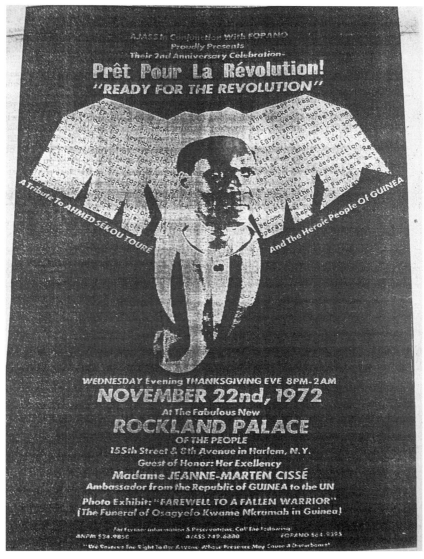

FIGURE 4. Flyer for "A Tribute to Ahmed Sékou Touré and the Heroic People of Guinea," reprinted in *Horoya*, 16 November 1972

neoimperialist and ensuring continued African subjugation at the hands of Europe. For proponents of both Senghorian *négritude* and militant African nationalism, however, culture and art were inextricably linked to politics. In this regard, two cultural festivals were held in the 1960s that defined the argument between these schools of thought (Dave 2009).

In 1966 Senghor hosted the First World Festival of Negro Arts, in Dakar. The festival was an affirmation of négritude and of Senegal's ongoing
relationship with France. At the opening ceremony, for example, one commentator noted that a young African artist threw open his "handsome tribal
robe" to reveal a Western shirt and tie underneath, while asserting to the
applauding audience, "I am African—but I come to you by way of Europe"
(Povey 1966: 104). This gesture illustrates the balance that Senghor sought to
achieve, culturally and ideologically. Yet it was precisely this inclusivity that
angered Touré and other militant African nationalists.

At the 1968 meeting of the OAU, it was decided that a pan-African cultural
festival would be held the following year. The First Pan-African Cultural Festival took place in Algiers in July 1969 and featured delegates and artists from
within the continent. In contrast to the Dakar festival, Algiers expounded
a Marxist, anti-imperialist view of African culture that was directly at odds
with the Senghorian view. The festival's cultural manifesto declares: "An imposed culture generally bred a type of African intellectual not at home in his
national realities because of his depersonalisation and alienation. The African
man of culture, the artist, the intellectual in general must integrate himself
into his people. . . . His action must inspire that radical transformation of the
mind without which it is impossible for a people to overcome its economic
and social underdevelopment."[51]

As one observer noted, in the charge against Senghor's négritude, "Guinea
led the attack" (Lindfors 1970: 5). Neither Touré nor Senghor personally attended the Algiers festival, but both leaders addressed the plenary session
through prerecorded speeches. While Senghor defended négritude as the best
hope for African progress and unity, Touré used his address to mount a forty-
minute attack on Senghor's ideas.[52] Some other Francophone delegates saw
Touré's attack as "too personal" and chose to focus on the concept rather than
the man behind it (ibid.). For Touré and the Guinean delegation, however,
their target was clear, and their addresses to the assembly were "an obvious
slap at the thinking of President Léopold Senghor" (ibid.).

In personalizing the criticisms of négritude, Touré sought to elevate himself as the true leader of Francophone West Africa. Beyond his own recorded
speech, Guinea's artistic and political representatives were charged not only
with showcasing the country's culture but with exporting Touré's personality cult to an international audience. The ethnomusicologist Gerhard Kubik,
who attended the Algiers festival, dismissively observed that "the delegation
of Guinée did nothing but carry huge pictures of Sékou Touré," as shown in
figure 5.[53] Musically, performance of the song "Regard sur le passé" served a
similar purpose. As a direct homage to Touré, with long recitative sections

FIGURE 5. Members of the Guinean delegation at the Pan-African Cultural Festival carrying pictures of Touré; photograph by Gerhard Kubik, reproduced courtesy of the International Library of African Music.

delivered in French, the song was a perfect vehicle for disseminating praise for Touré beyond Guinea.

Initially Bembeya Jazz was appointed to represent Guinea in the category of "modern music" at Algiers.[54] But Touré continually sought to diffuse the power of particular groups and individuals, and Kélétigui Traoré, the bandleader of Kélétigui et ses Tambourinis, was designated as *chef d'orchestre*. A number of musicians from the other dance bands were also added to the group, including the saxophonist Momo "Wandel" Soumah, the trombonist Pivi Moriba, and the singer Manfila Kanté. In its final line-up the band was reconstituted as the Syli National Orchestra, which was often appointed at such key performances in order to deflect attention from any particular group as the national favorite.

Bembeya's lead guitarist, Sékou Diabaté (a.k.a. Sékou Bembeya), was only twenty-four years old at the time, but he still remembers the band's feeling of excitement over representing Guinea at the Algiers festival. "We were there to show the revolution to the world," he recalls, "and all the other countries wanted to hear our music."[55] Guinea certainly had an impressive presence at the festival, with three hundred artists and delegates attending, including dancers, musicians, stage actors, and intellectuals. Guinea's contributions included four documentaries by the national Syli-Cinéma praising Touré's programs; a play by the national theater, *Et la nuit s'illumine* (And Night Turns to Day), on the last days of colonial rule; and the national choral and instrumental ensemble, led by the beloved jeli Sory Kandia Kouyaté. The exhibition hall also featured a stand with Touré's publications, while Syliphone issued a special-edition box set including an LP of his revolutionary poems and an LP of "Regard sur le passé."[56] Sékou Bembeya told me that English-, Arabic-, and Spanish-language versions of the central recitative text were also recorded so that the song's message could be understood well beyond Guinea.

The Syli National Orchestra's concert took place in the festival's main concert hall. On the day of the performance, fifteen musicians appeared on stage, dressed in black tie. Their set included a number of popular dance songs, including Balla et ses Balladin's "Sara" and Bembeya's "OUA," a song written in homage to the OAU (using the initials for the group's French name, l'Organisation de l'Unité Africaine). The centerpiece of the performance was an abbreviated version of "Regard sur le passé," as recommended by the PDG itself. Despite Kubik's observation, this performance was received enthusiastically, with the band winning a silver medal in their category. (*Horoya* was quick to observe that the gold medal was awarded to Algeria's own national philharmonic.) Guinea's other contributions were also well received, and the country won the festival's overall grand prize for its artistic contributions. This victory represented a triumph for Touré, who saw the award as a vindication of his ideology and rule. *Horoya* broadcast the point that the Algiers festival came on the revolution's first anniversary, thus affirming its righteousness. And for Touré the victory was particularly sweet for having occurred on an international stage and within the context of a heated debate with Senghor.

The Algiers festival was quickly woven into the narrative of Guinean exceptionalism and was—and still is—cited by the authorities as proof of its cultural and ideological superiority. Yet this victory was not attributed to Guinean artists and musicians. Rather, as one of Touré's ministers said to the party youth wing in 1970, it was a victory for the people, for Guinean youth: "The people of Guinea in particular won at Algiers by fighting imperialism on its favorite terrain: the terrain of Culture. At that meeting, the youth of Guinea proved that our way of cultural development, our mass direction, therefore of total development is historically just and objectively valid for all African people."[57] Yet for the musicians themselves, the Pan-African Cultural Festival represented a shining moment in their careers, as they gained recognition on a prestigious stage. In Sékou Bembeya's telling it was the band that triumphed, rather than the country or the revolution. For him and other musicians, the festival was above all a creative and artistic victory, one attesting to their place as modern, global artists. While the delegates debated liberation and anticolonialism, the musicians basked in the chance to sing, show off, perform, and play.

Pleasure and Pain

In the official eye, "Regard sur le passé" represented an apogee of revolutionary music, intended for focused listening to presidential praise. Yet despite party approval for the song, the national dance bands continued primarily performing dance music—and the government did not stop them. The regime commanded new directives for aesthetic and political control of music in August 1968, but this control was loosely implemented, and music carried on evolving in various directions. McGovern observes that, in Touré's Guinea, the state did not represent a monolithic force but rather was composed of various competing agencies, ministries, and institutions, each with its own policy interpretations and ideas. Yet despite being weak, it managed to create an *effect* that "many Guineans experienced as a coherent national identity organized by a strong state" (2013: 43). Revolutionary ideology looked to the past and the future, to youths and their elders, to scientific socialism and Islam, to modernity and tradition. Popular music was able to navigate these contradictions between old and new, past and future, pleasure and fear. Despite the emphasis on a march to the future, history lives in the present in Guinea, as ancestors and memories shape contemporary life and epic tales are discussed as current events. Revolutionary music evoked both, conjuring optimism and energy with its bright sounds and rhythms and referencing centuries-old narratives and knowledge. While musicians faithfully sang of Sékou Touré and the exigencies of his revolution, their melodies evoked pride in collective and cultural endurance and pleasure in self-recognition—being here and now, being in the world, being young and modern.

Musicians pushed back against the strictures of the revolution in many ways, experimenting with genre and style across political boundaries, cultivating individual personas and fan bases through their showmanship while occasionally ignoring government directives. But they cannot be said to have dissented. As Touré set out in a 1970 speech at the national arts festivals, the dance bands were to be judged first and foremost on their lyrical message. Praise was an essential component of state-sponsored art. Dissent of any kind was impermissible, representing crimes of the highest degree. In this context, musicians largely complied.

How real was the threat of violence facing musicians, and the population at large? As Martha Nussbaum notes, "In every society, rhetoric and policies work on ideas of what is dangerous, making danger salient where it really exists, but also constructing the perception of danger where it does not" (2013: 322). In Touré's Guinea, violence was real, but the main technology of rule involved the perception of danger. The regime fostered a climate of paranoia and secrecy in which neighbors were recruited to spy on each other, suspected traitors were arrested at night and detained in secret locations, and governmental action and accountability were cloaked behind the facade of the revolution.

By the late 1970s Touré, fearing plots against him, had become increasingly xenophobic, and Guinea cut off ties with other countries, becoming isolated and inward-looking. As a result, the country came to be defined by an atmosphere of guardedness, caution, and quiet, of strategic and meaningful silence, as people learned to keep the violence of the revolution a public secret. As Kaba wrote, "Most of those who had the ability to criticise [the regime] have been physically eliminated or imprisoned, and this has created a deep sense of insecurity among those who are still living, and has taught them to be prudent" (1976: 217–18).

This guardedness was in part an act of censorship enforced by the state. Critical Guinean writers such as Djibril Tamsir Niane and Laye Camara were either imprisoned or forced into exile, for instance, while all their works were banned. Yet, silence under Touré's revolution was also self-regulated. Cultural aesthetics in Guinea have long valued discretion and concealment, as illustrated by the Maninka proverb *Kuma tɛ kunan keba min kɔnɔ, ko tɛ diya wo la*: "An intelligent man keeps the words inside him" (a man whose stomach cannot suppress words will never succeed at anything). Under the revolution, these values gained new urgency as many Guinean people saw the importance of keeping quiet. Miriam Makeba observed that "as for challenging the president or offering criticism about anything, I never see a display of courage as great as this" (1987: 214).

There are strikingly few reports of artists (outside of literary figures) or musicians who dissented. Certain members of the Ballets Africains defected during their overseas tours. The guitarist Kerfala "Papa" Diabaté left Guinea for Abidjan in the 1960s for political reasons (Charry 2000: 254), while the kora player Jali Musa Jawara, the guitarist Manfila Kanté, and the singer Fodé Conté also left the country.[58] But almost no musicians in Conakry publicly criticized the regime or expressed opposition through song.[59] Rather, musicians were keenly aware of the potential rewards of state sponsorship and the dangers of angering Touré. The jeli M'Bady Kouyaté described for me the moment when state officials came to his village in northwestern Guinea to recruit him for national performance and bring him to Conakry. His mother, knowing only that Touré wanted to see her son, threw herself on the ground and broke down sobbing in fear for his life. The percussionist Papa Kouyaté similarly recounted that when he was first recruited as a state-sponsored musician, officials from the regime came to his house to tell him that Touré had summoned him. Not knowing the reason for the meeting, Kouyaté recalled that he was so terrified he could barely dress himself and arrived at the president's residence wearing two pairs of trousers, one on top of the other, before realizing his mistake.

Yet once recruited—as an accompanist for Miriam Makeba—Papa Kouyaté saw the benefits of state patronage. He and others recall that the regime paid for instruments for all the national bands and ensembles, that musicians were state employees and received regular salaries, and that many also received housing and monthly supplies of rice, fish, and cooking oil. It is understandable that such financial security would not be taken lightly. Furthermore, with jeli music as the model, the notion of performing praise in exchange for patronage had a deep historical precedent. Aesthetics and practices of guardedness further meant that it was "prudent" to keep one's criticism to oneself, as Kaba notes. The phrase "Yanfa man nyi" (treachery is not good) was commonly heard, from song lyrics to speech—an exhortation to keeping quiet. This stance was true not just for musicians, but for the population at large, although historical practices and aesthetics create particular discretion in music. If one wished to speak, the safest way to express oneself, whether one was a cabinet minister or a market trader, was to quote the president. Political silence in Touré's Guinea was filled with words, albeit words that were carefully chosen for their guardedness.

But what about the spaces in between these words? Much of the literature on African music describes metaphorical critiques in song, detailing the ways in which seemingly innocuous words can in fact be oppositional. Scholars have written of the use of humor, satire, and metaphors of love as veils for political attacks (Vail and White 1997; Olaniyan 2004; White 2008). In Touré's Guinea, the use of metaphor was also a common feature of popular music, but such devices did not necessarily constitute oppositional messages. For instance, Bembeya Jazz's song "Waraba" is an adaptation of a hunter's song about a lion. The lion in this case, however, is Sékou Touré.

Alongside prudent quietness and the perception of danger, the revolution also saw an expansion of public pleasure, as new sounds, new practices, and new spaces created opportunities for collectivity and effervescence. In particular, urban youth could experience new forms of modernity, night life, and cosmopolitanism. To some extent this revolution was the same as that of young people everywhere—rejecting old norms in favor of new. *Bardancings* provided a space for the erotic pleasures of couples holding each other tightly as they moved to the music, although the clothes, styles, and electrified sounds of the scene rocked older sensibilities. These opportunities were far more widely available to men than to women, as bars and night-clubs, being associated with alcohol and prostitution, were taboo for women (Durán 2000: 141). With its links to night life and social innovation, revolutionary music was greatly dominated by men. Exceptions included idiosyncratic women such as Makeba, and the all-female group Les Amazones de Guinée, a group founded and managed by a man, Fodéba Keita, who hand-selected women from the ranks of the *gendarmerie.* As Moorman notes of the Angolan case, musicians "produced a sense of nation . . . but they often did so in gendered terms" linked to male dominance and prestige in public life (2008: 87).[60]

Through experiences of listening, however, music of the revolution also allowed Guinean citizens more generally to be named and recognized—beyond the president, to hear their collective name broadcast widely and to feel at moments that the world was listening. The new practices of naming through revolutionary pop created pride in evocations both of a storied history and of the present. These pleasures for musicians themselves included the pleasures of showmanship, competition, creativity, and certain degrees of freedom. As other commentators on musical nationalism across Africa have noted, artists participated for many reasons beyond support for political agendas, including professional opportunities and the affirmation of older practices (Askew 2002: 199; White 2008: 228). Moreover, they felt great personal satisfaction in being called on to perform for the state (Gilman 2009: 72; Skinner 2015: 49). Musicians were able to carve out their own fame, glory, and fulfillment within an ideology of collectivism. Bembeya Jazz wrote praise songs to itself, such as "Bembeya," which celebrates the group as both "national and international" stars, and "Petit Sékou," an instrumental tune showcasing the talents of its young lead guitarist, Sékou Bembeya. As Salifou Kaba, one of the group's singers, says, songs such as these were advertisements for Bembeya Jazz in a competitive environment, as the dance bands tried to outdo each other to win over audiences and attract new fans.[61] Although Touré proclaimed that revolutionary art was made by the people, the dance bands expressed their own artistic agency as musicians with identities and objectives beyond the revolution. They remember their success at the Algiers festival not as a national or revolutionary success, but rather as an acknowledgment of their modernity, an affirmation of their inclusion in global culture. Touré knowingly overlooked such occasional intransigence because he needed musicians to bolster Guineans and broadcast his name. And in return for accommodating the regime, musicians were allowed to build careers, travel, perform, and create. In this, they acted knowingly—well aware of the regime's violence and brutality, but also of the spaces of pleasure and play that could be built within it.

Writing of ideology in late capitalist societies, Terry Eagleton argues that "there is no reason to assume that [the] political docility [of the exploited] signals some gullible, full-blooded adherence to the doctrines of their superiors. It may signal rather a coolly realistic sense that political militancy . . . might be perilous and ill-advised" (1991: 36). In Touré's Guinea, musicians and others took such a "coolly realistic" assessment of the situation and decided to act accordingly. Whether they did in fact revere Touré is impossible to tell, in light of the continuing opacity with which such topics are addressed. Members of the dance bands retain extraordinary loyalty to the former president to this day, an issue that I will address in the next chapter.

By the early 1980s, however, the system of revolutionary music and performance had largely collapsed. Economic decline, isolation, and the president's poor health made the system untenable as Touré faced increasing opposition at home and irrelevance elsewhere. An uprising in 1977 had greatly shaken the foundations of the regime when market women angrily protested food rationing and the unavailability of rice, Guinea's staple food (Kaké 1987: 182–83). The protests turned violent, and Touré countered with his familiar strategy of blaming them on outside forces (Pauthier 2010: 71). This tactic enraged the women present, who publicly denounced the president while shouting en masse, "Your handkerchief has become black!" (Kaké 1987: 185–86). This brazen mockery of Touré and his claims to power reportedly shook the president, who had never been faced with such direct dissent (ibid.). The regime responded with more violence, arrests, detention, and torture, but it never really fully recovered.

In 1983, a year before his death, Touré convened all the national dance bands to a meeting at the Palais du Peuple. Thanking them for their service, he granted the bands their autonomy. Each dance band was given a final payment and ownership of a Conakry nightclub so that it could continue performing privately. The following year Touré died in the United States during a medical evacuation. A coup d'état quickly followed in which the army lieutenant Lansana Conté seized power, and Guinea set course on another generation of authoritarian rule.

Yet Touré's revolution was the ever-present counterpoint to Conté's regime, and to successive regimes since. Exploring the key foundational moment of Touré's revolution allows us to understand the ongoing interaction between authoritarianism and music, politics and pleasure in contemporary Guinea, a subject I will explore throughout the rest of this book. As the next chapter shows, events following a military coup d'état in December 2008 set the historical moment of the revolution in play once again.

2

City of Musicians

In May 2009 the African Union (formerly the OAU) organized the Second Pan-African Cultural Festival, in Algiers. The timing of this festival was fortuitous for a new military junta that had recently seized power in Guinea. Exactly forty years after Guinea's victory in the 1969 festival, the new Guinean government was keen to evoke this episode in its bid to legitimize its rule and weave itself into the national story. The junta promoted the 2009 Algiers festival within its larger attempt to revive the sounds and perceived successes of Touré's revolution. Yet, such attempts were a simulacrum of an earlier historical moment, a moment that is increasingly contested today.

In this chapter I examine the afterlife of revolutionary music in Guinea, considering what music reveals about "the continuity of its subsequent history" (Treitler 1989: 74). The revolution continues to reverberate in Guinean public life today, even though its power structures had crumbled by the time of Touré's death in 1984. A recently painted mural in central Conakry, for instance, shows Sékou Touré alongside other pan-African heroes such as Thomas Sankara and Kwame Nkrumah. Yet concurrent with such official commemoration, public memories of the revolution are also being challenged and reshaped today, and an unprecedented debate has emerged over Touré's legacy. In private conversations and public forums, Guineans air conflicting views about the former dictator. Musicians from the revolutionary dance bands are largely absent from this debate, however. Despite the changing landscape, these musicians often continue to look to the past, both aesthetically and ideologically; "I am nostalgic," at least one of them told me directly.[1] As commentators remind us, nostalgia exists in many forms, sometimes reifying the past and sometimes "redeeming" parts of it in a self-conscious construction of culture (Stewart 1988). For Touré-era musicians, their adherence to past sounds and ideals is not passive complacency, but an active choice made in response to organized mobilizations of memory and past pleasures.

Since 1984 successive governments in Guinea have strategically turned to the symbols of the revolution, and in particular the music of the Touré-era dance bands, as fixed reference points of national pride. Revolutionary dance music continues to capture the official imagination as a means to mobilize public sentiment and solidarity and to bolster state credibility through evoking a shared sense of identity. The military regime in 2009 thus promised to revive these bands and the moment they represent. These attempts at a revival also come occasionally from private companies and individuals, such as international record labels and expatriate bar owners. Together these various actors frame bands such as Bembeya Jazz as emblematic of a glorious if faded legacy, but this representation largely ignores the politics of the revolution. Musicians from the Touré-era dance bands have responded strategically to these new opportunities, aware of their ephemerality, at times cautiously optimistic about new possibilities, at other times simply playing along. Their music still evokes certain public pleasures in Guinea, yet the pleasures for these musicians themselves today are less clear. Under the revolution, looking to the past was a future-oriented act. For musicians, it contained the pleasure of possibility and opportunity—of being here and now, in the world, and in the moment. Today these evocations of the past are simply that. And as some musicians wonder, what future, if any, do they promise now?

Modernity's Afterlife

By the time of Sékou Touré's death in 1984, the fortunes of the national dance bands were greatly in decline. With state support cut off and no real domestic recording industry to replace it, over the next generation these groups largely stagnated. The country's next president, Lansana Conté, quickly distanced himself from the symbols of the revolution. He pursued market reforms promoted by the International Monetary Fund and the European Economic Community and privatized Guinean art, definitively ending the era of musical nationalism. Nonetheless, the dance bands continued to exist, although they lost their official status. Over the course of his regime, Conté (who later promoted himself to the rank of army general) softened his initial antirevolution stance and came increasingly to reference revolutionary music and culture.[2] The bands themselves attempted to pursue careers in the privatized and precarious music scene. At the time of Conté's death in 2008, six of the great revolutionary bands were to varying degrees all still active in Conakry:

Bembeya Jazz, Kélétigui et ses Tambourinis, and Balla et ses Balladins, as well
as Horoya Band, the all-female Amazones de Guinée, and the 22 Band (formerly the 22 Novembre Band).

While their music can still be heard in Guinea today, a scroll through the
local radio dial shows that it occupies a shrinking place. Since the lifting of
a ban against private stations in 2006, at least two dozen new outlets have
emerged, showcasing a wide range of styles that can be overheard in street
markets and neighborhood bars, from taxicabs and hand-held transistor sets.
The national RTG programming still plays a good deal of Touré-era music.
But for most listeners, revolutionary dance music is only one of many genres
on the airwaves. Similarly, recordings from the 1960s and 1970s are still sold
in Guinean markets but are often crowded out by more recent hits. Bob's, the
bar with which I opened this book, was one of the only venues where I heard
old recordings played.

The best way to experience this music today is through live performances
at La Paillote, the Touré-era venue that remains the spiritual home of Guinea's
aging revolutionary musicians. Located in Conakry's Cameroun neighborhood, La Paillote consists of a large open-air courtyard dominated by a huge
mango tree, with a bar on one side and an enclosed performance venue on the
other. The area immediately surrounding it is known as the Cité des Musiciens,
and it is where many Touré-era performers were provided housing during the
revolution. Walking through the Cité you might pass the house of the late
trumpeter Mory Sidibé, formerly with Bembeya Jazz, and the renowned percussionist Papa Kouyaté. Around the corner from them is the house of Sékou
Diabaté (a.k.a. Sékou Bembeya, or "Diamond Fingers"), the lead guitarist
and *chef d'orchestre* of Bembeya Jazz, while Laye Dioubaté, the bass player
of 22 Band, lives just behind him. During the day, these and other musicians
gather at La Paillote to drink small cups of Nescafé or cold bottles of beer, play
checkers, rehearse, and talk. On Saturday evenings a mostly older crowd gath-
ers at the venue to dance to live performances by groups featuring different
permutations of the dance-band musicians, or to hear well-known jeli stars.
Most young people that I know, on the other hand, rarely drop in.

Musical change inevitably happens everywhere, and pop music audiences
can be notoriously fickle, captivated by the constant thrill of the new. Yet such
change creates confusion for former revolutionary artists, who once embod-
ied nationalist and future-oriented aspirations. They tell a common "narrative of professional crisis" that is also couched in terms of postnationalist and
postrevolutionary crisis (Skinner 2015: 49). As Moorman notes, musicians
contrast the ways in which they were valued and celebrated in the past with
"the ignominy and poverty they experience today" (2008: 97). On many long

afternoons I have spent at La Paillote, the conversation reflected these feelings of self-sacrifice, a sense that these musicians served the nation for more than two decades before being unceremoniously abandoned.

"Sékou's death changed everything," Mory Sidibé declared to me one day, airing a common view at La Paillote. "Art was completely trampled and . . . the new regime washed its hands of us." Like most of his contemporaries, Mory blamed the government of Lansana Conté, lamenting that under him, "for twenty-four years, culture was dead in Guinea."[3] I knew that the music scene in Conakry, although underfunded, was alive and well, with many exciting newer groups and genres gaining national and international popularity. Yet I understood that from the perspective of the Touré-era musicians, the particular model of culture they knew had been dismantled. La Paillote serves as a refuge to them now, as they wonder where they fit in and how they should navigate the new marketplace. Yet as regimes rise and fall in Guinea, they and their music are once again, predictably, called on in service of the state.

"Armée guinéenne"

On 23 December 2008, hours after the death of President Conté, a group of junior army officers seized control of the country, much as Conté himself had done a generation earlier. The move did not come as a great surprise to Guineans or to international observers, but the atmosphere was tense.[4] Branding themselves as the Conseil National pour la Démocratie et le Développement (CNDD), the new military junta quickly sought to dispel uncertainty by taking over government apparatus in a series of familiar moves: closing the airport and national borders, setting up roadblocks on major roads, and shutting down all radio and television broadcasts. In their place, the RTG played on a continuous loop a recording of the 1968 Bembeya Jazz song "Armée guinéenne" (Guinean Army).

The CNDD's choice of song was both inspired and obvious. Released shortly after Touré officially launched his cultural revolution, "Armée guinéenne" is based on the classic jeli piece "Duga." To those familiar with Mande music, "Duga" is instantly recognizable for its basic melodic structure, a repeating four-bar cycle. Figure 6 shows transcriptions of two versions of "Duga": the first is a flute melody from a 1961 recording by the Ensemble Instrumental de Guinée, and the second is a bala line from Bembeya's "Regard sur le passé," part 2, which turns to "Duga" at 12:46. The third is a variation of the same melody played on rhythm guitar in "Armée guinéenne."

Bembeya Jazz's version in "Armée guinéenne" slightly varies the basic

FIGURES 6A, 6B, AND 6C. Variations on "Duga"
6A. "Duga," Ensemble Instrumental de Guinée, 1961

6B. "Regard sur le passé," Bembeya Jazz National, 1969

6C. "Armée guinéenne," Bembeya Jazz National, 1968

melodic contour and rhythm, and adopts more of a pop format than its predecessors. The song begins with a solo by Sékou "Bembeya" Diabaté, a fast,
descending guitar melody that culminates in the band's characteristic wall of
brass instruments. Such ornamentation, known locally as *birimintingo*, is a
distinctive feature of instrumental jeliya, reflecting an influence from Islamic
music (Charry 2000: 168).[5] Here this line is played on electric guitar rather
than on a jeli instrument such as bala or *kora* (harp). Furthermore, the melodic pattern is used to mark a clear introduction to the song. The Ensemble
Instrumental de Guinée version of "Duga," in contrast, has no clearly defined
beginning, middle, or end, reflecting a cyclical music that has no fixed length
and that fades in and out. "Armée guinéenne," on the other hand, is clearly
structured, with a solo introduction, a chorus-verse-chorus form, and an instrumental bridge in the middle. In addition to this change, the rhythm guitar
in "Armée guinéenne" is slightly syncopated, as shown in the transcription,
lending a sense of freshness and excitement to the stately mood of "Duga."

A further change from "Duga" can be found in the lyrics sung by lead
singer, Demba Camara.[6] *Duga* means "vulture" in Maninka, a metaphor
for the patience and courage of hunters and warriors.[7] Although there are
many versions of the song, the original is said to have been composed by
Balla Fasèkè Kouyaté, the jeli of the Mande emperor Sunjata Keita, on the
eve of the great battle of Kirina, in which Sunjata went on to defeat his rival,
the Soso king Soumaoro Kanté (Kouyaté 2012: 70). The song is an homage
to warriors more generally, representing masculinity and military strength
(Diawara 1998: 90–92).

Building on these themes, the lyrics in Bembeya's song are adapted to pay homage to Touré's "revolutionary army," thus transforming "Duga" into direct praise of the regime:

Ah l'Armée guinéenne	Ah the Guinean army
Fabara makara ni kɛyə tɛ kɔrɔbɔlɔ	The fatherland's protection will not be exposed
Oh milisi guinéen	Oh the Guinean militia
Fabara makara ni kɛyə tɛ kɔrɔbɔlɔ	The fatherland's protection will not be exposed
Bureau politiki national ani gouvernement	The National Political Bureau and the government
La Guinée jamanadennu bɛ yɛ duba la i yɛ	The children of the Guinean nation bless you
L'armée nin tɛ mɔɔ kɛlɛ kwi telen ni	This army will not battle people who are just
L'armée nin tɛ mɔɔ kɛlɛ jɔnmaya	This army will not battle people with insult

"Armée Guineenne" was a huge hit in the 1960s and became something of an anthem, heard more frequently and acquiring more saliency than the official national hymn. By using the song, the CNDD sought to appropriate both its direct lyrical message praising the army and a general sense of optimism and pride that it evoked through memories of the revolution. Throughout the early months of 2009, the song featured heavily in CNDD efforts to allay public fears and represent the armed forces as advocates and defenders of the people. In one such tactic, during the spring and summer of 2009 a promotional video for the CNDD aired nightly between programs on the national television station. The ad featured images of CNDD soldiers in military fatigues and combat boots marching in the national stadium, and of the new president, Moussa Dadis Camara (known locally as Dadis), in his signature red beret and sunglasses saluting the troops, while "Armée guinéenne" provided the soundtrack.

I also heard the song in a number of spontaneous instances that year. One summer night while driving through Conakry with a group of musicians, we arrived at a military roadblock at the 8 Novembre bridge. True to form, the waiting soldiers pulled us over and demanded to see our identity documents and other paperwork. As I tried to sit as inconspicuously as possible in the back of my seat, the driver of the car began to cajole the soldier to let us go, telling him that we were all artists who were just returning from a performance. The soldier seemed unimpressed and continued to demand our paperwork, when suddenly the three musicians in the back seat all began singing "Armée guinéenne" in unison, laughing and persuading through song. The soldier stepped back and waved us on.

For the CNDD itself, its own use of "Armée guinéenne" was planned and

strategic, heralding a larger project of evoking Touré's cultural nationalism as
the new regime tried to generate optimism and national pride. Public pleasure was to be mobilized through both aesthetic and bureaucratic instruments. In early May 2009 the junta announced the creation of a new Ministry
of Information and Culture to replace the former Ministry of Culture under
the Conté administration. For Touré-era musicians, this change was met with
cautious optimism. A number of former musicians and cultural adminis-
trators from the revolution were appointed to high-level posts in the new
ministry. The minister himself, Justin Morel Junior, had previously been the
manager of the Touré-era band Camayenne Sofa. The new National Director of Culture, Jean-Baptiste Williams, was formerly the guitarist for Camayenne Sofa, while the newly appointed Director of the National Museum, Riad
Challoub, had been the same group's lead singer.

In addition, the new ministry announced early on a series of initiatives
aimed at reasserting state involvement in the arts. In late May, for example,
the Director of Culture, Jean-Baptiste Williams, spoke on the national radio
station about the CNDD's representing a "new era" in Guinean culture. In his
words, there was an urgent need for the "restoration of the state's authority"
in cultural affairs: "The authority exists. [The percussionist] Papa Kouyaté
and other artists must be aware that the state exists. . . . After long years of
rupture from 1984 to today, we're now reaffirming culture as a primary value.
The rebirth of Guinean culture is our cause. President Dadis has come and
he's recognized men of culture and the media."[8] Williams's radio appearance
was intended to signal a shift in tone in Guinean cultural politics, marking a
departure from the liberal policies of the Conté era and a return to the revolution's program. His language here directly references Touré-era discourse
on African modernity, citing a revitalization of a dormant, primordial culture. This statement was followed in subsequent days and weeks by the announcement of a number of proposed new programs, all closely resembling
those of the revolution. They included the organization of a new National
Cultural Festival and the creation of a national record label, Sonogui, to replace the long-defunct Syliphone.

At La Paillote, these announcements were met with some enthusiasm and
energy. "We must give these young soldiers their chance," Mory Sidibé said
to me as we chatted outside his house one day. Sékou Bembeya expressed
some guarded optimism with respect to the new regime, saying that former
president Conté had not been "a man of culture"—a line I often heard from
other musicians, one that distinguished Conté from the music-loving Sékou
Touré. Many at La Paillote felt that Guinean art had died on Lansana Conté's
watch. It was time, everyone agreed, for a change.

A week after Williams's radio appearance on the RTG, the new ministry held a formal event in early June to mark the "Official Launch of Artistic and Cultural Organisation in Conakry." The evening was a glittering affair, held at Bembeya Jazz's former venue, Club Bembeya, which is now a private nightclub. In attendance were well-dressed and high-ranking government officials and their wives, Touré-era musicians, and other VIPs. I was lucky enough to secure an invitation through one of the musicians and sat in the upstairs balcony watching the proceedings with interest.

The evening itself began with speeches by ministry officials, who spoke of their plans to renew culture in Guinea. As Minister Morel told the seated audience, "Guinean music has had a precipitous decline since 1984. But the talent is there, and the memories of the past are there." To underscore this last point, Bembeya Jazz then took the stage. As the group was announced to great cheering and applause, twelve musicians appeared, all sporting black dinner jackets and ranging in age from the white-haired trumpeter Achken Kaba to the young singer Mamadi Diabaté. The group began their set with the eponymous single "Bembeya," announcing their presence and claiming their name within the possibility of this new moment. Having demanded their recognition, they then launched into a rendition of "Armée guinéenne."

Although the evening as a whole felt like a largely civilian affair, with more suits than military fatigues visible, the act of performing "Armée guinéenne" at this particular event was a direct overture to the army, a statement of readiness and expectations. In return, the seated audience embraced the gesture. As the familiar opening strains of Sékou Bembeya's guitar solo rang out, spectators around me murmured their approval, while a number of government officials ostentatiously removed bundles of folded Guinean francs from their pockets and wallets. Throughout the song a steady stream of officials stood up to tip the musicians for the appropriateness of their performance. The singers in turn moved forward to greet each approaching dignitary, interrupting their dance routine with nods and bows. To my surprise, there was no audience dancing or more general overflow of joy; instead, the majority of spectators remained in their chairs, respectfully observing the duet between the musicians and their patrons.[9] Bembeya Jazz appeared to seal an agreement with the new CNDD government, both agreeing to name and recognize each other.

The younger musicians were elated at the end of the night, sensing an opening and a new space of opportunity and patronage for their music. Yet Sékou Bembeya, I noticed, was characteristically more subdued. "Yes, it was good," he said without emotion as we all drove home, and I suspected that he was reserving his judgment until official promises were realized. The ministry wasted no time in announcing a follow-up, however, and a second event in the official launch was held a week later. This concert took place at La Paillote and featured the band Kélétigui et ses Tambourinis. It was less formal than the first event but still featured many VIPs and was televised by RTG. The musicians were energized and optimistic, and the night was filled with cheering and dancing. In his opening speech, Jean-Baptiste Williams also celebrated La Paillote itself as "the cradle of Guinean culture" and, to thunderous applause from the musicians and audience of dignitaries, announced plans to renovate and promote the iconic venue.

A third *soirée de culture* was to be held a week later, on 20 June, featuring the dance band Horoya Band, among others. The event was canceled because of heavy rains, however, and in the end it never took place. Instead, as a sense of political crisis grew steadily over the course of the summer, the regime seemed to lose interest in music. Despite earlier plans for ongoing regular events featuring the dance bands, no such evenings materialized after the official launch. Moreover, after some initial painting of the walls lining the courtyard at La Paillote, no other renovation work was undertaken. A friend of mine who was meeting with Williams a few days after the La Paillote concert recounted to me what happened when the painters came to the Ministry of Culture looking for their fee. Arriving at the Director of Culture's office, the team of workers was told that Williams did not have any money to pay them for their work and that they should contribute "as patriots for the good of the country." The workers complained that they had spent two days painting and had previously been told that they would be paid for the job. Williams reiterated that there was no budget for paying them and, digging around in his pocket, grudgingly took out 50,000 Guinean francs (less than US$10 at the time of my fieldwork) to cover the team's transport and supplies.[10]

As the La Paillote example suggests, it quickly became apparent that, despite its big talk, the CNDD had no real structure, system, or commitment in place to create and implement a new cultural policy. After an initial burst of enthusiasm and planning, cultural initiatives became increasingly chaotic and ad hoc, and all talk of a national cultural festival soon dried up. Although Jean-Baptiste Williams had spoken about the "restoration of the state's authority" in public life, these initiatives in fact seemed based on little more than the personal whims and memories of a small group of officials at the new ministry.

Around this time I sat squashed into a shared taxi with five other passengers one afternoon in a massive traffic jam. The driver had long since turned off his engine and was staring morosely at the road ahead. As the passengers strained to feel some breeze through the open windows, they complained bitterly about the state of Conakry's roads, the lack of urban planning, and the state's incompetence. Shifting his weight, the man next to me sighed, "Ah Guinea, we're the last country in Africa."

This statement hit me hard. The CNDD was at that time actively evoking the story of Guinean exceptionalism, referencing the revolution as a stable symbol of nostalgia and pride. By turning to revolutionary music, the CNDD followed the long-established political instinct of "looking to the past." But while revolutionary music may evoke uncomplicated, happy memories of youth and optimism for a nostalgic few, most Guineans have decidedly more mixed feelings.

When I asked friends and acquaintances about their thoughts on "Armée guinéenne," I was often met with indifference. In some cases, people suggested that the song related to the post-independence armed forces and had no connection to the military today. One acquaintance told me that the song served as a continuing reminder to the current army about its obligations. For the most part, however, reaction to the recirculation of the song was a collective shrug. Even Touré-era musicians themselves were somewhat ambivalent about it. Because the bands have always competed with one another, there was some jealousy among the other bands that Bembeya's song should get so much renewed attention. But even the Bembeya musicians rarely spoke about the song and had little to say when I asked them about it, preferring instead to talk about upcoming gigs or complain about ongoing arguments.

These reactions reminded me that while "history continues" in Guinea, most people, including the former revolutionary musicians, also fervently wish to look ahead toward new ideas and solutions. Alongside an awareness of Guinea's pre- and postcolonial history, Guinean people today hold aspirations for change—in economic opportunity, in quality of life, in politics. They wish to participate in the modern world, rather than simply to relive past triumphs.

Céline Pauthier notes that Sékou Touré's own logic caught up with him as he arbitrarily detained, tortured, and killed his opponents in the name of freedom and liberation (2010: 71). Similarly, the temporal logic of the revolution—future-oriented and progressive—continually catches up with itself as the state continues to look to the past in an ever-exhausted gesture. As Svetlana Boym argues in her work on postsocialist Russia, "Communist teleology was extremely powerful and intoxicating; and its loss is greatly missed in the post-Communist world. Hence everyone now is looking for its substitute, for another convincing plot of Russian development that will make sense of the chaotic present" (2001: 59). Rather than creating a "convincing plot" for the present, the CNDD in Guinea turned toward Touré's ideas as a familiar fallback. After the risky and dangerous adventure of a military coup d'état, the regime appeared to flail around for safety, finally landing on the seemingly familiar ground of the revolution.

Algiers, 2009

Although the CNDD's own cultural initiatives fizzled out by early summer 2009, a lucky coincidence occurred to support their claim to Touré's legacy: in July the Second Pan-African Cultural Festival was held. Since the 1969 Algiers festival the OAU had largely overlooked cultural issues and events. Much of its earlier emphasis was tied to the role of culture and the arts in decolonization. By the turn of the millennium, however, little official action on culture had taken place in decades. The transition to the African Union saw some renewed attention, however, including the adoption in 2006 of a Charter for African Cultural Renaissance. Under the AU's auspices, the Second Pan-African Cultural Festival was organized, also in Algiers, and aimed to showcase the arts and performance of countries throughout the continent.[11]

For the new officials of the Guinean Ministry of Culture, the festival provided a perfect opportunity for renewing the discourse of cultural nationalism. In a radio address the National Director of Culture, Jean-Baptiste Williams, announced Guinea's participation in the 2009 festival: "From 5 to 20 July the Algiers festival will be held. The Ballets Africains and Bembeya Jazz are going to represent Guinea. It's a priority for us, and Guinea will be represented with dignity."[12]

In addition to the National Theatre Troupe and a traveling exhibit from the National Museum, the Guinean delegation to Algiers was to be composed of the two most celebrated artistic formations of the revolution: the Ballets Africains and Bembeya Jazz. Forty years after the first Algiers festival, the national delegation in 2009 was almost identical to the 1969 model.[13] When I asked Culture Minister Morel about this situation in the summer of 2009, he reiterated that the new regime was committed to promoting music. He then proceeded to list all the (Touré-era) groups that they were supporting.[14]

Within Bembeya Jazz expectations and excitement were boosted by the ministry's announcement. The opportunity to travel abroad and perform energized the group in its preparations for the festival. The younger musicians seemed bursting with pride, and even the more restrained Sékou Bembeya said to me with a smile, "We won the first time, so anything other than first place is unacceptable."[15]

STAYING IN THE FRAMEWORK

In the two weeks leading up to the second Algiers festival, Bembeya Jazz held rehearsals every morning in Sékou Bembeya's courtyard, next door to La Paillote (see fig. 7). Each day's set list included four or five songs, all Bembeya classics from previous albums. Recognizing most of these songs from recordings, I was struck from the beginning by how consistent the group's current sound was with its earlier style.

Bembeya rehearsals were a tangle of jokes, laughter, arguments, and instruments. Guinean social life is filled with comical insults and mockery, in part due to Mande joking relations or *sanakunya* based on ties across kin or clan groups (see Camara 1992: 43). The rehearsals were no different, with the instrumentalists playfully shouting across the room at one another until Sékou Bembeya would assert his presence and call everyone to order. The band was composed of twelve musicians, including a large brass section with trumpets, trombone, and saxophone, two percussionists playing congas and drum kit, and bass and rhythm guitarists. Diamond Fingers stayed up front with his guitar, commenting on the singers' footwork or a particular instrumentalist's solo. Three singers completed the sound with their replication of Trio Bazooka, a formation put in place after Demba Camara, the group's

FIGURE 7. Bembeya Jazz musicians rehearsing in Sékou Bembeya's garage. Photo by the author.

first and much-loved lead singer, died in a car crash in 1973.[16] Trio Bazooka
had been known for its tight unison singing and choreographed dance routines, a combination of rumba box steps and James Brown–influenced slides
and jumps. In 2009 the current trio's routines were rather more lopsided, as
the young singer Mamadi Diabaté danced energetically while his older counterparts, Alseny Doumbouya and the late Youssouf Ba, shuffled from side
to side. The beat was still unmistakably Cuban, however, with many songs
ending in rousing rumba rhythms in 6/8 time, even though this influence
had fallen out of official favor by the 1970s and tends not to feature in newer
Guinean popular music. Moreover, although recently there has been a re-
surgence of interest in traditional Guinean instruments, the instrumentation
remained firmly centered on electric guitar and brass instruments. Bembeya seemed to have returned to an earlier moment in Guinean pop, before
bala and other traditional instruments had been reincorporated and while
Cuban rhythms were still prevalent. Other similarities to the past included
song arrangements identical to those in the original recordings, with breaks
and ostinatos occurring at exactly the same moments. Even the timbre of
Sékou Bembeya's guitar, with its bright, echo-y tone and characteristic re-
verb, seemed straight out of an early album, nostalgically evoking the 1960s.
Perhaps the only remarkable changes were in the group's clothes, hairstyles,
and onstage acrobatics. Old video clips I have seen of Bembeya often feature
bell-bottoms and Afros, while Sékou Bembeya occasionally writhes on the
floor, Hendrix-style, playing guitar on his back.[17] The 2009 rehearsals and
performances were much more sedate, with Diamond Fingers often sitting
on a plastic chair. Yet if I closed my eyes I could hear, note for note, the music
of his youth.

   With little apparent distance between the recordings of yesterday and the
live performances of today, this strict adherence to an earlier sound has not
gone unnoticed. One Guinean music fan commented on a blog post that
"since Demba Camara's death, Bembeya doesn't shine like it did in its day. I
don't know that era myself, but what's certain is that I know Bembeya's reper-
tory by heart because every concert is the same. Nothing changes. We have to
reinvigorate the group by adding new blood and dancers. The old musicians
can't even dance anymore."[18] Other accounts, however, celebrate and reinforce Bembeya's choice to stick to its old sound. The music journalist Hélène
Lee writes that "if Bembeya has hardly changed its style, it's because it opened
up a path and continues to explore it. Can we ask the Rolling Stones to start
playing rap or funk?" (1988: 82–83; my translation). Lee's comments suggest
that the group cannot and should not deviate from its past sound if it is to
retain its authenticity. It is precisely this perceived authenticity that is also

of interest to its European and North American audiences, while Bembeya's attempts to try different sounds, such as the use of keyboards and drum machines in the 1989 album *Wà Kélè*, have been commercial and critical flops.[19] Jean Paul Cédy, then Secretary-General of the Culture Ministry, suggested to me that Touré-era musicians were "broken" by the end of the revolution and are no longer motivated to create anything new. Speaking of both musicians and the ministry itself, he acknowledged that "we're still traumatized by the revolution—there is still that hurt—we always take its ideas."

Yet, for the musicians themselves, the decision to recreate an earlier sound has been made deliberately. As noted in the previous chapter, Bembeya Jazz and the other dance bands evolved their sounds over the course of the 1960s and 1970s, incorporating new influences and ideas and shedding old ones. Moreover, many of these musicians are involved in newer projects beyond the dance bands and their nostalgic sounds. Sékou Bembeya has recorded two excellent solo albums in recent years, *Diamond Fingers* (1996) and *Guitar Fö* (2002), and is currently working on a third (currently untitled) in which he both sings and plays guitar in front of a backup band. Many of the younger musicians in his band are involved in other projects, such as the neotraditional group Djeli Den (Children of Jeli). For the past several years the *jembe* player Papa Kouyaté has organized and mentored a stunning dance and percussion group, the Petits Sorciers (riffing on Kouyaté's own nickname as the Wizard: *le Sorcier*). The saxophonist Mamadou "Le Maitre" Barry has built a successful crossover reputation as a contemporary African jazz artist and is often sponsored by the Franco-Guinean Cultural Center to perform and tour in Guinea and abroad. "If we always stay in our framework doing the same thing for forty years," Barry said to me with some concern, "it's not obvious that people will listen today."[20]

Returning to an earlier musical moment is not simply a case of these musicians only knowing how to do one thing; rather, they are doing it knowingly. For one thing, they recognize that the government in 2009 wanted a direct sound reference to the past in order to promote its own legitimacy. Moreover, these bands are competing for fewer and fewer resources and audiences, and the past offers a time-tested formula of success and popularity. Many of these musicians expressed a sense of vindication in the government's efforts, saying that they such efforts allowed them to continue doing "what they did best." Even though they received few financial rewards from the government, they felt "acknowledged and valued," as the late guitarist Lansana Condé told me. They framed their continued musical survival as an act of agency. As another guitarist, Lamine Camara, said to me, for example, "We refuse to die. We still consider ourselves as national bands, as cultural heritage, because you can't find better than us."[21] Yet despite such statements, my sense was that these musicians realized that the military regime's efforts were fleeting and superficial—that times had undeniably changed, and they could not recover the post-independence moment. They did wish to relive the pleasures of the past, but they also longed to experience the joys of innovation and change in the present.

In this regard, Bembeya Jazz's decision to recreate its older sounds can also be seen as a way of making meaning in response to political events in 2009. Bembeya and other musicians were interpreting these events as artists, rather than as ideologues, and continuing to search for pleasure and value in making their art. Yet, the regime did not treat them as living artists, but rather expected them to serve as static, unwavering symbols of a particular moment. Their capital, in the eyes of successive Guinean regimes, is as points of direct reentry to the past. As a result, in preparing for the 2009 Algiers festival, the state once again turned to Bembeya Jazz and its contemporaries to represent Guinea on this symbolically important international stage.

EXPECTATIONS AND ASSUMPTIONS

In late June 2009 Bembeya Jazz and the Ballets Africains performed before President Dadis and other members of the CNDD at a high-profile event held at the Conakry venue the Cases de Bellevue. The event was organized by the culture ministry in preparation for the upcoming Algiers festival. In addition to Bembeya and the Ballets Africains, three of the other former national dance bands performed (Horoya Band, Kélétigui et ses Tambourinis, and Balla et ses Balladins), along with the former national dance and percussion ensemble the Ballet Djoliba, and the former national Ensemble Instrumental de Guinée. There were also three newer groups, including a dance-and-percussion ensemble, Woï Loiny (Soul of My People), which is based in Conakry but represents performance from the Kpelle ethnic group in southeastern Guinea.

This concert and the composition of Guinea's delegation to the festival make clear that Touré's idea of national culture still informs official thinking. In a country of more than two dozen ethnic groups, one version of culture—heavily filtered through Conakry and privileging Mande performance—continues to dominate. In fact, I was surprised to hear that a Kpelle group was involved in the Bellevue concert until I remembered that Dadis is himself of Kpelle ethnicity. Cécé Paul Kolié, the leader of Woï Loiny, told me later that it was only once Dadis came to power that their group was suddenly invited to perform at official functions.[22] Until that time, *forestier* cultural groups—

from the southeastern forest region—had often been excluded from official events in the capital. I had long observed that the same holds true for Fulbe groups, even though Fulbe people are Guinea's largest and by many accounts economically predominant ethnic group.[23]

Many older Guinean people often say that one consequence of Touré's death in 1984 was that the nation has become fragmented, with each separate region wishing to express its own identity. This change has meant that the revolutionary version of a shared national culture has less resonance for younger people and those who were not brought up within Touré's party system. Dadis Camara, for example, joined the army in 1990, during the Conté regime and several years after Touré's death. The inclusion of Woï Loiny at the Bellevue concert and other official state events in 2009 suggests that he had not entirely subsumed his Kpelle identity into the Mande-centered national identity promoted by the revolution.

Furthermore, at the Bellevue concert, held just a few days before the start of the Algiers festival, Dadis was impressed by the performance of a young and largely Soso gymnastic troupe, the École des Arts Acrobatiques, who were not included in the official delegation. The president decided on the spot that they should also represent Guinea in Algiers. The French attaché at the Guinean Ministry of Culture later told me that the next seventy-two hours were spent frantically trying to obtain passports and visas for the group, as well as rechoreographing the Ballets Africains' routine so that the acrobatic troupe could be inserted into their performance. Clearly, although officials at the Ministry of Culture had long ago selected the national delegation, their notion of the best representatives of Guinean culture was not shared by the younger president.

In promoting the Touré-era representation of Guinean national culture, ministry officials revealed their own aesthetic and ideological biases, using the revolution to try to resuscitate the idea of the nation as a unifying concept and to cement their own political rule. This strategy is increasingly tricky to apply. Today multiple voices and identities openly challenge the notion that these groups represent the whole, or even that such a whole exists. In 2009 President Dadis Camara, as a non-Maninka and non-*révolutionnaire* from the Touré era, represented a powerful alternate voice, and ultimately the Ministry of Culture was forced to amend its coherent and tidy idea of national culture, hurriedly assembling a patchwork in its place.

Even despite these changes, outside of La Paillote most musicians and music fans in Conakry seemed largely indifferent to the Algiers festival, and beyond the official media it passed largely unremarked. In an analysis of the

Second World Black and African Festival of Arts and Culture (FESTAC) in Lagos in the 1970s, Andrew Apter notes that once-powerful symbols of national culture can become unstable over time as they are alienated from their original signifiers. In Nigeria official representations of the nation effectively collapsed in the 1990s following extended political and economic crisis. Although FESTAC aimed to present a nation of great culture and pan-African leadership, by the 1990s many outsiders equated Nigerian national identity with images of corruption and chaos (2005: 226–27).

Guinea in 2009 was faced with a similar problem. The country presented itself at the 1969 Algiers festival as a leader of African decolonization and cultural nationalism. In 2009, however, most observers saw Guinea as a marginalized and chaotic corner of the continent, caught in the grips of yet another military dictatorship. Perhaps aware of the country's public-relations problems, Bembeya Jazz chose not to play "Armée guinéenne" at Algiers, despite its ubiquity on the state airwaves at the time. This decision seemed to be one of the few concessions to contemporary reality—that a reminder of military rule in Guinea might not be well received by foreign audiences at a festival intended to dispel negative imagery about Africa.

In the end, contrary to the expectations of the participating Guinean musicians and officials, the Algiers festival did not include a judged competition, and there was no top prize for the national delegation to come away with. Calling me from Algiers, one of the musicians from Bembeya Jazz told me that their performance at the festival was a resounding success, and upon their return the other band members reported that they were received enthusiastically by audiences and the Algerian authorities. Nonetheless, I noticed on the festival's website and in press coverage on the Internet that there was no mention of Guinean performances and that news of the festival was instead dominated by larger countries such as Algeria, South Africa, and Senegal.

Guinea's absence from the Algiers website and other press coverage seemed to reflect its loss of political and cultural prestige and relevance in the forty years since the first festival. Just as the choice of Bembeya Jazz and other Touré-era formations seemed out of step with popular tastes in Guinea, its reception in Algiers suggested that the rest of the continent had also moved on. With the festival theme of "African Renaissance," audiences and organizers expressed an interest in looking forward to Africa's role in the present and future. The festival's foundation document explicitly stated that "the youth represent the majority of the African population. The key resources for contemporary creation reside in the youth."[24] In this context, there was little vested interest in promoting an ideology and music associated with the 1960s.

The Marketing of Nostalgia

Although audiences at Algiers seemed to have little investment in old Guinean music, other, non-state actors have periodically sought to mobilize memories and pleasures around the revolutionary sound. On a couple of occasions in 2009, for example, I visited a restaurant run by a Frenchman in Conakry. The restaurant had organized a regular weekend gig with Horoya Band, one of the great Touré-era national dance bands. The aim was to recreate a feel of mid-century tropical evenings by the sea, with Horoya Band faithfully performing its old hits for expatriate diners hoping to experience the past. Yet on my visits, the room was nearly empty: few people besides the musicians showed up.

Around the turn of the millennium there was also particular interest in revolutionary Guinean pop from a small but influential group of music fans in Europe and North America. In the 1990s and 2000s a handful of record labels, music festivals, and commentators on world music turned their attention to the Touré-era dance bands. Starting in 2004, for example, Sterns Africa released compilations of classic songs by Bembeya Jazz, Balla et ses

FIGURES 8A AND 8B. Two recent compilations of Guinean post-independence dance bands showing stylized cover art, © Editions Syliphone Conakry

Balladins, and Kélétigui et ses Tambourinis.[25] While these bands were losing audiences within Guinea, Euro-American world music fans embraced their sound and along with it evoked a nostalgic view of the Touré era.[26] This interest in the Touré-era bands reflected the world music tendency to spotlight groups of aging musicians in faded locales. Since the phenomenal success of the Buena Vista Social Club in the 1990s, music producers and fans have determinedly sought out similar stories. Within this broader context, Bembeya Jazz returned to the studio after a hiatus of thirteen years and steadily garnered attention in the world music press. In 2002 the group recorded the album *Bembeya* under the French label Marabi and conducted a U.S. and European tour the following year. As the music writer Banning Eyre observed at the time, "Bembeya Jazz's phoenix-like rise is part of a larger and long-overdue trend in African music today. The old guys are back!"[27]

Concert reviews, album liner notes, and interviews with the musicians frequently emphasized the idea that this music represents a "golden age" of African pop.[28] Consumers are offered the possibility of return to this moment, remastered and repackaged to maximize its nostalgic appeal. Figure 8

FIGURES 8B. (*continued*)

shows the retro imagery used on recent album covers, suggesting an unspeci-
fied tropical destination and borrowing from constructions in 1940s and
1950s American pop culture.[29] Although these images were originally used by
Syliphone in the late 1960s, they represent a fraction of the Syliphone album
covers, in contrast to the more common practice of using photographs of the
musicians or scenes of Guinean life, as shown in figure 9.[30] The decision to use
the stylized drawings rather than photographs suggests a conscious attempt
to abstract the particular Guinean or African identity of these bands into a
more generalized one. From the label's perspective, it is understandable that
the stylized images would be preferable because they are more marketable.
But for musicians and audiences in Guinea they work within a long-standing
set of feelings that Guinea has been forgotten and no longer occupies a dis-

FIGURES 9A AND 9B. Syliphone releases for Bembeya Jazz (1969) and Horoya Band (1971) showing
the more prevalent type of cover art used. © Editions Syliphone Conakry

FIGURES 9B. (*continued*)

tinct place in global consciousness. Nostalgia "depends on where you stand" (Stewart 1988: 228).

This particular moment of world music interest has faded, although, while I was conducting fieldwork in 2009, there was buzz at La Paillote around the Sterns recordings. As one might expect, the musicians felt gratified at the recognition of their talents and sensed new possibilities. Arguments and discussions arose among them about how closely to stick to their past musical formulas. Linké Condé, the guitarist and *chef d'orchestre* of the band Kélétigui et ses Tambourinis, explained to me that although Guinean music changed after Sékou Touré's death, market forces led musicians back to the sounds and styles they produced in the 1960s:

> That music that was on the rise during the twenty-four years of [the Conté era], people didn't consume it. Yes, it was consumed in the interior here in Guinea, but elsewhere, it didn't move an inch. But during that time, in the

FNACs [a chain of record shops] in France, little by little, that old Syliphone catalog that those old musicians had recorded in the 60s, '64, '68, all that, when you go in the FNACs, it's those records that are sold rather than the young ones. . . . So afterwards we realized that, oh no, no, because the music of young people doesn't sell, we should return back to square one.[31]

Condé suggests there was a trial-and-error experiment in which musicians attempted to change until external forces revealed that their earlier output was preferable. Interestingly, although he admits that post-1984 music did find an audience within Guinea, the preference of French listeners who chose the older music is held as vindication that this music really is better. As the anthropologist Adrienne Cohen notes, this evocation of elsewhere is a means by which postsocialist citizens "displace hope" (2018: 281). If we were to take Condé's words literally, it would seem that he overlooks the very success of younger Guinean groups that have gained popularity in France and elsewhere in Europe. But his statement is strategic: he is choosing not to engage with newer music while keeping future possibilities for himself and his peers alive. Some Touré-era musicians are often dismissive, and at times even hostile, toward the newer generations of musicians who have succeeded them. Even while they may teach and work with younger musicians, they sometimes rail against their own abandonment and loudly reject the validity of new forms.

The sounds of the Touré-era dance bands reference a moment that Guinean people are increasingly moving beyond. In emphasizing a past golden age, however, foreign representations have at times glossed over the politics of this music and the brutality of the Touré regime. An article on the BBC Radio 3 website states that "under the forceful unifying leadership of President Sekou Touré, performing artists were subsidised and encouraged to take pride in their local folkloric roots."[32] One music journalist describes Touré as a "poet before he was a politician" and "a music lover," while another calls him "visionary."[33] But these representations all clearly seem to take their cues from the musicians themselves. In interviews, they resolutely refuse to be drawn out on the subject of Touré's politics, as quickly became clear to me during my own research. Their guardedness is strategic. By remaining quiet on certain questions, by speaking of Touré in overwhelmingly positive terms, they reveal a wish to control the terms in which they are presented. Musicians from the Touré-era dance bands are aware of their status—however fleeting—as commodities and have to balance fulfilling expectations while protecting their own interests and maintaining their integrity. Caution, guardedness, and silence become important means by which they can do

both. Yet this silence becomes conspicuous, in contrast to a different, growing conversation about the past in Guinea today.

History Revisited

At La Paillote one June afternoon in 2009, the conversation turned, as it
sometimes did, to Sékou Touré. The bass player for 22 Band, Laye Dioubaté,
told a story: In the early 1960s Touré traveled to Saudi Arabia to perform the
Hajj. As he journeyed to Mecca, he noticed that there were no trees growing
along the way. Turning to the Saudi king, who was accompanying him, he
suggested that trees be planted to offer traveling pilgrims shade against the
scorching sun. The king replied that he had tried, but that no tree would
grow there in the desert. Touré considered the situation. He then found two
saplings, one of which he planted and the other of which he gave to the Saudi
king to plant. The convoy then continued on its way. A few months later, as
the king sat in his court, a messenger came running to report that the king's
tree had died, while Sékou Touré's was alive and thriving.[34]

Although not every story attested to such magical powers, Laye's account
illustrates the legendary status that Touré has acquired in the memories of
musicians and former *révolutionnaires* from the post-independence era.
When conversations at La Paillote turned to the past, they most often involved praise for Touré or laments at his passing, with the musicians expressing unwaveringly positive and nostalgic views. As Laye said to me on another
occasion, "We're only now beginning to understand the immensity of what
we've lost."

I did occasionally encounter oblique references to the terrors of the revolution. Speaking to me about Touré's love for art and music, for example,
Lansana Condé implicitly acknowledged that Touré wielded power as a personal toy. The reiterated emphasis here underlines that these musicians were
an exceptional and favored group: "The president had a particular affection
for art. He didn't like anything bad happening to artists. During his time,
artists never had political or moral problems. He never touched artists."[35]
Condé's careful response strongly suggests that others were not so lucky.
When I asked the dance-band musicians explicitly about the constraints of
the revolution, however, they uniformly declined to comment. On one occasion Papa Kouyaté said to me, "There are certain things that I can't tell you
because it becomes political."[36] Papa and his colleagues often separated the
categories of art and politics, declaring that they wished to express themselves
solely as artists. Yet elsewhere others openly grappled with the contradictions
of Touré's legacy.

Memories of the Touré era are a complicated affair in contemporary Guinea. While Touré is respected for his leadership in securing Guinean independence, he is also blamed for setting the country on its downward path. Counsel recalls one Touré-era administrator evoking to him the maxim that "the revolution eats its children."[37] Like other African liberation heroes turned autocrats, Touré is seen simultaneously as creator and destroyer, as having given to and stolen from the nation. In such a context, people often hold, and acknowledge, contradictory views on the former president. Toward the end of the rainy season in September 2009, for example, I arrived at the house of my *kora* (harp) teacher, Demba Diallo (the grandson of the jeli M'Bady Kouyaté) to find him and two friends from the neighborhood watching a DVD of a speech Touré gave in Paris in 1982.[38] The three young men, all in their twenties, watched in rapt attention as Touré spoke at length about Guinea's relationship with France and defended his human rights record. Whenever he made a particularly eloquent statement, Demba and his friends would shake their heads in admiration, laughing, and say, "Ah, there's a man who really could speak!" At the time this incident surprised me, because I had long believed that support for Sékou Touré represented a clear generational fault line in Guinea. Only a couple of weeks earlier I had sat playing kora in the courtyard with Demba and a neighbor while they spoke to me of the atrocities of Touré's regime, recounting horrific stories of political prisoners incarcerated at the Camp Boiro prison and executed by being hanged off the 8 Novembre Bridge in central Conakry. "It was butchery," Demba said to me. And yet, soon afterward, here were those same young men celebrating Touré as a refined and articulate leader.

Speaking to Demba on this subject over time, I came to realize that for him, as for many Guineans, Touré may have been a brutal tyrant, but he was also "a man of culture," to recall a phrase often heard at La Paillote. There is an abiding sense that during the revolution, and unlike today, Guinea occupied a place on the world stage. As Demba later told me, although Touré was ruthless, he also had certain priorities—art and music, for example—and he wanted above all for Guinean people to reclaim a sense of dignity.

Considering Demba's statements, it struck me that young people in Guinea today are growing up in an ideologically diffuse and complex environment in which it is permissible to say and feel many perhaps contradictory things. Although Guinea lurched in 1984 from revolution to antirevolution, with everything associated with the post-independence regime publicly repudiated overnight, there has emerged in recent years an attempt to historicize Sékou Touré in a more nuanced manner. This attempt represents not an outright rejection but rather an "undramatic accommodation" of the past

(Appadurai 1981: 218). The theater director Raliatou "Fifi" Tamsir Niane, daughter of the once exiled and imprisoned historian Djibril Tamsir Niane, suggested to me that Guineans were until recently not ready to engage in this discussion because it was "too close." But now, as she said, "We're beginning to acknowledge that the good and the bad of the [Touré] period are very much mixed up."[39]

This new discussion in Conakry appears to be taking place both in private conversations and in public, albeit unofficial, forums.[40] On the one hand, I often witnessed spontaneous conversations such as that between Demba and his neighbors. On the other, there were events such as Espace Culturel, a series of public discussions in Conakry organized by the private cultural agency Festi-Kaloum and featuring prominent figures in Guinean cultural life.[41] The format allowed for audience participation, and two of the three events held in 2009 ended with a lively discussion focusing on Sékou Touré and his legacy. At the first event, for example, which featured the former National Director for Culture, Telivel Diallo, a question from the audience sparked a debate about whether, and in what light, Touré should be included in the history books today. While Telivel argued that Touré should be written about alongside other great African intellectuals such as Kwame Nkrumah and Nelson Mandela, a member of the audience, the playwright (and future minister) Tidiane Cissé, countered that Touré could not possibly be equated with such individuals because of the crimes he committed in Guinea.[42] Both sides finally agreed that there was a need to engage in precisely such public debate in Guinea today and to reconcile the two faces of Touré's legacy.

At another event in the series, Fifi Tamsir Niane herself spoke about her experiences as an artist and the daughter of a famous survivor of the regime. To conclude her remarks, she read aloud the poem below, written by her father. It refers to Touré's famous 1958 speech in which he stood alongside Charles de Gaulle and publicly declared Guinea's intention to vote for independence in France's referendum that year—an event commonly referred to as Guinea's "No." The poem plays on the "No," and on Touré's iconic line in the speech to de Gaulle: "We prefer poverty in freedom to wealth in slavery."

> Djibril Tamsir Niane (1960): "J'ai dit 'Non'"
> Toi aussi tu as dit "Non"
> Et le méchant colon est parti.
> A sa place, Liberté est venue
> Escortée par Démocratie
> Responsabilité suivait d'un pas grave.
> J'ai dit "Non"
> Toi aussi tu as dit "Non"

Aussitôt, Richesse est venue,
Dans ta gibecière s'est logée,
Auprès de moi, resta Pauvreté.
Et pourtant, j'avais dit "Non."
Toi aussi d'ailleurs.

I Said "No"

You too, you said "No"
And the cruel colonizer left.
In his place, Freedom came
Escorted by Democracy
Responsibility followed with a heavy step.
I said "No"
You too, you said "No"
Soon after, Wealth came,
In your satchel it stayed,
Next to me was Poverty.
And yet, I had said "No."
You too, by the way.

The first version of this poem was written in 1960; Niane wrote a later one in 1961 while imprisoned in Camp Boiro.[43] The scholar and newspaper editor Souleymane Diallo described to me that the Voix de la Révolution broadcast Niane's poem in 1960 on the radio, intending to incite popular anger against him for his work in leading a strike by the teachers' union. Instead, secondary school students were ignited by its sentiments and led protests against the regime in Conakry and the highland town of Labé. According to Diallo, these marches represented the first public anti-Touré actions after independence. In choosing to read her father's poem, Fifi Tamsir Niane thus wished to underline that there have always been multiple points of view about Touré, even from very early on in his regime. What she did not realize at the time was that, at the Espace Culturelle event where she read her father's poem, Touré's own son, Mohamed, sat in the audience. In fact, Mohamed Touré attended the first two such events, although he did not speak publicly. When Fifi and I spoke about it later, she looked both shocked and amused at the idea of reading the poem and speaking as she did in front of Touré's son. "If I had known he was there," she said, "I certainly would have hesitated." Even to her, the idea of such forthright expression of voice was somewhat astonishing—although knowing Fifi, with her courage, intelligence, and eloquence, I felt quite sure that she would have spoken nonetheless.

Regardless of Mohamed Touré's presence, the open debate of events such as Espace Culturelle came as a great surprise to me, representing a new atmosphere of dissent and discussion that had not seemed possible even a few years earlier when I first moved to Guinea in 2002. McGovern suggests that this debate emerged in 2008 at the time of Guinea's fiftieth anniversary of independence (2010: 22). As conversation on the past coalesced around the fiftieth-anniversary celebrations, public memories of Touré began to be actively redrawn—perhaps because there was finally sufficient distance from the past, as Fifi Tamsir Niane suggested was needed. Today Touré's face is still seen on everything from monuments and murals to framed photographs in public buildings and private homes, but its meaning as a historical symbol is being disputed and reconsidered. One acquaintance pointed out that the bust of Touré at Conakry's national museum keeps being moved; it was long kept in a storehouse, then more recently brought out into the museum's courtyard, but relocated from background to foreground and back again.

Perhaps unsurprisingly, musicians from the revolutionary dance bands are conspicuously absent from this debate. At times these musicians seem quite nostalgic, remembering Sékou Touré as a mythical hero, as Laye Dioubaté did. At other times, they, like others, are mainly concerned with the social and political realities—and pleasures—of the present day as opposed to endlessly living in the past. During the post-independence period they sought to carve out their own expressive space within the strictures of the revolution, pursuing their careers, economic opportunities, and creative agendas as best they could. Today they continue to make music and revel in their endurance, in the occasional opportunities and recognition that comes their way, and in the friendship and camaraderie of their shared memories. Their statements and conversations often elide ideological revolutionary fervor to gratitude for their personal career opportunities. As other commentators have noted, part of what musicians recall as a "golden age" is their own ability to work and be acknowledged (Moorman 2008: 181; Gilman 2009: 72). More than one musician at La Paillote told me that it was thanks to Touré that they were able to become musicians at all—that they would never have been able to afford instruments otherwise.

Today they express bitterness at being "sacrificed"—at working hard for the revolution and in the end having little in return. In part, this situation is that of aging stars who no longer have their celebrity or their fans and find it hard to let go of the past—a situation intensified here by poverty and the hardships of life in Guinea. But these musicians are also caught in particular ways in the struggles and debates over Touré's legacy. They embody the period today, while many of them have also long struggled to move beyond it, and yet they are often pulled back into its orbit. The ongoing tendency to look to the past ensnares them more than others, while orientations toward the future are less available to them in a climate of rapid change. La Paillote has thus become a refuge for them, a home where they feel pride and experience recognition and are able to speak about the past without the judgment of others. The nostalgia that I often encountered at La Paillote is not simply a defensive or willfully blind gesture, but rather a way to reconcile their past with the present reckoning of the revolution. As Maria Todorova writes about post-Communist nostalgia, this feeling represents a way for people to "invest their lives with meaning and dignity, not to be thought of, remembered, or bemoaned as losers or 'slaves'" (2010: 7). Touré-era musicians recognize that they have a shrinking place in Guinean music and public life today. Choosing to meet the expectations of the government is tricky; nostalgia represents "a double-edged sword: it seems to be an emotional antidote to politics and thus remains the best political tool" (Boym 2001: 58). Sticking closely to the past is an attempt by these musicians to reclaim the pleasures they once enjoyed as symbols of the nation, yet by doing so they occupy shaky ground in a contentious historical moment.

3

Sweetness and Truth

Following the coup d'état in December 2008, an explosion of musical homage greeted the new military regime in Guinea. Praise songs to the junta circulated widely in Conakry over the next several months, from cheap cassettes flooding the marketplace to gala soirées at the prestigious Palais du Peuple featuring the most popular artists of the day. Music videos of varying quality rotated on the national television broadcasting station, while musicians scrambled to write and rehearse new, flattering songs. Many of the musicians involved were hereditary Mande jelilu, who specialize in praise singing, musically declaiming the names and virtues of powerful individuals. Others were musicians from different backgrounds and styles, yet who have absorbed the influences of Mande music. Across genres and generations, these musicians sang in adulatory support of the junta, even as public views of the regime became increasingly angry. As popular discontent was being increasingly voiced on street corners, musicians sang of lions and warriors, of brave soldiers renewing the country, of patriots and justice. And despite the widely publicized brutalities of the regime, and public anger toward it, ordinary citizens seemed largely to brush off this steady drumbeat of praise—and at times to find great pleasure in it.

How can we understand this public tolerance—even appetite—for dictatorial praise? Was this reaction itself a performance or dissimulation to placate the regime? Or can we look beyond the explicit texts of praise songs to consider instead how they might be varyingly experienced and interpreted?

Political theories of governance have traditionally examined the ways in which regimes seek to create legitimacy to ensure their rule. Yet, as recent theorists of authoritarianism have argued, legitimacy is not always the goal. In her work on the cult of Hafiz al-Asad in Syria, for example, Lisa Wedeen notes that the regime was more concerned with ensuring obedience and compliance with government dictates than with actually instilling a sense of loyalty among its subjects (1999). The regime worked laboriously to construct spectacles of power in which people were impelled to act "as *if*" they believed in the cult, whether or not they did in fact. The regime's concern lay solely with how people act rather than how they actually feel; its power was produced through disciplinary measures rather than affective ties.

In her analysis Wedeen seeks to understand the effects of political spectacle and to understand what and how people read, feel, and act in official displays of power. As Yael Navaro-Yashin similarly asks in her study of political culture in 1990s Turkey (2002), why do ordinary citizens participate in and perpetuate rituals of state veneration? Building on these analyses, I consider in this chapter the ways in which the spectacle of praise performance involves not just top-down political theater, but also the varying interpretations, values, and meanings assigned by participants. In examining both an instance of live performance and a popular recording released in praise of the regime, my discussion of spectacle here goes beyond the visual to focus primarily on vocal aesthetics in Guinean public life. How do the sonic and aesthetic qualities of voice capture various strategies to negotiate political crisis in Guinea today? How does voice create meaning and feeling? How is it varyingly heard?

As discussed in chapter 1, Sekou Touré was ambivalent about jeliya, the verbal and musical art of jelilu, and during his regime praise singing was tightly controlled in support of the revolution. Since his death in 1984, however, the landscape has changed greatly. Free-market reforms have led to the professionalization of music and the emergence of a new culture of individual stardom, or *vedettariat*. These changes are central to the post-1984 economics of music in Guinea, in which powerful individuals tip singers in increasingly ostentatious displays. Jeliya is a "generic resource" for professional musicians who wish to channel its affective power (Skinner 2015: 67).

Praise performance today involves glittering spectacles of power, yet this is not simply a representation of propaganda and obedience to the ruling class. Instead, musicians, the patrons for whom they sing, and the audience together create the show, one in which the powerful voice creates a shared space in the immediate moment. While the singer projects her voice outward, broadcasting as loudly as possible, the patron and various audience members command center stage to extravagantly display their wealth and status. These vocal and visual acts of amplification serve to publicly recognize and affirm not just the patron but the entire community of participants, reminding them of their glorious shared past. Although politicians embrace the opportunity to have their power actualized through the spectacle of display and the act of being named, it is the immediacy of performance and the pleasurable feeling of community and pride that are at the heart of the show. Jeli praise performance involves the transformation of public power to collective intimacy.

Taouyah

When I returned to Guinea for fieldwork in 2009, a friend suggested that I meet the family of the great jeli M'Bady Kouyaté. I vividly recall first visiting them at their home in Taouyah, a popular Conakry neighborhood—walking in the blazing heat from the bustling market and quickly leaving the tarmac road behind, winding through what seemed a maze of dusty unpaved lanes, past the mosque and corner stalls and rusted cars rattling along the potholed alleys. I suddenly noticed the cacophony of the main streets fade away and, turning a corner, found myself in a leafy, sun-dappled courtyard (fig. 10). At one end a group of women sat on low chairs chatting and cooking over an open fire, while at the other tiny children ran riotously in a game of chase. Between them, seated by the wall of the house, were an old man in a white *duruki-ba* (robe, or *grand boubou*) and sunglasses and a young man in dreadlocks playing kora.

The family of M'Bady Kouyaté represents four generations of jelilu and is one of the best-known musical lineages in Guinea today.[1] The patriarch,

FIGURE 10. The family home of M'Bady Kouyaté, with Fallaye Kouyaté playing kora. Photo by the author.

M'Bady, who passed away in 2016, was one of the great kora masters of his generation, while his nephew Ba Cissoko, also a kora player and leader of an eponymous group, has had a successful career on the world music stage. M'Bady's fourth wife, Diaryatou (fig. 11), is well-known locally as a *jelimuso* (a female jeli; pl. *jelimusolu*; So. [Soso], *jeliguinè*), specializing in the vocal artistry of jeliya, while many of the younger men in the family are busy performing and recording locally and internationally as they make names and gain fame for themselves in their own right.

M'Bady, known affectionately in the family as *le vieux* (the old man), was born in 1934 in the Gabú region of Portuguese Guinea (later Guinea-Bissau) and eventually settled in Koundara, a village in northwestern Guinea. The family primarily speak Mandinka, the language of the music of the older generation, but the younger men perform more commonly in Maninka or Soso.

FIGURE 11. Diaryatou Kouyaté. Photo by the author.

The older women in the family are now largely retired from music, although they are accomplished musicians and performers in their own right. M'Bady's second wife, Mama, plays the kora, unusually—very few women jelis in the region play instruments in public. Mama Kouyaté was also a dancer with the Ballets Africains for many years. M'Bady's fourth and youngest wife, Diaryatou, has performed widely in Guinea and has performed in France. Few of the younger women in the family are pursuing musical careers, however, reflecting the overall gender imbalance in Guinean popular music and related conservative views about women's roles in public life (see Dave 2019). When women do perform, singing is considered their appropriate role, and the singing voice is often gendered as female (Durán 2007). Because vocal music is the highest form of the art of jeliya, however, women's musical roles are central, although men are given the most prestigious role of reciting historical knowledge. In the past, jeliya often featured the pairing of husband-instrumentalist and wife-vocalist. As the tradition has evolved, young urban *jelikè* (male jelilu; So. *jelixamè*) rarely perform this way. Nonetheless, while few of the family's women perform publicly today, their voices can often be heard in the Kouyaté household.

The surname Kouyaté is an indicator of jeli credentials of the highest order (Cherif 2005: 156). The epic of the first Mande emperor, Sunjata Keita, prominently features the figure of Sunjata's own jeli, Balla Fassèkè Kouyaté. According to the story, Balla Fassèkè enchanted the sorcerer king and Sunjata's rival, Soumaoro Kanté, by playing a bala that the king had created. Soumaoro was bewitched by this performance and allowed Balla Fassèkè to escape captivity (Niane 1995). Balla Fassèkè's descendants became hereditary jelilu, and although other jelilu families emerged—including those with the surnames Diabaté, Cissoko, Kanté, and Kamissoko—Kouyaté is acknowledged as the most authentic jeli name. It carries particular musical prestige because of its association with Sunjata Keita. In fact, the instrument that Soumaoro Kanté created—the famous Sosso bala—is still preserved and guarded by another Kouyaté family in the northern Guinean town of Niagassola. The classic Mande piece "Lamban" celebrates the Kouyaté lineage in an homage to jeliya itself. The lyrics—in Mandinka here, from the version I learned from Diaryatou—state, "I yɛ jaliya, Ala lɛha jaliya da" (Oh jeliya, it is God who created jeliya). As Diaryatou told me proudly, this is a song of the Kouyaté clan.

Alongside ties to history and legend, jeliya is also an evolving tradition, and the family of M'Bady Kouyaté exemplifies some of its varied aspects today. Like many jelilu in urban areas today, their role focuses largely on music rather than other forms of oration. Yet even within music, the family reflects some of the traditional, rural roots of jeliya. While different jeli families are associated with different instruments, including bala and *koni* (lute), the kora is central to this particular family. M'Bady is descended from a long line of *korafòlalu* (kora players) and from a very young age learned the instrument by accompanying and listening to his older male relatives.

But jelilu have long incorporated non-jeli influences, including mixing with other genres and traditions and using new instruments such as the guitar. Diaryatou Kouyaté even sang on a hip-hop album by the local group Degg J Force 3. In M'Bady's view, the openness and possibility of modern jeliya is entirely due to Sékou Touré. "Sékou gave us everything," he once said to me. In the years after independence, M'Bady was recruited by Guinean government officials to perform with the Ensemble Instrumental de Guinée in Conakry.[2] He later performed with his second wife, Mama Kouyaté, and toured throughout Guinea and overseas, traveling to Europe, the United States, and Asia.[3] He became used to performing onstage in concert settings and to playing in ensembles with musicians from other traditions. M'Bady often spoke of Touré as a great man, and indeed Touré's photo still hangs on the wall inside the Taouyah house. Many of the young men in the family also continue to venerate the former president. M'Bady and Diaryatou's son Kandia (also known as Kandia Kora), who has recently found crossover success as a kora-playing pop star and singer, has composed songs about Touré.

As Kandia's example also suggests, many of the younger men in the family mix up their musical practice. Kandia and his brother Séfoudi have both played frequently with a popular neotraditional group, Espoirs de Coronthie. Séfoudi and his cousins Soundjoulou, Demba, and Diamadi also played for a while as the Étoiles de Mandingue, a neotraditional group with kora, Mande-style guitar, and singing, as well as such non-jeli instruments as *bolon* (bass-harp), *horde* (half-calabash drum), and *jembe* (hand drum). These young men spend many long afternoons in Taouyah in neotraditional sessions, with songs ranging from jeli classics such as "Duga" and "Kaïra" to reggae songs, Congolese guitar tunes, and, on one occasion I sat in on, even a kora rendition of "Careless Whisper."

Jeliya has never been a static art, and recent innovations do not undermine what for many musicians constitutes an ancient hereditary practice. The Kouyaté family consider themselves guardians of a glorious tradition, yet they embrace change and innovation. However, the wider discourse around jeliya has long been one of a continual loss of tradition and corruption, of too much change happening too fast.

Vedettariat

Toward the end of Ramadan in 2009 I accompanied M'Bady's grandson Demba Diallo to the home of the jelimuso Djeli Kani Fanta Diabaté. Djeli Kani Fanta lived in the Cité des Musiciens, just next door to La Paillote and near many musicians from the revolutionary dance bands. While most of them reside in small and rather faded houses provided by the Touré government, her house was visible and distinctive—a brand-new structure with gleaming pink walls and a shaded courtyard to the side. On the day of our visit, the courtyard was filled with musicians and others who had come to speak about Djeli Kani Fanta's upcoming *sumu*, an extravagant musical party popular in neighboring Mali. Djeli Kani Fanta was to hold a sumu at La Paillote to mark the end of Ramadan and had asked Demba to play kora in her backup band. As Demba spoke to another musician about the arrangements, a regal woman in heels and a saffron-colored robe strode out of the house toward us. This was the jelimuso herself.

A relatively new culture of vedettariat, or stardom, has emerged in Guinean music over the past generation. While Touré framed his musicians as "poets of the revolution" who were organized into ensembles and bands, the scene in Conakry today is dominated by individual celebrities, or *vedettes*, seeking their personal careers. The privatization of the arts in 1980s Guinea created new opportunities, as music making was suddenly open to anyone who could crack the market, not just to those chosen by Touré. Writing about similar patterns in Mali, Ryan Skinner notes the emergence of *artistiya*, the condition of being an artist, in an urban, neoliberal space (2015: 54–55). Artists in this context are bound neither to the hereditary lines of jeliya nor to the exigencies of socialist cultural production. It is the "value of the individual person" who is showcased and who pushes practice forward (Cohen 2016: 651).

In today's competitive marketplace, solo vocalists stand out as the stars of Guinean music, whether in hip-hop, R&B, or jeliya, and in line with older aesthetic values that have long privileged the singing and speaking voice. Kandia Kora performed as an accompanying instrumentalist for years but only hit fame once he started to sing himself. In contrast, most of the other young men in the Kouyaté family work as session musicians for vedettes. At Djeli Kani Fanta's house, Demba had a brief chat with the jelimuso and then spent the next hour or two mainly haggling over terms and arrangements with her manager (and husband) and the other musicians. While instrumentalists tend to dominate world-music markets, they are rarely the vedettes of the local scene. Singers, on the other hand, move and capture local audiences with their powerful voices and their role in giving praise.

Yet this role also carries longstanding moral opprobrium. In Mande culture *fasa*, the highest form of praise, is the sole provenance of the jeli. Fasa is sung by a jeli to his or her patron or host (*jati*) and involves the evocation of deep historical and genealogical knowledge of the noble's family. According to tradition, the practice involved a social contract in which the patron would protect and provide for the jeli in exchange for the jeli's praise, and at stake was the patron's honor if they did not fulfill their side of the bargain. In its modern incarnation, jelilu may sing not just to nobles or kings, but to whoever holds power and wealth at the given moment. Moreover, other musicians across genres also emulate this practice today, and often concerts feature the singer pronouncing a litany of names, with enough pauses in between to let each person enjoy the spotlight for a moment. As noted, being named creates great pleasure and pride—the Maninka phrase *ka kasi la tɔɔ lefe* can be translated as meaning "to cry to have one's name sung." Even in this adapted form, however, the practice is one of social and moral affirmation for all involved, symbolically evoking past structures of authority and sociopolitical order. Those who share the same last name as the person being sung about will also feel recognized, as will others who claim solidarity with that person. As Paula Ebron notes, jeliya historically exists within the "economic and political webs of dependence and difference" that make up Mande social life (2002: 129). Praise singing, with its exchange of words for patronage, illustrates this connectivity more than any other aspect of jeliya. But this connectivity also leads to resentment and sometimes hostility toward jelilu, who are often accused of greedily exploiting their traditions, particularly as traditional structures of authority have changed. A number of commentators have lauded the Malian jeli Banzumana Sissoko as an exceptional figure because of his public criticism of the 1960s ruling elite (Keita 1995: 185; Hopkins 1997: 59–60). In contrast, other jelilu are seen as having sold out to their baser instincts.

As a prerevolutionary source of authority, jelilu represented a particularly complex group for Sékou Touré. In the early years of his rule, he had celebrated their role as guardians of African cultural memory, stating in 1960 that "In the tranquility of our villages, in the shade of our forests, on the shores of our rivers, our griots [French word for *jelilu*] patiently, lovingly rewrote our history and thus contributed to the greatness of the future Africa."[4] In poetic and sentimental terms, Touré here associates jelilu with the unspoiled rural sphere, evoking Herderian images of folk patriotism and ideals of a precolonial Africa. Yet, as his revolution intensified over the next two decades, these

"African poets" became a target of his reformist fervor. By 1968 the government had adopted a resolution calling for "griotism," which took on negative connotations of backwardness and moral corruption, to be abolished.[5] Touré also played on existing discourses on the social and moral inferiority of jelilu, vilifying them for their "greed, idleness and begging" (1972: 431; my translation). Evoking socialist rhetoric, he further added accusations of jelilu as antimodern and antirevolutionary, condemning their "unscientific" and "feudal" practices.[6] Such ideas also circulated in post-independence Mali, which saw calls to end social distinctions and related practices (Hopkins 1997: 55–56; Hoffman 2000: 53). In Guinea, the Touré regime took steps to divest jelilu of their traditional power. For instance, the 1968 resolution explicitly overlooks artistry and heritage by announcing that hereafter the president or a high-level party official will take over the ceremonial role of jelilu. The regime also attempted to ban praise singing to individual patrons by denouncing the practice, and the best-known jelilu were recruited into formations such as the Ensemble Instrumental de Guinée, whose mission as Touré outlined in 1972 was to "give a collective form to musical expression" and to "kill griotism."[7]

All this changed with Touré's death in 1984. Individual musicians were now free to pursue solo careers without the encumbrance of a twelve-person band, and singing the praise of powerful individuals became an important professional and artistic opportunity for musicians across the stylistic spectrum. As official sponsorship of culture dwindled, an atmosphere of individualism, competition, and virtuosic spectacle intensified as musicians, both jelilu and non-jelilu, sought to promote themselves to secure the support of wealthy patrons. Today, praise singing proliferates well beyond jeliya, and praise singers can come from any genre or background, including hip-hop, reggae, and R&B.

Government officials in Guinea continue to monopolize wealth and power—and a great deal of praise performance is still directed toward them—but Guinean musicians today are less involved in "performing the nation" (Askew 2002) than in singing the state: singing for the largesse of wealthy and powerful individuals rather than for a revolutionary and seemingly unified cause. This shift is not simply one from collective effervescence to dispassionate capitalism, however. While national sentiment and revolutionary fervor play a much smaller role than in earlier times, vedettariat still provides ample space for musical emotion and pleasure. For musicians, particularly singers, vedettariat allows for greater public recognition and opportunities for virtuosic display as individual singers compete for patronage. For audiences, these performances combine thrilling, sensual spectacles of wealth and power with the continued evocation of older ideals.

Power Aestheticized

Despite the familiar, anxious talk frequently heard in Conakry about excessive individualism, corruption, and moral decline in music, a trip through town any day or night of the week shows that jeli praise performance is thriving and hugely popular. In addition to concert venues, many of these performances occur at street parties or at weddings and other celebrations at spaces such as La Paillote. In this context, women jeli singers—*jelimusolu*—dominate, while women also often dominate the audience, where they revel in collective pleasure.

The music here is most often jeli pop rather than deep jeliya—a singer and female chorus accompanied by modern or traditional instruments. Jeli pop songs seldom draw from the classic jeli repertoire but instead are newly composed; they are often about love or God or social counsel and very often sung to particular individuals. For these singers, rampant music piracy in Guinea means that the only sure way to make money through music is either through concert ticket sales or patronage.[8] Any musician who is able will thus hold a grand album release party, or *dédicace*, and invite all his or her patrons to attend. Traditionally, jeli praise performance is about the arousal of cultural and collective memories through listening and watching. But in modern contexts such as a dédicace, praise performance also rests on the social pleasures of seeing and being seen, dressing up, commanding attention, and any performance is as much if not more about the audience than about the musician. The singer's voice dominates the event, while the spectators and patrons complete the thrill and immediacy of the show.

The aesthetics of Guinean vocal music value power and projection, with singers commended for their shifts in dynamics and their ability to command space. As discussed in chapter 1, an emphasis on volume is tied to the power and authority of the jeli's voice to secure their patron's name and place in the past, present, and future. By broadcasting the patron's name and virtues widely for all to hear, the jeli extends the patron's recognition and social role. As a result, the best jelilu are prized to a large extent for their vocal intensity, their ability to shift from soft phrases to ringing declamations. Diaryatou Kouyaté, for example, is often lauded for her ability to project her voice all the way across a room. To achieve this ability, young singers in Conakry often practice on the rocks along the city's beaches, singing out into the sea so that water spirits can hear and give further power to their voice. As Hoffman notes, volume and power are proof of the ability to produce and control high levels of *nyama*, a fundamental and potentially dangerous natural force or energy (2000: 247).[9] Vocal power and intensity showcase the social identity and power of jelilu.

A few years ago I attended a concert at the Palais du Peuple featuring Sékouba Kandia, the son of the great Touré-era singer Sory Kandia Kouyaté. Sékouba's performance clearly evoked his father: the singer opened with Sory Kandia's well-known 1973 song "PDG." As the opening bars of the song rang out, a familiar, almost operatic voice sounded offstage, at first suggesting a recording until, moments later, Sékouba Kandia strode forward to ecstatic applause. Dressed and sounding very much like his father, Sékouba Kandia gave an impressive performance that was received enthusiastically by the audience. Yet this reception did not prevent the emcee from promptly undercutting the artist, triumphantly declaring, "The difference between him and his father is that his father could do it without a microphone!"

Singers are admired for their ability to project naturally, shifting from soft to loud and moving higher in pitch until their voices ring with strident authority and demand the listener's full attention. Nonetheless, for public events musicians rarely perform acoustically, preferring instead to supplement their own abilities with as much amplification as they can afford. At concerts, speakers and microphones are often set to the highest level until they punctuate the event with piercing squeaks and squeals. At times the volume is set so high that the sound is completely distorted, with accompanying instruments rendered entirely inaudible. In addition, a noisy generator is often added to the mix. Few people seem to mind, however, and the liveness of the event is not compromised. Instead, the presence of sound equipment is proof of the event's prestige, while the deafening volume is accepted as part of the show.

Tied up with these sound aesthetics of the powerful voice is the visual spectacle of the performance, which rests as much if not more on the audience and patrons as on the performers. The line dividing audience from performer in Guinea is extremely porous. Concerts most frequently feature a continuous flow of people moving back and forth from the stage to dance or to tip the musicians. If a concert is successful, the musicians themselves are at times completely obscured by audience members, who crowd the stage to dance, shower money on the singer, and be publicly recognized. These interactions are key to the concert's liveness, a spatial call-and-response allowing deeper engagement in the show.

At Djeli Kani Fanta Diabaté's sumu at La Paillote, for example, the jelimuso turned periodically to face a row of spectacularly dressed women seated in a special section of the open-air venue. These VIPs included wives of govern-

ment ministers, and Djeli Kani Fanta knew exactly whom among them to
single out for praise. At one point she faced the group and, as the instrumentalists receded and a hush grew, raised her hands above her, her voice rising
and falling with melismatic ornamentation as she sang out: "Soliyooo . . . Soli
Silamakanba Koita." This short melodic phrase is from an important jeli song
that represents a "call to the horses," evoking the steeds historically owned by
nobility. As a lyrical and musical device within another song, it intensifies the
mood and power of the performance.[10] For Mande listeners, it immediately
indicates jeli praise to individual patrons and as a result was seldom used
in Touré-era recordings, when the practice of praise was tightly controlled.
Many Touré-era musicians complain that "the only thing jelilu know how
to do today is sing soliyo." For others, however, singing soliyo is intrinsic to
the jeli's heritage and allows her to express her vocal and aesthetic power to
move people.

At the sumu, Djeli Kani Fanta captured the full attention of the quietly
seated audience as her voice rang out, filling the sound space entirely. A short
while later she launched into a series of full-throated staccato declamations
of family names, punctuated by instrumental flourishes from Demba and the
other backing musicians. The women in the VIP section looked on impas-
sively yet with full attention, only their jaws moving as they slowly chewed
gum. Finally a woman in brilliant yellow *basin*, a highly prized damask tex-
tile, subtly gestured to those around her, and the group rose. The woman
in yellow, whom one of my friends named as Madame Sylla, the wife of a
high-level CNDD official, slowly approached the stage. With her entourage
encircling her, Madame Sylla moved forward, her face remaining coolly de-
tached as she opened her purse. By this point she and the jelimuso were facing each other, the jelimuso calling out her virtues as well as those of her
husband. Cameramen swooped around, filming from every angle, their images simultaneously projected on a screen behind the stage. Madame Sylla
began taking out bundles of folded Guinean francs from her purse, handing
each one to a woman in her entourage, who in turn handed it to one of the
jelimuso's backup singers. With her entourage swaying gently to the music,
Madame Sylla remained still while casually producing bundle after bundle,
displaying for all the seeming endlessness of her generosity. The entire duet
between jelimuso and patron lasted for several minutes until, finally satisfied that the praise had been sufficiently reciprocated, Madame Sylla and the
other women abruptly turned on their heels and briskly walked off the stage.

The sumu at La Paillote was a particularly refined occasion, with an audience composed primarily of middle-class women. In such settings emotional
restraint conveys social status and dignity, and while jelilu are traditionally

exempt from these expectations because of their low social status, nobles—
and those aspiring to noble traits—are bound by them, because they must
maintain control over their bodies and speech (Hoffman 2000: 87–88; Schulz
2001: 146). Women in particular are expected to show physical and emotional
restraint (Hoffman 1995: 38; Durán 2000). Just as the patron herself displayed
no emotion, audience members also sat in cool, reserved silence through
much of the concert, speaking among themselves while nonetheless taking
in every detail of the performance before them. Watching the stage and the
projected screens, the women around me noted exactly who had paid and
how much, how the patron had behaved, and what she and her entourage
were wearing, and at the end of each exchange there was a palpable sense of
satisfaction that things had been done correctly. As Madame Sylla emptied
her purse, a woman next to me almost let her excitement get the better of
her as she speculated that the jeli's gift may have exceeded 1,000,000 Guinean
francs—approximately $200 at the time of my fieldwork, and more than the
monthly salary of most Guineans.

In less refined settings the audience will not be so contained in its reactions. Spectators may roar their approval as a patron generously tips the
singer, perhaps tucking money into the jeli's collar or showering the jelimuso
with fistfuls of Guinean francs, which are quickly swept up by an assistant
standing to the side of the stage. At large concerts the emcee may take the
microphone to announce a patron's tip, and if it is particularly impressive,
the cheers can be deafening. Audience members often jump to their feet in
ecstatic dancing, moved by the powerful voice, its poetic allusions to the past
or to proverbs, and the patron's act of recognizing and reciprocating these
shared references.

Yet even in more elegant settings, the audience's participation is vital to
the performance, in which pleasure is made palpable. From street parties to
sumus and other lavish concerts as these, audiences participate in many ways:
by close listening and watching, by dancing and clapping, willing a patron to
respond to praise, cheering and stamping their approval at the response, discussing among themselves the amount given, and probably gossiping about
it the next day. These reactions produce the performance just as much as the
music itself does. While people listen to the jeli's words, they also drink in the
clothes, the colors, the sounds of the instruments, and the visual spectacle
of tipping. This tipping, or *jeli son wodi* (jeli praise money), represents a climactic moment in which all three parties to the exchange are moved—the
jelimuso amplifying her voice, the patron affirming the sung references, and
the audience signaling its approval in subtle or direct ways. The display of
wealth in part heightens the experience both quantitatively and qualitatively.

Yet more important than the spectacle of money itself is the act of recognition that it allows. The patron's name has been broadcast for everyone to hear and for its bearer creates an immeasurable sense of social wealth and pride in being publicly recognized. The cultural administrator and historian Mamadi Koba Camara told me that if he hears his family name sung in praise, "N'kun bara na fuula fa" (my head fills up my cap). The sense is expansive, of someone bursting with pride (see Hoffman 2000: 83; Skinner 2015: 99). These feelings spread beyond the individual and are felt by the whole at the moment of naming—the individual is recognized and, by virtue of the shared understanding and shared structures of feeling of the moment, so is the collectivity.

Of course, patrons have a key role to play in the performance. They must make their pride and pleasure manifest for all to see (Hoffman 2000: 84). As the example of Djeli Kani Fanta's sumu illustrates, patrons often draw out the act of tipping, performing their role carefully and deliberately. From Madame Sylla's expensive clothes to the studied detachment of her demeanor, the spatial arrangement of her entourage, and the slow and public production of money from her bag, she was presenting her wealth and status for all to see. Such displays strongly counter long-standing taboos against women's economic power.[11] By proudly and publicly flaunting their wealth, such women are also flaunting their independence and their "shamelessness" in transgressing social norms (Skinner 2015: 40).

These displays are further heightened by the suffocating attention of the cameramen, who crowd in closer to capture the exchange, projecting it outward for the seated audience. Patrons often stretch out the act of public recognition by self-consciously working the physical space. A patron will rarely rush up to face a singer; rather, the patron will start from afar, approaching and drawing out the act in slow, deliberate motions in order to take up space and time. As the patron and her entourage approach the singer, there eventually comes a moment when the various individuals—singer, patron, entourage, cameramen, people collecting the money that is gifted, perhaps someone whispering the patron's family names to the singer, others also crushing closer to join in—all converge into one larger mass that becomes the focus of the performance. This coalescing of individuals, energy, and feeling underlines the importance of people, of being surrounded by and recognized by others. Status and standing are measured to a great extent in this part of the world by "wealth in people" (Osborn 2011: 7–8). These social / spatial dynamics also mirror the dynamics of the voice in performance, projecting outward from the individual, conquering space, demanding that all present see and hear the individual and the wider group.

In theory, praise singing can be done for anyone whom the singer wishes

to acclaim, and even a poor woman or man can be made to feel rich by having his or her name sung. But in practice, there is also a particular recognition and space that is granted to elites, and praise singing is not a purely
democratic form in which anyone can be equally recognized. These practices
developed in highly structured societies, and hierarchy matters, setting the
parameters for social order and equilibrium. Today, while patrons do not
necessarily protect or provide for jelilu as social ideals dictate, the overall
structure of hierarchy remains. Elites today, whether political leaders or foot-
ballers' wives, occupy the role of the noble and jati of the past, and have significantly more means to capture this sociomusical space. In this way, praise
singing is also about the actualization and recognition of relations of power.
But the practice also illustrates some of the contradictions in these relations,
between secrecy and spectacle.

Secrecy and guardedness are key social features in Guinea. Money, posses-
sions, words, and plans are all things to be closely guarded, in an atmosphere
that often feels heavy with suspicion, fear, jealousy, and vulnerability. At times
extraordinary effort is made to conceal the exchange of small amounts of
money. A friend once handed me a 500-franc note (worth about ten cents in
U.S. currency at the time of my fieldwork) wrapped in a piece of paper, which
was in turn wrapped in a cigarette package. Such a desire to keep things hidden permeates everyday life, stemming from the residual paranoia of the
revolution as well as from older norms of secrecy. Such norms hold that traditional power is maintained through esoteric practices, its sources hidden
away behind the surface of the everyday. These ideas, both old and more recent, reverberate in Guinea today. Even among friends, people often conceal
from each other what their plans are, where they are going, whom they are
meeting, and what they hope to achieve. The Guinean social world is a precarious place where people must protect their interests as best as they can.

Yet this "aesthetics of discretion" (McGovern 2013) works alongside what
Achille Mbembe has termed the "aesthetics of vulgarity" in the African postcolonial state, in which politics becomes extravagant spectacle, "turning
prodigal acts of generosity into grand theatre" (2001: 102, 109). The aesthetics
of vulgarity—perfected by dictators such as Mobutu Sese Seko and emulated
by others—is a marker of power at the top levels of society and politics, a case
of flaunting what you have. While hiding the sources and instruments of their
power, those at the top nonetheless reveal their strength through grandiose
and public display. Charles Piot argues that political power in West Africa re-
alizes itself "through demonstrating its capacity to act—and through making
itself visible for all to see" (2010: 42). Political leaders do not seek to identify
themselves with average citizens. Instead, it is precisely the transcendence of

the average, the sheer un-ordinariness of power, that actualizes it. In twenty-first-century Conakry, government officials speed through the city in brand-new Land Rovers and Humvees, sirens blaring as they push aside battered taxis and crowded minibuses. Official functions are choreographed to maximize their theatricality, with speeches, praise songs, dancing, VIP seating areas, and supporters wearing t-shirts printed with the leader's face. Through such display the elite stake out their political, economic, and social territory, spreading themselves out to occupy as much space as possible.

Entangled with the "aesthetics of discretion" is the sense that power is also naturalized through its display, that it must be performed to be rendered real. John William Johnson notes that power in Mande cosmology is not a process but "an entity to be stockpiled" (1999: 10), while Dorothea Schulz argues that political power in the Mande world has always been "justified by and in itself" (2001: 59). Once one occupies the seat of power, it is seen as rightfully held. This idea also extends beyond political power. Those who are wealthy, for example, are seen as somehow rightfully so, even if there is gossip about how that wealth was obtained. Banning Eyre (2000) cites the example of the Malian businessman Babani Sissoko, whose onetime almost mythic wealth was an enormous source of gossip and intrigue in Bamako, even while its rightfulness was never really questioned. Similarly, in Guinea it often struck me that it is not the most successful vedettes who are most criticized for their individualism or corruption, but rather the aspiring ones. They are often labeled as aggressive self-promoters and pretenders, while the biggest stars, such as Mory Kanté and Sékouba Bambino—almost all male—are seen as occupying a well-deserved place.

Political authority and social status in Conakry are increasingly made tangible through an aesthetics of showmanship, in which ostentatious displays of wealth and influence are both expected and often rewarded with approval. Such showmanship is common in other parts of the region as well. Sasha Newell details the ways in which status in Côte d'Ivoire depends on public display, just as urban youth perform "waste" by splashing out cash to publicize their status (2012). The context of poverty and precariousness, the fact that onlookers know the young men are bluffing their wealth, are all key to the thrill of this show. As Newell writes, audiences delight to the artifice itself, which in turn can "produce real social transformations" in relations among people (ibid.: 144).

In Guinea, vedettariat similarly upped the stakes to public showmanship by injecting more and more money and flashiness into the spectacle. Yet praise performance does more than simply create fantasies of acquisition and consumption. Newell notes that in urban Côte d'Ivoire, collectivity is at the heart of public displays of waste. Similarly, praise performance in Guinea rests on an enacted agreement by singer, patron, and audience to be together and to recognize the shared ethics of the community.[12] At Djeli Kani Fanta's sumu, Madame Sylla played her role in exaggerated gestures, stretching out the act of tipping both spatially through her entourage and temporally through her drawn-out motions. The praise was intensified by the sudden hush of the instruments as the jelimuso sang out her declamations. The audience reciprocated with close attention and subtle acknowledgments that things were proceeding as they should. The pleasure of the event was found not in a vicarious consumption of other people's wealth and status, but rather in its elicitation of collective, cultural order and endurance. Rather than a performance imposed on a passive audience, the moment was one that engaged everyone present, a moment of shared unspoken pleasure as the community was bound closer together. As Manthia Diawara notes, jeliya works by mobilizing this feeling of individual and collective recognition shared by descendants of the Mande empire. Jeli songs "keep telling us to return to Mande, for there is no place like it. No other people know us as well as the people in Mande; no other place welcomes us as fully as Mande" (1998: 116).

Praise performance has never been a fixed, stable site. In the volatile political context of Guinea, old concerns about the opportunism of praise are continually given new urgency. How do audiences and listeners negotiate between anxious talk about praise singing and the unapologetically straightforward songs themselves? The unspoken pleasures of praise performance may be manifest; but how do we account for the words of praise it carries?

We Sing for Those in Power

Throughout the summer of 2009, a subject of intense political debate in Guinea was whether or not the junta leader, Moussa Dadis Camara, would stand as a candidate in the presidential elections to be held later in the year. At the time of the coup d'état in December 2008, Dadis, as he is commonly known, had swept into office with the words "Je ne suis pas affamé de pouvoir" (I am not hungry for power). He had proclaimed that he would oversee a transition to civilian rule and then step down. Over the next several months, however, it became clear to all observers that he was becoming increasingly settled in his seat. As a result, by the late summer opposition parties had begun to mobilize their supporters, while the CNDD and its supporters made repeated statements about their right to run the country. A Mouvement Dadis Doit Partir (Dadis Must Leave Movement) was organized to put pressure on the government to hold free and fair elections. In return,

CNDD supporters created their own Mouvement Dadis Doit Rester (Dadis Must Stay Movement) to encourage the president to remain in power.

In this climate, I spent long afternoons in Taouyah with the young men in the Kouyaté family talking about the elections and Dadis's obligations to the country. Over kora melodies and small frothy cups of gunpowder green tea, almost everyone agreed that the military should step down and there should be a return to civilian rule. But in a country of more than eighty political parties, the real question was who should lead the new government.

In mid-August a musician friend, Balla Kanté (the son of the jeli star Mory Kanté), announced that he was organizing a rally and concert in support of an opposition candidate. Alpha Condé led the Rassemblement du Peuple de Guinée (RPG; Guinea People's Party) and was at the time a popular figure particularly among Maninka-speakers because of his long history of opposition to the previous president, Lansana Conté. Many of the young men in the Kouyaté family were enthusiastic supporters of Alpha Condé and were pleased when Balla asked them if they would perform for him. One of them told me that he himself was not a supporter of Alpha Condé but would sing for whoever paid him to do so. For the others, however, it was an uncommon opportunity to perform, to earn a bit of money, and to support a political leader in whom they believed.

A few days before the event, Balla came to the Kouyaté household in Taouyah to ask the patriarch, M'Bady, if he would also come to perform for Alpha Condé. Sitting in the courtyard, M'Bady heard him out, then politely declined. After Balla left, however, M'Bady called the young men before him and forbade them from participating in the rally and concert. "We are *jalolu* [the Mandinka term for jelilu]," he said. "We support whoever is in power, and we don't perform for political campaigns." Despite a long precedent of jelilu playing for candidates, M'Bady wished to make clear that they would only support the sitting president.

But the young korafòlalu were intent on performing for Condé, although they did so discreetly rather than openly defy the old man. Torn between a fear of displeasing the patriarch and a desire to see art and politics at work, I agreed to accompany them, and on the day itself we headed to the RPG headquarters with kora and *bolon* (bass-harp) in tow. The headquarters were housed in a large single-story concrete building with a stage at one end; the rest of the room was packed with well-dressed men and women sitting in rows of white plastic chairs. When we arrived a jelimuso was just finishing her song, accompanied by female dancers, all dressed in long boubous made from material printed with RPG party slogans and Alpha Condé's picture. Next came two reggae groups, one of whom received particular enthusiastic applause for a song calling for political change. Our turn followed, and we took the stage to perform, with bright lights shining on us and cameramen swooping around to record the event. With two kora and a bolon providing the accompaniment, the younger M'Bady, one of the patriarch's grandsons, and I stood in the center of the stage and sang the classic jeli song "Ala l'a ke" (God Has Done It), M'Bady singing the solo in his deep young voice while I contributed the chorus. The Mandinka lyrics, which say that God is responsible for all things and that no one can go against his will, suggested that Alpha Condé had divine favor on his side.

Ala l'a kɛ	God has done it
Kuwo bee kari bayi le	All things can be blocked
Ala baro jonte bayi la	God's work cannot be undone

In the middle of the song, M'Bady stepped forward to sing a praise section to the candidate, articulating in short, staccato bursts that he is a great leader who has the people behind him. The audience roared and stomped their approval, particularly when one of the RPG party leaders stood up to tip us, publicly affirming the song's words.

For the young men in the Kouyaté family, the event was a success, and they beamed with pride as people came to shake our hands after the performance. Sitting down later in the evening with Demba and another friend, Cheick, we spoke about the music: whether the kora was audible, whether we should have performed two songs instead of one, whether the young M'Bady's solo had been long enough. The conversation then turned to the candidate himself, and Cheick explained to me the reasons why he supported Alpha Condé. Trying to understand the role of jelilu, I reminded him and Demba about the patriarch M'Bady's earlier stated position against singing for campaigns and asked whether he would ever play in a similar context. Demba repeated what M'Bady had said: "He won't perform for politicians, only whoever is in power."

"What about if he doesn't agree with whoever is in power?" I asked.

"Then he won't perform for them."

"So, what about the CNDD?"

Demba and Cheick looked at each other and shrugged their shoulders, laughing.

Sounding Truth

Praise for the new military regime took over much of the national airwaves throughout the spring and summer of 2009 as music videos filled with refer-

FIGURE 12. Concert in support of Moussa Dadis Camara at the Palais du Peuple, 2009. Photo by the author.

ences to the militarization of daily life in Guinea were regularly aired in trib-ute to the junta. The video for Hadja Aminata Kamissoko's "CNDD" featured the jelimuso singing in front of ministerial office buildings in Conakry, in-terspersed with clips of President Dadis and other officials at public func-tions.[13] Images in the video included scenes of soldiers dancing with machine guns strapped to their chests. Similarly, the video for the Ivorian-style *coupé décalé* singer Aubin Thea's "CNDD" features troops in red berets and com-bat boots dancing and conducting drills. Aubin Thea is himself dressed as a soldier, and much of the video is filmed inside an army barracks. Members of the regime are thus allowed to perform their power, much as they would during live performance. The imagery also attests to the close relationship between singer and patron, as the vedette is allowed access to official spaces and symbols.

The best example of such reciprocity, and the song that made the biggest splash that year, was "CNDD la mansaya" (CNDD Kingship [or Rule]) by the popular jeli Kerfala Kanté. Kerfala Kanté became a star in the 1990s and, though not well-known outside of Guinea, has long been a top-tier singer in the country. His celebrity meant that the song was particularly well received by the regime—and was often played on state television and radio. The video for "CNDD la mansaya" features images of the jeli meeting Dadis and other high-level officials of the regime in the presidential palace in Conakry's mili-tary Camp Alpha Yaya. In one scene Kerfala is shown being escorted into the palace, where he is filmed shaking hands with Dadis. Other scenes feature

him chatting with Vice President Sékouba Konaté and dancing in a plush office with soldiers from the presidential guard. The regime's cooperation and
enthusiasm for the song is apparent. This enthusiasm was also demonstrated
in material terms. In late July 2009 Conakry was buzzing with the news that
at Kerfala Kanté's album release concert, a group of senior military officials
took to the stage at the Palais du Peuple to announce they would reward the
jeli with a brand-new house.

Musically, "CNDD la mansaya" typifies many of the elements of jeli pop
in Guinea today. The song is set to a 4/4 drum-machine beat overlaid with
synthesizer, which is seen as modern—and, on a more practical level, is
cheaper than using live musicians. Live instrumentation does also play a role,
with bass guitar, bala, and jembe adding to the background rhythm in a discrete repeating two-bar cycle. The overall emphasis, however, is strongly on
the vocals, beginning with a female chorus.

Ka nin fuɲɛ, Fama Ala da k'i ɲe	Let me tell you this, Almighty God will make it happen for you
Ala ba ko min kɛ mansa la ko la dan nin wo te tiɲan na	Who God makes king can be broken
ko sabu le mɔɔya kolu la	People need God's mercy in their relations
Tuɲa fɔla ba min fɔ wo kɛ to le	What the truthful man says, he does

Kerfala Kanté joins in at one minute, coming in on B-flat and maintaining
a steady register and pace for the next two minutes as he sets out the lyrical
themes. About three minutes in, he suddenly leaps an octave to launch into
the song's climax, a praise section listing the names of the top officials in the
CNDD and, in some cases, their wives. This melodic contour is a common
feature in jeli music: it is used to intensify the declamation of praise. Kanté
adds to this effect by elongating each syllable with added vibrato. As the song
draws to a close, Kanté cools down again, dropping to a lower register and
allowing the chorus singers to join in, with vocal lines alternating until the
song's end.

The Maninka lyrics of "CNDD la mansaya" relate to common themes
in jeliya of honor, responsibility, and God's will. But the praise sections are
distinct from traditional jeliya, for the singer has no specific knowledge of
Dadis's family history. Rather than presenting deep historical knowledge,
Kanté inserts the new president into the genealogy of past Guinean leaders.
In this way he both crafts a personal history for Dadis—whose ancestors he
does not know—and legitimizes Dadis's role as a successor to the former
presidents Sékou Touré and Lansana Conté.

Oui, alu ma wuya fɔ	Yes, you did not lie
Fama Ala ba ko menfo	What Almighty God says
wo tɛ tiɲan la	cannot be broken
Oui, se bɛ Ala ye	Yes, God has the power
CNDD la mansaya, Ala le nɔ	CNDD's kingship, God wills it
Président Sékou Touré ka mansaya kɛ	During the reign of President Sékou
la Guinée a la wati yado	Touré in Guinea
Wo mi son yanfa ma fɛwo	He didn't betray at all
Général Conté ka mansaya kɛ	During the reign of General Conté
la Guinée a la wati yando	in Guinea
Wo mi son yanfa ma fɛwo	He didn't betray at all
CNDD la mansaya mi la Guinée ko bɛ	Now it's the rule of the CNDD in Guinea
na wati	
Dadis ko a tɛ yanfa kɛ fɛwo	Dadis says he does not betray at all

"CNDD la mansaya" was not a particularly big hit in Guinea, but its re-lease did create a stir, mainly on account of the jeli's lavish reward. A few weeks after the release party I was sitting in the courtyard at La Paillote when the song started playing on the radio. One of the men seated next to me, a nonmusician named Monsieur Diallo, laughed derisively that Kerfala Kanté was only doing *mamaya*, a term often used to signify shallow, opportunistic praise.[14] Mamadi Diabaté, the younger singer from Bembeya Jazz, jumped to his defense, saying that jelilu had no other choice but to sing praises today because since the death of Sékou Touré they had been abandoned by the government. The problem, he argued, was that musicians were excessive today, whereas during the revolution the government had "controlled" them.

"Not controlled," the bass player and older musician Laye Dioubaté quickly interjected, "but *organized.*"

Mamadi continued that jelilu must sing for patrons because they have no other sources of income. "How are we supposed to support ourselves and our families if we have no other means?" he asked.

At this point in the conversation a number of the musicians jumped in, claiming that it was not a question of singing for money but rather of respecting the strictures of Mande culture. Laye argued that it was his role to educate people about Mande history through singing, just as it had been his father's role before him.

"Jelilu are supposed to sing the truth," Monsieur Diallo countered, "not just *Yamaru O* [flattery]."[15]

The conversation then took another turn as everyone began to speak about how music had operated in the revolution, but this question of "singing the truth" stayed with me. The idea of truthfulness is one that features frequently in talk about jeli praise singing. There is a common Maninka dictum: "Ni jeli ma tuɲa fɔ, kuma da fa" (if a jeli does not tell the truth, his words will eat him). In conversations about music, both jelilu and other people often spoke to me about the importance of *tunya* (truth), and the idea features frequently in song texts. When I asked friends about the notion, however, the responses I received were rather vague. Balla Kanté, the young singer who had organized the RPG rally, told me that singing the truth entailed "advising people, supporting the nation, unifying African people."[16] Others described it as "raising people's awareness" or, more simply, as "the reality, what's good for the country."[17]

Yet, despite this seeming vagueness, the notion of truthfulness is pervasive and deep-rooted. The Kurakan Fuga, a charter believed to originate shortly after the founding of the Mande empire and that set out social codes for Mande people, states in its Article 2 that "the *nyamakalas* [the artisan class, which includes jelilu] must devote themselves to tell the truth to the chiefs, to be their counselors, and to defend by speech the established rulers and order throughout the whole territory."[18]

The idea of truth here has been interpreted as "immunity of speech," which corresponds with other usages that I encountered.[19] Truth is associated not so much with factual accuracy or a lack of deception, but more with facing up to one's duties rather than avoiding them, with not "skirting the issue." Jelilu are charged with speaking plainly to leaders, giving honest criticism about the political, economic, and social realities of their societies. As "masters of the word" (Camara 1976), they are licensed to say to the leader what other members of society cannot. Telling the truth in this context entails an ethics of community, social responsibility, and interdependence. This responsibility can be dangerous for the jeli and serves as a test of his or her integrity. In a fascinating study of *ngaraya*, the most powerful and skillful display of jeli speech, Lucy Durán describes how such mastery is dependent on fearlessness. As the Malian jelimuso Kandia Kouyaté says, to be *ngara* is to tell the truth without concern of angering or offending one's patron (2007: 581). Truthfulness is said to reside at the core of ethical behavior, signifying concern with the social order and the collective good over concern with one's own immediate interests. Jelilu are faced with the competing obligations of honesty in exercising their voice with deference in respecting the social and political hierarchy (ibid.: 583). They must mediate between ideals of truthfulness and the expectations and constraints of their own positions within the "webs of dependence and difference" that Ebron describes (2002: 129).

As the literary scholar Cheick Mahamadou Chérif Keita notes, truthfulness represents "an ideal" (1995: 190), one of social balance in which power and its techniques are shared and distributed. One of the most legendary tales in Guinean musical history is of Sory Kandia Kouyaté singing truth to the presidents of Mali and Burkina Faso (then known as Haute Volta). In July 1976 Touré hosted both leaders in Conakry in an attempt to mediate a border dispute. During this purportedly tense visit, the leaders attended a concert at the Palais du Peuple, where Sory Kandia Kouyaté sang the famous jeli piece "Kéléfaba," which warns against the dangers of war. According to stories that still circulate in Guinea, it was this sung counsel and warning that caused both leaders to set aside their differences and pledge to work together toward peace.

Yet while historical legend may be full of the actualization of such ideals, the contemporary moment seems to suggest a stark gap between discourse and practice. Jeli songs to the CNDD did not provide the regime with honest criticism in 2009; instead, Kerfala Kanté and others offered extravagant, straightforward praise. And for the most part this praise was shrugged off, even, in the moment of performance, much enjoyed.

In her work on Malian jeliya, Schulz argues that the value of praise singing is based not on the perceived truthfulness of a song, but rather on the cultural knowledge that is shared by the "community of listeners" (2001: 157). Jeliya works through skillful play on historically rooted emotions, evoking both the ongoing jeli-patron relationship and the poetic allusions to a collective past for all those present. And while, in Guinea today, the patron and jeli often have no long-standing relationship, the performance nonetheless symbolically conjures both the precolonial Mande past and the revolutionary practice of praise singing to the nation. Even in its modern variant, where the jeli, or indeed non-jeli, singer may sing to whoever currently holds power and wealth, allusions to a shared history of the group add to the efficacy of the performance and ensure its truth effects.

Yet the pleasure of participation and collectivity that comes from this affirmation of a shared past does not by itself wholly account for the seeming discrepancy between the direct meaning of words and their reception. Time and again, when I asked friends what made for a good performance or a good voice, I was told that it was the meaning of the words that gave the voice or the performance its value. At concerts, friends and strangers have many times spontaneously translated song lyrics for me, wanting to make sure that I get the full impact of the words. Yet, as Barbara Hoffman notes, Mande-speakers may control their words but "cannot control how they are understood" (2000: 33). Hoffman observes that words in Mande speech are inherently ambiguous and polysemic, and their meaning depends on social context and the expressiveness of communication. In this regard, a sense of how words and voices can be *heard*—materially as much as semantically—provides under-standing of the aesthetic work happening in praise performance.

In Guinean cultural ideologies, the notion of truthfulness is closely linked with vocal production. Local knowledge holds that words originate in differ-ent parts of the body—the stomach (Mn. *kono*), the throat (Mn. *kan*, which also means "voice"), the mouth (Mn. *da*), and the tongue (Mn. *nen*)—and are associated with the characteristics of these organs (Camara 1992: 248). The stomach is responsible for self-control, for keeping words in check. If a person is morally upright, then words that should not be spoken remain in their stomach. On the other hand, words that are said to come from the mouth and tongue, particularly from a dry mouth, are dangerous because they have not been regulated (Cherif 2005: 117). Someone who speaks from the tongue or from the mouth cannot be trusted because they are not able to control themselves (Camara 1992: 249). This understanding of the body corresponds with ideas about surface versus interior: the idea that surface appearances can be misleading or unstable, while real meaning is concealed further within, in the "underneath of things" (Ferme 2001).

There is also, moreover, a sonic and aesthetic component to this under-standing. Words that come from the mouth can be sweet or beautiful in their sound or in their poetry, but are not always trustworthy. In contrast, words that come from the throat are trustworthy but not necessarily sweet. As Sory Camara notes, and as I heard in reference to Diaryatou Kouyaté, Maninka-speakers may say admiringly that "jelimuso a kan waɲanɛ" (the jelimuso has a rough, hoarse, or scratchy voice) (1992). Durán points out that the ngara, the jeli with the highest form of mastery over words, is prized for having such a voice, associated with age and wisdom, rather than a smooth, sweet one, associated with youth (2007: 580). This rough timbre signifies knowl-edge and authority, as well as mastery over the unruliness and deception that words can contain. Interestingly, this kind of timbral preference can also be found in instrumental music in Guinea, which often prizes buzzy, resonating layers of sound over clean or "pure" tones. These sound ideals correspond with values of obscurity and ambiguity over transparency, prizing the core, the internal, and the hidden over the surface and the immediately apparent (Hoffman 1995: 41).[20]

Mande aesthetics value both a beautiful and a knowledgeable voice (Charry 2000: 94), but these two characteristics are not necessarily present together. In "CNDD la mansaya," for example, Kanté's vocal timbre through-out is velvety and smooth, ranging in dynamics from quiet to powerful. Pop-ularly known as the songbird of the town of Sankara (*sankaran kono*), Kanté sings with a beautiful or sweet voice (*kan duman*). He exhibits the qualities that friends suggested constitute beauty in the male voice—warmth, resonance, intensity, alongside skill with poetic allusions. His voice is not, however, historically authoritative, as Kanté is not a ngara, a specialist of deep jeli traditions and knowledge. He may move people with sweet, poetic, or religious references, but his voice is not considered to convey the highest authority over truth and knowledge—the authority of a true ngara.

From this distinction—this dual nature of words and their sounding—we begin to understand how jeli song and speech can be heard and interpreted. Audiences may be able to find pleasure in the sweet and beautiful voice of a singer such as Kerfala Kanté without assuming that it is authoritative or even necessarily trustworthy. They can distance themselves from his worded praise even while immersing themselves in the poetry and sound of his voice. Here it is not just the referential meaning of words that matters, but the way and context in which they are delivered. Hoffman notes that in traditional jeli speech, phrases are often incomprehensible to audiences—uttered like "verbal gunfire, bombarding the noble with more sound than can be assimilated, causing confusion" (1995: 42). It is this ability to create layers of meanings in the experience of the voice and the transmission of words that creates the power of jeliya.

Even authoritative voices can be heard and appreciated from a critical distance. The scratchy, rough vocal timbre of a ngara such as Diaryatou Kouyaté may add a further layer of authority, but that does not mean that audiences uncritically absorb or accept the literal meaning of her words. Rather, they are able to find various pleasures in different aspects of the performance—the timbre (whether sweet or authoritative), the poetic allusions and references to God and the past, the overall sense of self-recognition. All these elements may deeply move listeners even as they distance themselves from the direct political message of the text. It is this estrangement from the literal meaning of the words that makes their appreciation, and the appreciation of the performance, possible. As Hoffman notes, listeners ultimately respond to the power of jeli speech—power that manifests itself in volume, expression, content, and knowing when and how to use it. The jeli's aim is "to stir, to move, to arouse strong emotions, to evoke that which is possible, not necessarily to describe that which is verifiable" (2000: 65).

Taken together, the various sensual and social elements create the performance and its effect: the power, amplitude, and timbre of the jeli's voice; the poetry of their sung references or the skillful telling of historical knowledge; the visual spectacle of power, social order, and reciprocity; the splendid colors and clothes; the instrumental melodies and rhythms that inspire people to dance; and the overall sense of participation, of seeing and being seen, in the event. In the moment of the performance, even if the jeli's voice is not heard as historically authoritative and truthful, it may still be beautiful and pleasing, appreciated for its power and sweetness, which add to the liveness and immediacy of the show. These various aspects lead people to attend concerts, to watch music videos, and to find pleasure in the performance. In such circumstances, the literal veracity of praise words themselves is often unimportant as cultural insiders understand and revel in the multifaceted dynamics of jeli pop.

Feelingful Politics

The day after Djeli Kani Fanta's concert, I asked Demba whether it had been an enjoyable night. "We're not happy," Demba said, speaking for himself and the other backup musicians. "Did you see how much the jelimuso made? And we got almost nothing." Demba complained that the musicians had been told that they would get paid more, but in the end they received only a fraction of what they had expected. But then he continued on more cheerfully, saying that Djeli Kani Fanta had been pleased with his playing and had asked him to accompany her at an upcoming ceremony. "She's good," he said of the jelimuso. "Did you see that woman who tipped her? She was very happy that everyone could hear her husband's name. She wanted to show Djeli Kani how happy she was by giving her so much."

Despite his personal disappointment, Demba was nonetheless fairly excited about the evening. The performance had been a success, as attested by the audience's reaction and participation. Demba attributed this success to Djeli Kani Fanta's voice and was pleased to have been asked to accompany her again, hoping for more opportunities for musical showmanship and reward. When I asked Demba about the praises Djeli Kani Fanta had sung to a member of the military regime—a regime I knew he did not support—he laughed off my questions, much as I had come to expect by that point. I was already beginning to understand the dynamics of praise and realized that my earlier preoccupation with the veracity of words obscured the relationship between politics and pleasure that it entails.

Praise singing does not constitute an act of persuasion in the usual, political sense of the word. Rather, it operates by creating a "feelingful" space (Feld 2005: 91), in which history, pride, collective memory, and continuity are evoked in a spectacle of sound and sight. In this way, the political work that it does—producing political power as well as broadcasting and amplifying the leader's name—is transformed into a pleasurable, sensual act that in that moment goes beyond the individual patron to draw the community together. Through the ostentatious spectacles of performance today, including displays of wealth and musicianship that would have been unimaginable in an earlier time, political power is rendered real. The sounded and seen performance provides proof of the patron's authority and power through the jeli's voice, the visual display, and the public recognition of it. Yet beyond state power, the political also operates here in a broader sense, as affective ties bind the community of participants together.

While I have described the ways in which audiences maintain distance from political messages in song lyrics, I do not read this estrangement as an act of protest or resistance against the message. Instead, it represents an act of quiet accommodation to a jeli singing praise to a dictator. As Lila Abu-Lughod argues in her work on Egyptian television, TV serials create "an excess of meaning" whose interpretations are impossible to control (2005: 235). In the case of jeli praise, the performance creates an excess of both meaning and feeling. Pleasure in the event is affected less by the literal messages of political praise than by the shared sensorial event and evocation. The effects of the event on the participants are found in a "mix of intimacy *and* distance" (ibid.: 239; emphasis added).

In her work on Syria, Wedeen emphasizes the role of bodies and movement in regimes of discipline, with bodies serving as "the apparent and immediate site upon which participation is enforced" (1999: 21). Public choreography and regimes of movement keep bodies in motion, as they are continually compelled to enact reverence to the leader. Yet while Wedeen emphasizes the "politics of pretense" in Assad's Syria—the boredom and exhaustion of bodies mobilized in his cult—the example of jeli praise performance in Guinea illustrates a slightly different dynamic. Like political spectacle in Syria, praise performance serves to substantiate state power: state officials are able, through the public display of their status and wealth, to claim their position within the hierarchy, as well as to compel bodies to act publicly in their support. What the authorities are not able to do, however, is control the excess of meaning and feeling that the performance creates. Praise performance makes power publicly visible and audible, yet, importantly, it also transforms it into something aesthetic, intimate, sensual, social, and feelingful.

In post-coup Guinea, the CNDD military regime did not design a new strategy of dictatorial praise. Rather, it grafted itself onto well-worn practices and ideas, from the traditional art of the jelilu to Touré's totalitarian cult. Ordinary citizens were at times keenly aware of the absurdity of President Dadis's pretensions in seeking to promote himself as a great leader.[21] Yet the public sense of pleasure derived from praise sung to his regime was nonetheless meaningful and real, as the examples in this chapter illustrate. Praise songs to the CNDD evoked power at many levels—the political power of the state and its elites, but also the power of the voice, the power of words to move people, and the power of the collective to claim space and recognition. Their performance serves as a site of "symbolic intensity where people's experiences of political and economic life are brought into being and made vividly legible" (Larkin 2008: 170). Performances recreate an intensified account of public life in which the powerful and wealthy display their power and wealth in grandiose fashion, aestheticizing structures of authority while also affirming community.

Yet, alongside pleasure and pride, praise songs also illustrate the ephemeral nature of power in this context. Like the successive authoritarian regimes in Guinea abruptly cut off by coups d'état, so the exaggerated and drawn-out act of each patron in a praise performance ends swiftly and unceremoniously, quickly replaced by the next patron, who becomes the jeli's, and the audience's, object. At Djeli Kani Fanta's sumu, for example, shortly after Madame Sylla and her entourage returned to their seats, another group took the stage to play out the same ritual.

Moreover, in the context of a cultural practice extolling history, continuity, and endurance, praise recordings are often startlingly ephemeral. By the time Kerfala Kanté's album was released in 2010, for example, President Dadis had been deposed and the military regime had imploded. The album still retained the song "CNDD la mansaya," but its title was discreetly deleted from the track list. Furthermore, a new praise song to the interim president, Sékouba Konaté, was hastily recorded and tacked onto the end.

Here we see a balancing act between the ephemeral praise of a dictator and the evocation of sensations and emotions that are much older and more durable. Dictatorship seeks to impose the face and voice of the dictator onto everyone and everything, as the image of the dictator presides over public space. The jeli is presented as his voice, his loudspeaker—a vocal embodiment of the leader, magnified and re-presented. Yet audiences and listeners do not simply *hear* the jeli as the dictator's voice. Instead, they hear their own names; they feel and recognize the evocation of their own shared past and the possibility of cultural endurance in the future.

4

Warriors for Peace

As the political emergency in Guinea escalated, by the late summer of 2009 the sounds of dissent became louder and more insistent. From angry callers on radio phone-in shows to impassioned protesters marching in the streets to genial debates in neighborhood courtyards, voices could be heard throughout Conakry expressing uncertainty about the country's future and frustration at the military regime's intransigence. Elections were to be held later that year, but no one knew whether the military would actually cede control to civilian rule. "Fifty years of misery" was the popular refrain, a reference to Guinea's half centenary of dictatorship and chronic poverty. Yet, in this environment of contestation, as conversations on street corners and in the private media echoed the growing crisis, musicians remained largely quiet.

In this chapter I examine quietness and guardedness in Guinean music, considering the meanings and feelings that such stances convey. As noted throughout this book, the act of naming is integral to both local music and politics, by publicly recognizing particular individuals and their place in history and the present. These acts sit in constant counterpoint with long-standing norms of silence and discretion, however, in which words are to be carefully controlled. The tension between naming and not naming is an ongoing feature of Guinean social life, from everyday encounters and conversations to heated public debates about the legacies of Sékou Touré. Jelilu and other musicians have long been in the crosshairs of this tension, as their roles vis-à-vis the wealthy and powerful are much debated. This situation becomes particularly precarious for musicians at moments of political crisis, as they must balance social ideals with material realities, discourse with practice, and pleasures with fears—whether of physical pain or social censure.

My discussion here focuses on the ways in which young musicians in particular negotiate aesthetics of quietness in Guinea. Under the revolution, Touré imagined both musicians and young people more generally as transformative agents, with the capacity to remake the world. He championed musicians as revolutionaries while periodically warning of their backwardness and, privately, fearing their influence. This notion of young musicians as rebellious and revolutionary continues to reverberate today in the ways in which this generation often speaks of itself in Guinea and is spoken about by others. Local and foreign commentators frequently imagine young Guinean musicians as rebels and dissidents who are plainly outspoken in their criticisms. For the artists themselves, however, the relationship with political power is not so straightforward. Young artists position themselves as alternatives to the perceived complacency and corruption of their musical elders. Yet, while they are frequently highly critical of the state, their criticisms are often cautiously grounded in local understandings of discretion and keeping quiet. Talk about music—whether by the state, by fans and commentators, or even by the musicians themselves—often seeks to present clear-cut identities and politics; but in practice, music is much more polyvalent, and its pleasure is found in part in these mixed meanings. My discussion in this chapter focuses on young, mainly Soso musicians engaged in a youth-oriented genre of urban traditional music in Guinea. Crucially, these musicians know when and when *not* to name, and their popularity, relevance, and the many pleasures of their music lie precisely within this careful balance.

Stars and Hopes

Boulbinet is the name of a neighborhood at the very southern tip of Conakry, home to a lively port and market where fishermen set off in wooden canoes to catch monkfish in the warm Atlantic waters. The neighborhood is mostly populated by Soso people, a Mande language group who make up the main population of the coastal region, including Conakry and the nearby archipelago, the Îles de Los, and extending northward to the lower edges of the Fouta Djallon highlands. Also found in neighboring Sierra Leone, Soso people represent the third largest ethnic group in Guinea, a group that existed at the fringes of the Mande empire and over the past five hundred years was pushed down to the coast by its more powerful northern neighbors, Fulbe- and Maninka-speakers (Thayer 1983: 119; see also O'Toole 1995: 151). While their culture and music are closely related to that of Maninka- and Mandinka-speakers, Soso people self-identify as a distinct group, with social features such as language setting them apart. Soso social organization recognizes categories and differences, but in practice musicianship is less

bound by classification, and music making is relatively open to nonheredi-
tary artists.[1]

Besides the fishing port, Boulbinet is well-known today for a musical
genre that has emerged on its streets over the past two decades. This genre,
referred to generally as urban traditional, or Soso music more generally, is
closely associated with the group Étoiles de Boulbinet (Boulbinet Stars).
Many of the musicians credit the genre to a local Soso man and former ballet
musician, Vieux Coca, who undertook to teach traditional Guinean instruments to young people in his area. As the boys and young men would play,
others would add songs or join in with percussion on jembe and shakers, and
thus the group was born. Vieux Coca and his son, Kerfala Coca, organized
this group of neighborhood musicians into Étoiles de Boulbinet, which began playing locally and by 1997 had recorded its first album, *Wâa Mali*, in
Côte d'Ivoire.

The emergence of this style of music contradicts the narrative often put
forward by older people that younger Guineans are only interested in imported genres such as hip-hop. Rap, R&B, dancehall, and reggae are the
dominant sounds of youth music in Guinea, but the neotraditional scene
has a large and enthusiastic fan base. Moreover, the genre has made its presence felt in others, which regularly introduce traditional instruments alongside electronic beats. Since the appearance of Étoiles de Boulbinet, a number
of other urban traditional groups emerged, all largely following the same
model of young, mainly Soso men with mixed instrumentation.[2] The most
successful of these groups is the Espoirs de Coronthie (Hopes of Coronthie,
also a Soso neighborhood at the southern end of Conakry). While Étoiles de
Boulbinet are considered the originals, Espoirs de Coronthie have the largest
following and have found success on the international stage, spending several months of the past few years touring Europe. I had first seen them perform in Conakry in 2005, and during my return trip to Guinea in 2009 their
album *Tinkhinyi* (a Soso word meaning "honesty") provided much of the
soundtrack. Today the band plays weekly at their popular seaside bar Fougou
Fougou Faga Faga, their Sunday-night gigs packed with fans.[3] As their lead
singer, Aly "Sanso" Sylla, said to me, "Music is the one thing that everyone in
this country has!"

Many of the young men from the Kouyaté family, though Mandinka
themselves, are closely associated with neotraditional music. M'Bady and
Diaryatou's son Kandia played kora and toured and recorded with the
Espoirs for several years, while others in the family created their own group,
the Étoiles de Mandingue (Mande Stars). Demba has recorded a single with
Étoiles de Boulbinet, and in 2009 he performed regularly with the band at

their weekly gig at a neighborhood bar, Glonglon. He often spoke with enthusiasm about the group, so on a wet Saturday evening during the middle of
the rainy season that year, I went to see what it was all about.

The now-defunct Glonglon was a tiny bar-restaurant tucked away in the
Manquepas neighborhood of southern Conakry, just next to Boulbinet. The
venue, run by an Ivorian expatriate, consisted of a small, walled-in courtyard
with a thatched bar on one end and a performance space on the other, partly
covered by a corrugated tin roof. On my first visit to Glonglon, I arrived to
find a dozen musicians playing under the leaky roof, while the rest of the
courtyard was filled with customers sitting at plastic tables. Throughout the
evening, as the rain fell in intermittent bursts, everyone would pick up their
chairs and dash under the tin roof, huddling inches away from the musicians
and their equipment, until the rain subsided and the audience could retreat.
This back-and-forth movement continued all night, the musicians barely
seeming to notice the constant invasions of their "stage."

The Étoiles struck me immediately for the sheer variety of instruments
they played, representing different regions and traditions from throughout Guinea (fig. 13). As noted, the music of Soso people closely overlaps the
Mande music of Maninka- and Mandinka-speakers. The group featured the

FIGURE 13. Alya Camara (*left*) and Demba Diallo (*middle*), two of the musicians with Étoiles de Boubli-
net. Photo by the author.

jeli instruments kora and bala, alongside the Mande hunter's instruments
bolon (bass-harp) and jembe.[4] At the same time, the *kongoma* (three-key la-
mellophone) from coastal Guinea and the *krin* (slit-drum) from the forest
region added further percussive layers.[5] In addition, three or four male singers took turns providing powerful vocal solos, mostly in Soso.

The group's innovation has been to create urban dance music that incor-
porates a variety of older instruments. Although electric guitars and drum
kits are used, the sound is dominated by instruments representing all four
of Guinea's regions, many of which had not been previously played together
in pop formats. The incorporation of these instruments created new textures
in Guinean popular music, characterized by the distinctive timbres of bala,
kora, bolon, and various percussion instruments. Played together, they create a thick, buzzy texture, distinct from the synthesized instrumentation of
much jeli pop music. Many of these instruments, including bala and bolon,
have gourd or tin-sheet resonators (*sese*) attached to achieve a buzzing effect,
while shakers and rattles add to the percussive density. Such a drone often
runs counter to Euro-American preferences for clear sound and marks a contrast with the consciously cosmopolitan sounds of many other local genres.
These groups are built on intergenerational flows of musical knowledge and
readily acknowledge their debt to their musical elders. Espoirs de Coronthie
are even recording an album, *Légendes*, that pays homage to the revolutionary
dance bands. Yet, at the same time, with their distinctive instruments, members of Étoiles de Boulbinet and similar groups set themselves apart as young
musicians doing something different from past practices. Alya Camara, the
group's talented bolon player, has even created his own technique of playing
the instrument upright and slung across his body like a bass guitar, as well as
further innovating by building an electric bolon.

The idea of Soso music as an alternative for urban youth is key to its popularity and success, and to the pleasures it holds for audiences and musicians
alike. Groups such as the Espoirs and the Étoiles revel in their innovative
sounds and their rebellious looks, with musicians often sporting dreadlocks
and other Rastafarian styling—looks that are often met with disapproval by
older Guineans. But for young musicians, the look signals solidarity with such
outspoken reggae artists as Bob Marley and the Ivorian star Alpha Blondy,
and the ideals of youthful protest and resistance that they represent. As the
late Mohamed "Branco" Camara, one of the lead singers for the Étoiles, said
to me: "Young musicians, young artists, we're the real warriors for solidarity and peace in this country. When there's a problem, we stand up. We tell
people, Stop. Ethnocentrism isn't good. War isn't good. We're all Guineans."[6]

Similarly, Balla Kanté, a young jeli singer engaged in urban traditional forms, told me, "I think that music can really help our country, can unify it, because there's still ethnocentrism in our country and everyone wants power, so young people were divided. But today, thanks to music, music is beginning to ease young people. . . . Music is helping our country through the crisis. And that same music is undoing the political crisis." Branco and Balla both described a landscape in which young Guinean musicians lead the charge toward political change. They are able and willing to stand up and express their views freely and for the collective good, echoing the ideals promoted by Alpha Blondy and others. Yet, while their statements reflect aspirations of music as a vanguard and of the political agency of young musicians, it is less clear that they represent lived reality in Guinea today. When I asked Branco and Balla for examples of songs or lyrics, for instance, both suggested to me that they were speaking "in general" rather than in reference to specific cases. My own observations were that very few songs by local musicians, young or old, were directly critical of politicians or the CNDD. While a flood of praise songs across the musical spectrum greeted the new military regime in 2009, examples of musical critique or opposition to the regime were much harder to find.

This is not to say that the music of Soso and other youth-oriented genres is not political or topical. These songs are animated with vivid references to everyday life, its hardships and its joys. While jeliya traditionally emphasizes history, the past, and the high politics of the Mande empire and modern state, Soso music often speaks to the low politics of the street today. Like almost all musicians in Guinea, urban traditional singers do frequently offer praise to politicians and powerful figures, and Étoiles de Boulbinet even performed at a concert in support of the CNDD in May 2009. Other songs by these groups celebrate love, family, and the vitality of urban life. But notably, these songs also movingly evoke the struggles of ordinary people, recounting the deprivations of poverty on the postcolonial citizen. As the Espoirs sang in "Torrè" (Suffering), a popular recording in the summer of 2009:

Iyo tɔɔre mu fan, wo tɔɔre gere, tɔɔre mu fan	Yes, suffering is not good, let us fight suffering, suffering is not good
Banna xa saabi nan setarera	The rich uses the poor like his key
Banna xa saabi nan setarera, duniya	The rich uses the poor like his key, oh life [the world]
A nati nadeyoma nan na nabima passe-partout	If he puts him in the door, it opens like a master-key
Kɔno mixi mu fan, Ala nan fan	But people are not good, God is good

Ala nan fan	God is good
Gine dimɛdi sarɛmati bara gboo to soge	There are too many young girl sellers nowadays
Gine dimɛdi sarɛmati bara gboo, Y'Ala	There are too many young girl sellers, oh God
Kuyɛ nu yiba nde plateau rafɛ marché mato	When the sky is clear some will be washing plates [working] at the market today
Kwɛ na so sexy kangrɛ sac tongo, tɔɔre gbalu	When night falls, the sexy take their bags to go out [prostitute themselves], because of suffering
Dii ma bari ma, baba me hebɛ, 10,000 xa fe	Children born, without a father, for the sake of GNF 10,000
Kɔnɔ tɔɔre mu fan	But suffering is not good

The frank portrayals of social hardships in such songs would have been impossible during the revolution, when music was required to convey optimism and pride. Today, however, young artists are not afraid to sing directly about injustice, corruption, and the difficulties of life in Guinea. Yet, despite their rich depictions, these songs also tread rather carefully around the subject of state politics and politicians. The Espoirs in particular have released songs about young people killed by police violence, and about the endless corruption of the state and the exhausting nature of Guinean politics. At the same time, however, no one is named directly in these songs, no leader or party is singled out as accountable; in this way the songs offer stirring critiques of the situation rather than of those who are responsible for it. In a highly personalistic musical and political environment, one in which musicians routinely sing the names and stories of individuals, these songs are largely left impersonal and nameless. Musicians thus deftly interpret the parameters of voice and quietness, of when and when not to name, in Guinea. For local listeners, the criticisms are clear, even when they are not explicitly made.[7] Yet this careful balance becomes particularly fraught in moments of political crisis, as the events of 2009 show.

First, however, a brief return to Glonglon. The crowd responded with enthusiasm to Étoiles de Boulbinet's performance. Each piece started with a solo on either kora or bala, usually a fast, descending melodic line that would settle into a steady cycle as the other instruments joined in. The musicians would then alternate between slower, melodic passages during which a succession of singers would take the microphone, and loud, faster tempo passages during which a member of the audience, or indeed one of the musicians, might jump up to dance. As the music heated up, the singer would periodically shout, "Climatiseur!" (air conditioner!) to cool down the instrumentalists so that he could resume singing. At the time I left, well past 3:00 a.m., the music, and the rain, showed no signs of abating.

28 September 2009

By late August 2009 the sense of emergency in Guinea was palpable. The CNDD had initially been greeted with enthusiasm as an alternative to the hated Conté regime, and there was widespread agreement that the country needed a change. President Dadis was hailed as "Obama Junior," and for the first few months of the new regime people would line up to cheer as its military convoys drove down the streets of Conakry. The regime launched street-cleaning campaigns and vowed to crack down on petty crime and illegal construction on public land. For a time its commitments could be seen in teams of street sweepers and the smashed skeletons of buildings around town. But these campaigns quickly dissipated as the president turned his attention toward consolidating his political power, and talk about a transition to democratic elections became increasingly fraught. Despite his claim of not being hungry for power, Dadis soon became defiantly silent on whether he would step down from office. At a press conference on 19 August, a local reporter asked the president whether he would stand in presidential elections that had long been discussed, to which Dadis replied that the decision was between himself and God. He then shouted that he did not want to be asked that question again and threatened to prosecute the next person who put it to him.

Everywhere but the state media, the conversation seemed to veer toward the elections, the CNDD's plans, and the rumors of total disorder in the army. Although it was still Ramadan, traditionally a time of no political or musical activity, the first protests against the regime were held in Conakry's suburbs. The government responded by blocking all text-message services, which had been used to mobilize demonstrators. Liberia and Senegal sent their presidents to Conakry to negotiate with Dadis and reach a peaceful solution. The government organized the Ballets Africains and other musicians to entertain the visiting dignitaries and show their unwavering support. Opposition politicians began making increasingly vocal statements about their plans to run against Dadis. The CNDD paid young people and women to march down the city's main thoroughfare while chanting pro-army slogans.

This pattern of political call-and-response intensified over the next few weeks as the regime grew increasingly defensive, and expectations were high that something would happen after the end of Ramadan. As the holy month drew to a close, four opposition parties announced plans to hold a joint rally on 28 September. The date is an important symbol in Guinea, marking the anniversary of Guinea's vote for independence from France in 1958. The rally was to be held at the National Stadium, also named in honor of the original 28 September, and opposition supporters were called to join together there in a show of popular discontent against the military regime. In the days leading up to the rally, Conakry seemed caught in a fevered grip of anxiety, excitement, rumors, fear, weariness, and the everyday concerns of keeping afloat. The government announced a national holiday on the twenty-eighth in an attempt to keep people at home and off the streets, and many people warned me to stay indoors. In any case, two days before the planned rally there was a noticeable increase of military roadblocks and convoys throughout town, adding further obstructions to the already chaotic and gridlocked city streets.

On the morning of 28 September I awoke to the sound of thirty or forty antigovernment demonstrators cheering and marching on the street below, calling out "Democracie!" and "Non à Dadis!" From the balcony of the fourth-floor flat where I was then staying in downtown Conakry, I could see that the center of town was quiet—shop fronts closed, street vendors and taxis absent, no noise or movement except for the military vehicles that regularly sped past and the groups of youthful demonstrators marching toward the National Stadium. Thousands of people from across Conakry were converging at the stadium, and over the course of the day my flatmates and I heard sporadic reports of what took place there. While the rally was peaceably under way later that morning, government soldiers surrounded the stadium and, without warning, opened fire on the unarmed civilians inside. At least 157 people were killed in the ensuing massacre, while a further 89 are disappeared and remain unaccounted for ([FIDH] 2018: 299). Fifteen hundred others were beaten and savagely brutalized by the security forces. More than a hundred women were gang-raped by soldiers in unthinkably vicious assaults, and some died from their injuries or were simply killed. Opposition leaders were swept up in arrests and later tortured in detention. Many reports also held that the army gathered the bodies of the dead to be burned at their military camp, while sealing off the stadium and local morgues so that panicked and grieving families could not find out what happened to their loved ones.[8]

The massacre of 28 September left Guinea shocked and reeling. Over the next few days, as the markets slowly reopened in Conakry and people cautiously emerged, the city felt eerily subdued. Many businesses remained closed, and few people could be seen outside after sunset. Military vehicles continued to rip through the city streets. Many friends living in the outer suburbs of the city later told me that they spent several days indoors, not wanting to encounter the rampaging soldiers who were searching their neighborhoods for those involved in the demonstration. Some people expressed great anger and indignation at the army's actions; some seemed resigned to the situation; almost everyone was deeply anxious about what would happen next. Two friends from the Kouyaté family, Hadja and Diamadi, left the country in a shared taxi headed to Mali, while Diaryatou made arrangements to join her sister in Dakar. Another friend, a Liberian woman who had originally come to Guinea as a refugee from the Liberian civil war a decade earlier, told me that she now wanted to return to her home country rather than face yet another war.

Alongside these anxieties and fears, however, normal life began to resume, much quicker in fact than I would have thought possible. Within a week the city's streets were once again bustling with life, albeit with even more soldiers and armed vehicles than usual. Moreover, the initial feelings of anger and shock that my friends had conveyed seemed to be quickly tempered. For the first time in my own experience of living in Guinea—almost four years at that point—I noticed a palpable, public sense of outrage directed at the military. I remember walking down the main Avenue de la République in Conakry a few days after 28 September. A soldier in fatigues and combat boots stood in the middle of the street laughing at something, while around him passers-by turned to stare with unusual and unmistakable bitterness and anger in their faces. Yet the soldier was heavily armed and swaggered about self-confidently, and public expressions of anger were pushed no further at that moment. I assumed that a tipping point had been crossed, that people would rise up to storm the military camp and demand an end to the CNDD's brutal rule. Instead, Conakry and indeed the rest of the country remained tense but mostly quiet. In 2006 and 2007 the crises prompted by violent repression of dissent dissipated over time, and Lansana Conté succeeded in remaining in power until his death.[9] Similarly, as horrified families frantically searched for the bodies of their loved ones, the days immediately following the massacre were marked by sporadic protests and a two-day general strike, but within a fortnight these signs of popular dissent had died down.

While people were shocked and grieving over the killing of so many innocent civilians, there seemed to be little belief that the government could be removed from power—and in some cases even that it should. Some friends told me they doubted the government's responsibility for the attack. Rumors circulated that Dadis had recruited mercenary fighters from Liberia and Sierra Leone to bolster his forces, and it was argued that these recruits had committed the worst crimes.[10] Dadis himself claimed to have "lost control" of the army, thereby confining the problem to a renegade group. A number of people told me that Guinean men could never sexually assault women, that foreigners must have been responsible because Guinean culture did not allow such things, even though I knew of course that such crimes took place.[11] But through reasoning such as this, many people in Guinea attempted to create distance from the atrocities of the day, to separate themselves—and their leaders—from the massacre. Yet where was the outrage and demand for accountability, I wondered. How could people be so seemingly complacent about what the government had done?[12]

Musically, the long-standing practices of praise and accommodation for the military soon resumed as well. Less than a week after the massacre, I went to Glonglon to hear Étoiles de Boulbinet play at their usual Saturday night slot. The bar was as lively as always, with no hint of the turmoil that had ravaged the country. As the band played, I noticed that a table of soldiers in uniform sat near the stage. The soldiers were regulars—I had often seen them when I went to hear the Étoiles—but that night the sight struck me as particularly jarring. No one else seemed to mind, however, and as the music continued, one of the singers took the microphone and began singing in a mixture of French and Soso, "*Wo nu wali,* thank you, CNDD! Thank you, Guinean Army!" The soldiers cheered and danced, tucking folded Guinean francs into the singer's collar. Demba, sitting with his kora behind the singer, caught my eye, knowing how I struggled to understand such dynamics. "That's just the way it is," he said to me later during a break in the music. "Everyone knows that the singer will earn his bread by singing for the soldiers."[13]

That same week, there appeared on RTG a music video for a new song. Filmed at La Paillote against a backdrop of a large Guinean flag, the song featured a number of Touré-era musicians as well as a few younger vedettes. Singing in unison to a synthesized backing track, the musicians delivered messages in Maninka and Soso for peace and unity in Guinea. These messages coincided with the CNDD's call for a national unity government in the days after the massacre, an initiative that was furiously rejected by opposition parties, who demanded that Dadis step down. The RTG song seemed rather bare and functional, with no solo singing and none of the melodic leaps and dynamics that otherwise create heightened emotion in Guinean song. This was music made purely for putting forward a message. Moreover, no one was named in the song, either in praise or by indirect reference, despite the presence of several musicians who had sung for the regime in the past.

The RTG song suggested to me that there was little public appetite for praise to Dadis so soon after the massacre. While the singer at Glonglon sang directly to the soldiers present, the musicians at La Paillote strategically chose

not to. Such a public and high-profile declaration of praise and of the regime's power would have been excessive at a time when the political situation was so tense, and the normal dynamics of praise performance seemed
off-balance. The audience may have shrugged its shoulders at the low-profile
praise at Glonglon, perhaps because of fear, or familiarity with the soldiers
in an intimate setting. But audiences did not seem willing to participate in
a higher-stakes performance at the national level. By limiting the RTG song
to general themes of reconciliation, the government seemed to acknowledge
this feeling, knowing that this was not the time for an ostentatious display of
power and prestige (see also Dave 2017). The government thus deployed abstract and neutral language—in this case about reconciliation and peace—as
a means of glossing over the particular facts of the moment. Nonetheless,
the song's implicit message was clear: Guineans should support the government and keep quiet for the good of the country, rather than engaging in
further protest. And, it seemed to me, this was precisely what most people
were doing.

Vedettes and members of the revolutionary dance bands have never held
themselves out as protest musicians, and while I was surprised that they
would wish to ally themselves with the government at so sensitive a moment,
I understood that their participation in the RTG song was part of a well-
established practice. The reaction of the Étoiles and other urban traditional
groups, however, caused me much greater confusion. These musicians explicitly position themselves as activists firmly placed on the side of urban
youth—indeed, at the vanguard of urban youth—rather than the state. Yet,
through the praise at Glonglon and the distinct lack of protest, it seemed to
me that they were bending to the regime's will just like everyone else.

Quiet Positions

When I spoke to Branco, the Étoiles' singer, in the weeks after the massacre, he appeared exhausted and downbeat. While normal life had resumed
in many ways, the situation was still strained, and many opportunities for
playing and earning money had dried up. Branco was both angry at the government and resigned to its actions. For the moment he just wanted things
to settle down so that some semblance of stability could return. A prolonged
state of emergency was simply not economically sustainable for him—nor
for most Guinean people, who do not have savings accounts and regular pay-
checks to fall back on. The vast majority of the population rely on the informal economy—producing and selling goods at the market, doing favors for
people, providing informal services. Within days of the massacre, most of

these activities had resumed as people attempted to continue their economic lives and stay afloat. The feeling of wanting to get back to the day-to-day and leave politics aside was an acknowledgment that people need to buy, sell, cook, and eat in order to survive. And that included musicians.

A few weeks after the massacre, for instance, the French-Guinean Cultural Centre (CCFG), one of the only reliable sources of regular support for many local artists, announced that it was closing its doors in response to the political crisis. At the time many expatriates were leaving Conakry, and embassies were cutting funding to the Guinean government because of the state-sponsored violence. Musicians were dismayed by the closure of the CCFG, however. Kandia Kouyaté (a.k.a. Kandia Kora), one of M'Bady and Diaryatou's sons, echoed a common view that "what happened on the twenty-eighth of September is terrible, but politics should not impinge on culture."[14] Kandia understandably wished to distinguish Guinean artists and everyday citizens from the criminal elite. Yet, for the CCFG and other foreigners, the situation was too volatile, and no semblance of support could be given. Ties needed to be cut.

For many people, including some musicians, it was the protesters who were at fault for the instability and resulting fallout. As information circulated about a general strike led by the opposition in early October, a Soso percussionist friend of mine, Alya Bangoura, was adamant that he would never participate in such actions: "I don't go out in the street [to strike]. Other people will go out. Artists don't have anything to do with that. If there's a strike, we stay at home. We can't work. There's no music. That's not good for us. People speak about change, but artists don't care about that. What we care about is to do our work. It's not politics."[15] For musicians who are paid by the performance, support for the status quo, for a sense of steadiness and predictability, is vital to ensuring that they have work. Like most people in Guinea, Alya's pressing concern was to simply stay afloat, to earn enough money to survive and possibly a little more if he was lucky. Politics for him was an intrusion, an interruption of the flow and familiarity of regular life. In a context in which political change has historically been achieved through coups and violent upheavals, people are understandably wary of such situations. Many people told me that it was only the unemployed who protest because they have nothing to lose, even though I personally knew working people who do so. But in Guinea, as everywhere else in the world, people's foremost concerns are with their immediate stability and security, with ensuring a degree of certainty in their lives.

Statements by Kandia, Alya, and others also resonated with a distinction I commonly heard drawn between art and politics as musicians attempted to separate the two domains. Described in abstract, idealized terms, the distinction was never really convincing, yet over time I understood why musicians felt the need to distance themselves from the complexities of the political sphere. Many musicians in Guinea have responded to an increasingly vocal and critical public by tightly circumscribing their roles, framing themselves as apolitical artists who transcend the messiness and corruption of politics. In the days and weeks after 28 September 2009, I heard this distinction more than ever. For instance, Alya's friend and fellow percussionist Gali Camara stopped by his house during one of our conversations on the subject and was also unequivocal on the protests: "Artists don't demonstrate because they love their country. If you're the president, all the artists are behind you. . . . Whether you're good [or] you're not good, that doesn't concern us. What concerns us is peace."[16]

In addition to such statements, moments of conspicuous quietness abounded. Over the next several weeks and months, no songs were released criticizing the CNDD or even mentioning the massacre. Moreover, two weeks after the massacre, once the protests and strikes had died down and things seemed to be slipping back to the status quo, the reggae star Takana Zion gave a concert at Rogbané beach, a favorite meeting place for young people in Conakry. Takana Zion is one of the biggest stars in Guinea, and a huge crowd gathered to hear him. Throughout the afternoon concert audience members shouted out their requests for "Crazy Soldiers," a song that Takana had released in 2007 and that criticized members of the military for their daily abuses of power. Each time a yell was heard for "Crazy Soldiers," however, Takana demurred, repeatedly calling instead for the audience to "unite."[17]

On another occasion I sat in the courtyard at La Paillote a few weeks after the massacre. Around the table were several musicians, some of whom had been involved in the recently aired RTG video. The subject of conversation varied, from concerts and recordings to family life and everyday concerns. After a while a professional-looking woman appeared and asked to speak to some of the musicians from the revolutionary dance bands. She and her assistant were invited to join us, and she pulled up a chair and introduced herself as a journalist from the BBC. The musicians were pleased and smiled welcomingly as they began to introduce themselves and tell her about their backgrounds. The journalist sat poised and ready to listen, but within a few minutes it became clear that she had not come to interview them about their music: she wanted to ask about their views on the massacre. Specifically, she wanted to speak to Sékou Bembeya, the best-known of the revolutionary musicians today, and someone stood up and volunteered to take her and her assistant to his house.

After the journalist had left, the remaining musicians all turned to face each other in shocked disbelief. "But she's come to ask us about *the events*," one of them said with indignation. The others shook their heads in dismay. Another responded that "in Guinea, we don't comment on such things, and that's the way it's been since Sékou [Touré]'s time." As I listened, a heated discussion developed on the proper role of Guinean music. The musicians all agreed that it was not their role to get involved in politics. As one said, "You can ask me to speak about art, but I'm not interested in the rest of it." He argued that artists in Guinea do not criticize the government because their role is to support whoever is in power. The others all echoed this last statement, agreeing that Guinean art is about promoting peace. "We sing about peace, not politics," said one musician, echoing the familiar theme, "and we're not going to get involved in other things."

I left La Paillote that day, and for a long time afterward, feeling dejected and confused. My musician friends seemed at times almost indifferent to the carnage of 28 September. By separating art from politics, they seemed to be relinquishing any moral responsibility to the broader public. As Gali had said, whether the president is good or bad "doesn't concern us." Yet hundreds had died or been raped and assaulted at the hands of the national army. How could it be that such an act was of no concern?

Thinking back on these moments, however, it is clear to me that I imposed my own expectations on my Guinean friends, rather than acknowledging the cultural parameters of guardedness and discretion, the understandings of local history as well as of musical pleasure that shape their choices. These norms do not exclude the possibilities of other emotions, such as anger or outrage. Rather, they act alongside them, yet require a necessary forbearance.

In her work on Uduk-speaking people in Sudan, Wendy James writes:

> The academic discourse on feeling tends to assume as a starting point a normal human being "in neutral," untouched by appetite, or memory, let alone love or worry. But real people are never in a state of *normal* emotionless abstraction, nor even of *average* fleshly comfort; they are always either hungry or satiated, optimistic or depressed, rested or tired. Nor are they alone; they are always entangled with others and infected by the social exchange of feeling. (2003: 116; emphasis in original)

James describes emotions not as distinct and isolatable categories, but rather as utterly mixed up in the everyday experience of being human. For Uduk people who have fled from war, the fear of violence is mixed up with day-to-day feelings of hunger, cold, fatigue, and a long-standing wariness of government officials. Fear may later be remembered and distinguished through words and memories, but at the time this and other feelings are experienced all at once—people are "hit by them all together" (ibid.: 121). In Guinea people often seemed to me resigned to and even complacent about the daily presence of soldiers, rifles, and rocket launchers. While I was routinely enraged at being stopped at military roadblocks, my Guinean friends laughed at my reactions and shrugged off the hassle, even though they were subjected to much worse harassment than me and did not have the option of easily flying out of the country. What I did not recognize in their statements and reactions was the layers of feelings and memories of past experiences that were all present together, even if not manifest to my eyes. With a long history of violent dictatorship and a lifetime of dealing with the constant presence of the military, Guinean people have learned to accommodate state power, to avoid antagonizing it where possible, and to take a low-key approach when forced into confrontation.[18] In 2009 fatigue with the reviled Conté regime meant that many Guineans at first embraced the new military government and held out hope even after its violence became apparent. They had long coexisted with the military, with many Guineans holding the institution in respect, and in general people were both wary and impatient for change. Their desire to keep things quiet did not mean that they did not experience other feelings, such as anger and grief. Rather, Guinean people are able to situate their feelings within a broader understanding of the need to sometimes keep a low profile, to get on with life in order to stay afloat.

The decision to keep quiet does not negate or exclude other feelings; rather, it is a particular way of being and doing that is intimately rooted in local understandings and experiences, from both deep history to more recent times. As Keith Basso shows in his work on silence in western Apache culture, this stance often involves a culturally guided decision not to speak, and must be interpreted as such (1970). Michael Herzfeld examines the ways in which Greek women keep quiet as an expression of irony as well as a means of protecting themselves from social censure (1991), while Hélène Neveu Kringelbach similarly explores the unspoken transgressions of women's participation in Senegalese *sabar* dance performances (2007). Kay Kaufman Shelemay suggests that the public silence of Syrian Jewish women exists in fluid relation with their private musical lives, whose affective power should not be underestimated (2009). In these examples silence exists as a dense presence, both intensifying and complicating existing structures of power.

In Guinea, long-standing norms hold that words must be kept in check and carefully controlled, that they must not spill out dangerously and excessively (Camara 1992: 252–53). And while local ideals suggest that jelilu—and, according to some, musicians more generally—have poetic license to criticize leaders and transgress these norms, political exigencies in Guinea have long dictated otherwise. Since the revolution, musicians have understood the need to be prudent and discreet, and they have seen that keeping quiet can allow manifold musical and public pleasures to be enjoyed, while too much voice threatens an altogether different outcome. Guardedness nods to the past and to certain appropriate and distinctly local ways of behaving musically. Rather than being a void or a submission to the violence and volatility of successive authoritarian regimes, it conveys a particular set of aesthetics and understandings.

In Guinean music, this politics of silence involves the crucial distinction between knowing when and when not to name, and the understanding that music should serve the greater social good by creating collectivity. As Sanso says, music is "the one thing everyone has." Its codes must be respected. Sanso's manager, Alya "Espoirs" Camara, expressed a sentiment I heard from other musicians: that "tradition (*naamunyi*) —that's our Guinean culture." As Alya pointed out, presidents in Guinea see this culture around them everywhere: "ceremonies, spectacles, people singing their name. They understand the importance of it. They know that's what the culture is, and that it matters to people." Once again, praise singing is not simply thoughtless propaganda, but a deeply meaningful, value-laden practice that speaks to the heart of what it means to be Guinean. Understanding the value of this practice, the pleasures that it allows for everybody, musicians also understand when it is not right to name someone—when speaking or singing about someone becomes an act of division and discord, when it threatens the collective.

Musicians may feel anger toward the regime, but they also understand that their words must be controlled. Declining to speak or sing at certain moments or on certain topics is a way to create space and time for multiple interpretations and possibilities. Quietness itself is therefore an expressive mode—a way to acknowledge culture, history, and tradition while also recognizing the political and material realities of the moment. Like praise, it should be read alongside other actions and behaviors. Young Soso musicians strategically keep quiet—and sometimes even sing praise—as a gesture of guardedness while also performing other stances, from their rebellious looks and matted hair to their old instruments and their self-identification as "warriors for peace and solidarity." These various acts may strike us as contradictory, or perhaps as cynically calculated, but they can also be read together as ways in which musicians maintain an "open stance" to the possibilities around them (Makhulu, Buggenhagen, and Jackson 2010: 8). By playing with these various stances—what they say, how they look, what they do and do not sing—they deliberately elude any one category in favor of a more fluid position across a spectrum of feelings and expressions.

King Liar

A few weeks after the 28 September massacre, three well-known Guinean musicians based in France released the song "Manguè Woulefalè" (King Liar), a scathing indictment of the military junta. The song largely follows a reggae format, with slow, off-beat rhythm guitar, vocal harmonies, and a bouncy bass line. The reggae singers Alpha Wess Bangoura (known as Alpha Wess) and Alseny Kouyaté provide alternating solos in French, while the singer Bill de Sam adds a narrative section in Soso. His story recounts a traditional morality tale about a man named Moussa, a reference to the junta president Moussa Dadis Camara. While this section offers a veiled metaphorical critique, the passages in French are more direct, with forceful words against the military regime.

Tu nous as dit que	You told us that
Tu es venu pour libérer le peuple.	You came to free the people
On ne te croit pas, on ne te croit plus.	We don't believe you, we don't believe you anymore
Un chef d'état qui tire sur sa population	A head of state who shoots his people
On ne le croit pas, on ne le croit plus.	We don't believe it, we don't believe it anymore
Il faut quitter le pouvoir.	You have to step down.

Dadis is not explicitly named in the song, but the message is unmistakably directed at him, with references to the head of state and the military. In the chorus the musicians sing, "We don't want any more soldiers in power, no more killers in power." In addition, the video for "Manguè Woulefalè" features shocking images captured on mobile phones on the day of the massacre and in the following week, documenting the abuses committed by soldiers outside the national stadium. Shots of bloodied bodies and corpses wrapped in white muslin are interspersed with clips of Guineans demonstrators in Paris, marching along the streets with anti-Dadis slogans and banners. With these incendiary images and lyrics, "Manguè Woulefalè" offered a bitter attack against the government, directed toward the president and telling him in unambiguous terms to leave.

In the aftermath of the CNDD's atrocities, the contrast between Alpha Wess's song and musical responses to the crisis within Guinea is striking. While "Manguè Woulefalè" pointedly denounced the regime, musicians in

Guinea either continued to support the CNDD, as did Étoiles de Boulbinet and the musicians in the RTG clip, or kept largely quiet, as did Takana Zion. This difference is understandable when one considers the everyday pressures and longer histories of practice within which local musicians operate. Musicians in the diaspora, on the other hand, sing from both a physical and cultural distance, in which not just the same threats of violence and hardship, but also the norms of guardedness exert less influence. Yet as songs such as "Manguè Woulefalè" travel via YouTube and other media, musicians within Guinea face greater pressures to similarly exert their voice. Young musicians in particular are caught between competing expectations as their fans consume music and culture from other, less guarded places and artists. This process creates tensions for musicians and consumers alike. One Guinean friend told me, for example, that the images of violence shown in Alpha Wess's video were from Rwanda, even though distinguishing features of Conakry life are clearly visible. Such a reluctance to accept the images as local resonates, however, with long-standing norms to keep state violence a "public secret," to keep certain things opaque and unsaid. At the same time, the circulation of such images, and the direct and pointed criticisms against the regime, inevitably raise the stakes for musicians in Guinea.

As one of the groups most known outside Guinea, Espoirs de Coronthie in particular illustrate the ways in which expectations are placed on musicians. The group has been variously described in the European press as "activist musicians," "the spearhead of a generation of youth who begin to dare express their frustration," "the loudspeaker of Guinea's fed-up youth."[19] This notion that musicians are the "spearheads" of political change and voice in Guinea reflects widespread assumptions about music's role vis-à-vis politics—that music is a progressive force for change—rather than an understanding of the realities in Guinea. Undoubtedly, the changing climate in Guinea today underlines the fact that local people wish to have a say in their politics. While expressions of oppositional voice have long been silenced, both through censorship and self-censorship, over the past ten or fifteen years in particular Guinean people have begun to express dissent publicly, as I will discuss in more detail in the next chapter. Although the threat of political violence and instability remains, the recent flood of political commentary and oppositional voices on radio airwaves and private newspapers shows a public hungry for new perspectives and ideas. Yet, in most cases it is actually young protesters who are spearheading musicians. The vast majority of musicians in Guinea so far seem to be one step behind the changes in political culture as they continue to respect traditions and past practices. In part, they wish to support the status quo, to stay afloat, and to have opportunities to perform and, if they can, earn some money.

Moreover, musicians in Guinea have a more nuanced and rounded understanding of what Guinean music is and does. While the music of Espoirs de Coronthie does certainly speak of poverty, injustice, and deep frustration in Guinea, it also speaks of love, religion, and football. As Sanso told me, "You have to sing about things that touch you. We sing everything that we feel. At times that means happiness. At other times, it's about pain. We sing about suffering, poverty, about love, about daily life." Their music represents the experiences of urban youth in all its totality, including hardships and joys. Fans are moved by their tender songs of love and their praise songs to wealthy businessmen, just as they are by songs about suffering. At their weekly gig at Fougou Fougou, the audience thrills to the beats as well as to the acrobatic antics of Kassa, a dancer who regularly performs with the band.

When the Espoirs do address questions of politics, they do so in ways that resonate within local aesthetics. For instance, a few months after the 28 September massacre, the group posted an announcement on its MySpace page: "Les Espoirs de Coronthie sends their condolences to the families of the victims of the 28th September 2009 demonstration, who were bloodily repressed by the Guinean army. Conforming to its promises, the CNDD must cede power to civil society, protecting its citizens, and not the contrary."[20]

Unlike most musicians in Guinea, both young and old, Espoirs de Coronthie responded directly to the massacre. Their words were clear and confrontational, directed at the CNDD and siding firmly with the victims and their families. Yet the medium of this message is deliberate. Rather than delivered through song and in a local language, the message was written in French and disseminated through the group's website. They expressed their view, but in a way that would not exacerbate tensions in Guinea.

Through song, the group has continued to address themes of politics and suffering without naming names. Two years after the massacre, the group released the song "Justice," a depiction of a country lagging behind the rest of the world and a critique against an indifferent government. Like most of their songs, the recording is much cleaner than live versions, with a simple background of acoustic guitar and layers of percussion. Sanso sings in his deep, resonant voice about the fear that Guinean governments inflict on their population, about the greed of politicians while the people are left with nothing. Ultimately, "Justice" is a song about sadness rather than anger. Heavy with feeling, it succeeds in moving Guinean audiences because of the poignancy of its melody and words, which paint a picture of sadness and suffering, eschewing the explicit, pointed attack of a song such as "Manguè Woulefalé."

In distinguishing between "Manguè Woulefalé" and responses within Guinea, however, my aim is not to suggest that the impulse to speak out originates in Europe. Alpha Wess was in fact a vocal opponent of the regime of Lansana Conté while he lived in Guinea and reportedly left the country because of pressure from the authorities.[21] But the fact of being in the diaspora meant that he and other Guinean musicians in Paris were able to sing against the regime immediately following the 28 September massacre. Their desire to do so is not European or foreign, but rather the product of physical safety and cultural distance. Protest also exerts a particular currency for musicians in the diaspora, where Euro-American audiences often expect African musicians to be political and oppositional. As Stokes observes, the "romance of resistance" has often led world music stars to present themselves as political rebels on the international stage (2004: 61).[22] Thomas Turino cites the example of the Zimbabwean guitarist Thomas Mapfumo, who has been celebrated in the world music press more for his politics than for his music. Political activism during the *chimurenga* liberation struggle in the 1970s became key to Mapfumo's international commercial success: "Worldbeat fans—white, liberal, college types—wanted a musical hero . . . Mapfumo was quite possibly pushed to emphasize a political point in foreign interviews, largely due to the orientation of his foreign interviewers and his awareness of the desires of his worldbeat audience" (2000: 339).

Yet even for Guinean musicians in the diaspora, the value of guardedness and accommodation still hold sway. By the end of 2009 the CNDD regime was in freefall in the aftermath of the September massacre, and in early December Moussa Dadis Camara was shot in the head in a dispute with his aide-de-camp, Aboubacar "Toumba" Diakité. Dadis was flown to Morocco for treatment, and in early 2010 he agreed to step down from office in favor of an interim government. His vice president, Sékouba Konaté, took over as head of state, presiding over the transition. A few months later, and a year after "Manguè Woulefalé," Alpha Wess released a new song, "Bravo mon général," which praised the interim president for agreeing to democratic elections.[23] Wess's example suggests that musicians in Guinea and in the diaspora are in fact acting within parameters that are more similar than a casual glance suggests.

Conclusion

Guineans live with the consequences of their country's image overseas, and for musicians this image creates particular constraints. Their songs need to circulate well beyond Guinea's borders in order to capture new audiences.

But even if those audiences are found, how can a three-minute song over-come stereotypes and perceptions that are reinforced by continual reports of violence and coups? Guinean music speaks to joy and suffering, pleasure and pain, and is heard locally in all its fullness and complexity. Yet how to translate these songs to audiences that know very little of the country, that only hear stories of its problems and not of its joys? For artists, this question is a vexing one, linked to material opportunities and to a sense of wounded pride and frustration that their country and culture are so little known or understood by so much of the world today. If Guinea and its culture did have a place on the world stage during the revolution, there is a feeling today that it has fallen off the map. As one of the singers from Espoirs de Coronthie, Man-gué Camara, said in an interview with Radio France International, "Guinea is not [a place in] the bush! We're here to show that great things can happen in our country!"[24]

Playing with categories of voice and quietness, of protest and accommo-dation, are creative coping strategies within such an environment. But some-times these stances are insufficient. The last few years of the Conté regime saw thousands of people taking to the streets in protest against the government's abuse of power. Similarly, the fall of the CNDD regime saw mass demonstra-tions in Conakry and other Guinean cities as citizens vociferously expressed their anger and desire for material change. As I show in the next chapter, the increase in public protest in recent years has opened up new spaces for musical protest in Guinea. These developments have also created new uncer-tainties and new possibilities around the public pleasures of Guinean music.

The Risks of Displeasure

Following the implosion of the CNDD regime, Guinea tentatively set out on a new path toward democratic rule. Dadis Camara's second-in-command, Sékouba Konaté, presided over a handover period that formally culminated with presidential elections in 2010. But concerns remained, perhaps even intensified, in the months and years that followed—about divisions within the country, the ongoing threat of violence, and the relationship between citizens and the state. What does it mean to be a democracy? How should democratic subjects behave? What are the limits of state authority, and of popular dissent? In the context of a protracted and uneasy transition in which such questions hung in the air, an emergency meeting was held at La Paillote in March 2013. The meeting was called by a concerned group of citizens who were alarmed at recent developments and divisions in the country's public life. Speakers at the meeting railed urgently against the current "crisis" and called on the Guinean government to work with them to find a solution. The state for its part affirmed its determination to halt the tide. Yet it was not violence or electoral fraud that the participants wished to address that day, but rather a musical crisis—a crisis stemming from a protest song.

In this chapter I consider the ways in which music and musicians negotiate the tensions of postauthoritarian transition. My discussion focuses in particular on a recent instance of musical dissent in Guinea, considering official and popular reactions to an inflammatory song released in 2013 by one of the country's biggest stars, Takana Zion. As I show, musical protest creates anxieties among musicians, officials, and ordinary citizens alike, signaling changes in long-standing cultural and political norms, and a shift to a new, uncertain mode of public action and being. The displeasure I evoke here references not just the anger of Guinea's newly elected regime in being

THE RISKS OF DISPLEASURE

publicly criticized, but also the loss of popular pleasure as protest becomes increasingly vocal, and as older aesthetic forms become increasingly problematic and unstable.

As Guinea attempts today to step beyond its authoritarian past, anxieties simmer about what the future holds for the country. Starting with antigovernment protests in the 1990s, the need for democratic elections provided focus and concrete goals to the opposition movement over the past two decades, as hopes were pinned on the popular outcomes of a credible vote. Yet today, years after the country's first democratic elections in 2010, the ongoing trouble in Guinea has become difficult to name. Many speak of ethnocentrism, others of a new age of authoritarian rule. Regardless of the label used, the continued sense of uncertainty is audible and palpable on the street.

Recent discussions of post-socialism and postauthoritarianism highlight the everyday experiences and subjectivities of citizens grappling with rapid political, economic, and cultural change. Such accounts interrogate the idea of seamless shifts from violence to order, from closed to open societies, and instead explore the paradoxes and contradictions of regimes and their legacies (see, e.g., Boym 2001; Yurchak 2005; Pitcher and Askew 2006). Moreover, as Sharad Chari and Katherine Verdery have noted (2009), discussions of the various "posts," whether -socialist or -colonialist, invariably tell partial accounts, shaped by scholarly histories and preoccupations. Instead, local storytelling and the accounts of people living through such shifts tell us that change is more difficult to name, and does not occur in neat analytical frameworks or trajectories. In a study of praise performance through dance in Malawi, for instance, Lisa Gilman traces the ways in which reformists loudly reject and then reinstate older practices of political dancing and music (2009: 83–84). As Gilman notes, dance is caught between narratives of exploitation and celebration, often invoked by the same actors at different historical moments. Writing of postsocialist transition in Bulgaria, Donna Buchanan describes the struggles of everyday people contending with the unleashing of free market forces, in which shops suddenly sell everything but citizens cannot afford to buy any of it. As one musician friend tells Buchanan of the situation, "This isn't [democracy], this is . . . crazy-ocracy!" (2006: 430).

Guinea has long been transitioning between a number of posts: postcolonial since 1958, postsocialist since 1984, postauthoritarian (maybe) since 2010, "post-optimist" (Appiah 1992) since much longer ago. Contrary to the hopes and representations of commentators, both local and foreign, these transitions have not occurred in smooth, linear inevitability. Rather, at every moment the past seems to have come into closer contact with the present and future.

Once again, popular music provides an intensified account of these dynamics. Protest music has emerged in Guinea over the past two or three decades as musicians began to address issues of poverty, social injustice, and corruption. As noted, previous songs largely avoided singling out particular politicians or parties and were instead impersonal in their critiques. The current shift points to an altogether new action of naming—directly calling out those with power and responsibility, and not through metaphor or title, but personally, by name. In the context of jeli praise singing as well as attendant norms of guardedness and discretion, the act of naming has suddenly taken on stark new possibilities: naming not as an act of collective recognition or an evocation of a shared past, but rather as accusation. This naming directly challenges the politics and aesthetics of quietness in Guinea, destabilizing older understandings. Genres such as hip-hop and reggae offer forms that revel in such destabilization and create new pleasures for their fans as they listen subversively. Yet older ways of singing and doing, older codes of ethics and aesthetics, and older forms of public pleasure also continue to matter to musicians and listeners across generations. The seemingly radical break of protest music, the seeming transition from silence to voice, is more ambiguous than it first appears.

Voicing Protest

In June 2010 Guinea held its first-ever democratic elections, following fifty-two years of authoritarian rule in the postcolonial state.[1] The electoral moment was the most visible marker to date of a shift that had been under way over the previous two decades. From street protests since the 1990s and rising popular discontent with the regime of Lansana Conté, to the proliferation of private radio stations, newspapers, and websites at the turn of the millennium, to anger against the CNDD junta, dissent has been increasingly and publicly voiced. Mike McGovern notes that a particular breaking point occurred in 2007, which saw government crackdowns on strikes called by labor unions against Conté's regime: "The political center of gravity in the country had shifted" (2017: 171). These changes in political participation in Guinea—from quiet accommodation to protest—have continued since the election of President Alpha Condé in 2010. Ongoing violence, electoral chaos, and abuses of power did not end with the elections, as many hoped, and clashes and protests continue on an insistently regular basis throughout Conakry. In this new atmosphere of unease, a particular voice has been amplified—young, angry, hoarse, often male—and public debate has escalated as both official rhetoric and rebukes against it are hurled at each other on the street and over the airwaves.

For many Guineans, the elections have led to a new uncertainty in which tension and crisis are palpable, yet difficult to name. What is democracy, and what are its implications? Commentators on African politics have sought to answer these questions in various ways. Although political scientists measure democratic success or failure against a set of indicators, such as GDP and strong political institutions, they also increasingly consider various local and historical factors that lead to a diversity of democratic experience. Richard Joseph (2014) argues for a "prismatic" approach to these questions, considering the interplay between local expectations and anxieties and national and international forces. Such an analysis shows that what might constitute good governance by international standards does not necessarily translate to stability and security in everyday life.[2] At the same time, Nic Cheeseman (2015) notes that social relations in Africa have long been marked by expectations of reciprocity and interdependence, which provide a local reference point and precedent for political accountability. His analysis suggests not that African culture is inherently democratic, but that local sets of conditions must be recognized. For anthropologists, the task involves describing and analyzing what these conditions may look and feel like. Piot notes, for example, that in the final years of the Eyadéma regime in Togo, "liberalization spread across political and cultural fields like brushfire," with new political parties, opposition newspapers, new churches, and the telecommunications revolution existing within the dictatorship (2010: 33). Yet despite these changes, he notes that most Togolese people experienced a worsening of crisis, a "loss of hope and of a sense of political possibility" (ibid.: 34).

In a study on African postsocialism, Anne Pitcher and Kelly Askew recall that socialism eluded definition and varied greatly in its forms across the continent (2006). This point suggests interesting parallels between the past and present. At both moments, the state and its citizens have looked to a seemingly fixed point—revolution then, and elections today—which held the promise of closing one chapter and opening another. For this reason, the Touré regime continually evoked revolutionary affects and language, but in reality it oversaw an inconsistent, drawn-out project that long wore out its welcome for many Guineans. Similarly, the current Guinean administration evokes the 2010 elections as proof that authoritarianism has finally been vanquished and "Guinea is back!"[3] As Pitcher and Askew note, democratic transition does not occur on a blank slate following the end of socialism. Rather, an understanding of the socialist past is key to interpreting the postsocialist present (ibid.: 3). Understood in these terms, ideas of transformation are re-configured, and it becomes clear that elections and "democratic transition" do not occur as if on a *tabula rasa* but instead build on past experiences and strategies. In this regard, Gilman writes of a Malawian politician who justified buying gifts and spending money on supporters with the claim that "this is democracy. It is an expensive system" (2009: 115). While elections are framed as a clean break from the past and a turning point, the politician's words suggest that democracy is just a different label for a familiar set of practices.

In Guinea, the country's first democratic elections provided a seemingly clear goal, yet their realization has been complicated and extraordinarily messy. Even several years later, the electoral results and the fairness of the vote continued to be debated and challenged. Moreover, legislative elections were to follow the presidential race in a smooth series of mechanisms that secured Guinea's democratic present. Yet the legislative elections in 2013 were consumed by violence, ethnic and regional hostility, and anger, much as the presidential campaign had been in 2010.[4]

These dynamics resulted in part from the close nature of the vote between Alpha Condé and his main opponent, Cellou Dalein Diallo of the UFDG (Union des Forces Démocratiques de Guinée) party. Diallo, who is of Fulbe ethnicity, had won 44 percent of the vote during the first round, while Alpha Condé had come in third, after the former prime minister Sidya Touré. Fulbe people are the second largest and, by some reports, the economically dominant ethnic group in Guinea. With a string of Maninka, Soso, and *forestier* presidents in Guinea, many Fulbe people have long expressed the sentiment that it is now "their turn" to ascend to power. As Cheeseman notes, multiparty politics have at times aggravated ethnic tensions because campaigns consciously play to ethnic identities and divisions (2015: 151–52). Both Cellou Diallo and Alpha Condé campaigned heavily in their ethnic constituencies and regions, although Diallo also courted Soso voters during the campaign by speaking their language. For this reason, and despite earlier corruption scandals, Diallo was seen by many as a charismatic and effective candidate.[5] Nonetheless, Alpha Condé won the runoff elections in November 2010 and was declared president.

Among his supporters, expectations following Alpha Condé's victory were high. Condé is often referred to as *le professeur* because of his doctorate in public law. As an opposition figure he held excellent credentials. Exiled from Guinea during the Sékou Touré years, he studied and taught law and economics in Paris, before returning to Guinea in 1990 under the military regime of Lansana Conté. Alpha Condé established an opposition party, the RPG, and ran unsuccessfully in three presidential elections. During this time

Lansana Conté frequently targeted him for his political activities, earning
Alpha Condé the nickname of *le grimpeur* (the climber) for a famous episode
in which he scaled the walls of a local stadium to escape one of his rallies when
state authorities came to stop him.[6] In 1998 President Conté finally arrested
Alpha Condé for allegedly attempting to destabilize the government, and he
was imprisoned without a trial. He remained in prison for three years and
became something of a *cause célèbre* among the opposition. During this time
the Ivorian reggae star Tiken Jah Fakoly even released a song titled "Alpha
Condé" (2000), comparing the leader to Nelson Mandela and calling for his
liberation. And as noted, Balla Kanté and many of the young men from the
Kouyaté family had actively supported and sung in his honor during the contentious summer of 2009.

With his long history of political involvement and opposition, his exile,
his imprisonment, and his education, many (particularly Maninka) Guineans greeted Condé's election with enthusiasm. Yet disenchantment soon
followed. Returning to Guinea in 2013, I was surprised to see the extent of
anti-Condé sentiment among many of my friends who had enthusiastically
supported him. One friend, who had previously posted a Facebook picture
of himself standing next to Alpha Condé, described the president as "a good
politician, but not a good leader"—able to gain power but not able to wield it
effectively. Another said that there had been great hope upon Condé's victory,
but it had all evaporated in light of the violence, tension, and suffering that
Guinean people were enduring. There was a widely expressed sense that life
had worsened under Alpha Condé's rule, with exacerbated ethnic and other
divisions in the country and degraded material conditions of daily life. Power
outages, lack of running water, and filthy streets with overflowing sewage
ditches are long-standing and endemic problems in Conakry, but it did seem
that conditions were worse in 2013 than I had remembered. Even in central
Conakry there were often days on end with no power or water. For many, it
seemed that President Condé was entirely unconcerned how these hardships
were affecting people's lives.

Among members of opposing parties and ethnic groups, the anger was
fierce.[7] The Opposition Radicale, as the coalition of antigovernment parties
was called, had organized a series of protests and strikes in the run-up to
legislative elections in the spring of 2013 that had turned violent. The main
point of contention was the credibility of the legislative elections, and the
opposition had steadfastly refused to participate in the vote until Condé met
a number of conditions that would allow the vote to be fair. In response, the
police and army reportedly used brutal tactics to crack down on the protesters, and over the course of the summer the opposition held many funerals for

members who were killed in this violence. The situation became so dire that UN Secretary-General Ban Ki-moon appointed the UN Special Representative for West Africa, Saïd Djinnit, to mediate. The long-overdue elections were further postponed, eventually being held in September 2013; the official results showed Condé's RPG party to have won a plurality of seats. Unsurprisingly, the opposition claimed electoral fraud, and the country remained deeply divided across political and ethnic lines.

Around that time I sat with two acquaintances, Kaba and Bah—childhood friends themselves, but today divided in their support of opposing parties—as they debated the situation. Bah, a UFDG official himself, was livid that Condé was subjecting its members to such violence. "He is killing our *militants*," he said.

"Call them Guineans, my friend, not *militants*," said his friend Kaba, who supports and works for Condé's RPG.

"No," insisted Bah. "They are *militants*, opposition members, and for that they have been killed."

Kaba and Bah remained friends despite the deep ideological and political differences between them, but Bah was unequivocal in his condemnation of the government, accusing it of placing political interests over national ones. It was the government, according to this view, that was abandoning and abusing huge swaths of its own population.

At the same time, many Guineans also saw other causes at play besides government failure. The legislative elections created mayhem in Conakry, with the outer suburbs of Bambeto and Hamdallaye periodically engulfed in tear gas, renewed military roadblocks set up throughout the city, and businesses closed during the strikes. People wondered whom to blame. In conversations and in the media, the "international community" was a common target of anger because of its perceived meddling and its preoccupations with "free and fair" elections at any cost, as well as its history of violent interference and extraction in Guinea. Another target of the current anxieties was the private press itself. Media reforms from the 1990s have meant that the airwaves today are a sea of incisive political commentary, arguments, diatribes, and satire. Yet all this loud, public dissent sits uncomfortably with many. One afternoon, for example, I sat in a crowded shared taxi in central Conakry as RTG, the national broadcasting station, aired a program criticizing (private) talk radio. The presenter likened radio call-in shows to drunken arguments at street bars, stating that they often begin with some clarity, then quickly degenerate into sloppy name-calling and vulgar jokes. In response, one of my fellow passengers nodded and said, "Yes, it's true. Journalists are the ones who are burning down Guinea."

This view is not an uncommon one: many people blame those who are loudest in calling for change. While the international community operates insistently yet from a distance and the state takes familiar measures to consolidate power, it is protesters and journalists who are seen as shaking things up at home and in new ways. Many believe they are to blame for naming those with power, for seeking to reveal too much about power and authority. Yet even as journalists and protesters stand as accessible scapegoats who are lower down the rungs of public life than state and international officials, the shifts in political life they represent are irrefutably under way. How, then, to respond to these changes?

"OUA gagnera"

For the state, unsurprisingly, at least one answer to this question was found in looking to the past. As strikes, demonstrations, and street violence consumed Conakry and other parts of the country, the government found some diversion in celebrations for the fiftieth anniversary of the OAU. Guinea had been active in its creation and early years. The OAU was founded in 1963 in Addis Ababa, Ethiopia. A Guinean lawyer, Telli Diallo, was one of the founders of the organization and served as its first secretary-general. This connection meant that the Touré regime could and did claim the OAU as proof of its own power and influence, and as noted in chapter 1, Touré even tried to move its headquarters to Conakry. Revolutionary cultural productions from the 1960s frequently celebrated the organization, including regional choral songs such as "OUA vaincra" (The OAU Will Vanquish) and "OUA," as well as a popular dance-band number by the same name.[8] And a praise song to the organization, Bembeya Jazz's 1965 "OUA gagnera" (The OAU Will Win), featured in Guinea's contribution to the 1969 Algiers festival.

In 2013 Alpha Condé's new government saw the organization's fiftieth anniversary as a moment to mobilize public pleasure again around these familiar stories of triumph and pride. In May of that year the Ministry of Culture organized an event at the Palais du Peuple to mark the anniversary. The artists invited were a familiar line-up: Bembeya Jazz, the Ballets Africains, the Amazones de Guinée (the all-female *gendarmes* troupe that Fodéba Keita had first formed in the 1960s), Kélétigui et ses Tambourinis, and the Ballet Djoliba. In the lead-up to the concert, Bembeya Jazz held rehearsals in Sékou Bembeya's garage, mainly focusing on a rendition of "OUA gagnera" sung by the duo of M'Bemba Camara and Youssouf Ba. But Sékou Bembeya himself was particularly invested in a second set he was scheduled to play, in which he would perform material from a solo album that he was working on at the time. One song in particular stood out, an homage to Sékou Touré titled "Manguè" (King [or Leader]). The song was in Soso and Maninka, with Sékou Bembeya not just on guitar but also singing—in fact, the first time I had heard him do so. The first part of the song featured a poignant, slow-tempo melody in which Sékou Bembeya sang of Touré's courage while a young woman with a low, gravelly voice, M'ma Condé, added harmony. The guitars and drums remained softly in the background. But after a few minutes an instrumental bridge suddenly shifted the song to full modern Mande sound, with interlocking guitar loops and an uptick in the rhythm as Sékou Bembeya and M'ma Condé switched to a lively call-and-response pattern. It was gorgeous. I remarked to Sékou how different the song was from anything of his I had ever heard before, and he said that was entirely his intention—to do something different and new.

The concert itself was held on a Saturday, and I arrived early at the Palais that evening to sneak in unnoticed, since I did not have a formal invitation. But I need not have bothered. Despite all the fanfare in the state media trumpeting the event, the great hall was only sparsely populated. Well after the concert was supposed to have begun, a slightly harried organizer ushered those of us sitting in the back to move closer to the stage in order to create some presence before the dignitaries arrived. Much later still, the music began with the Amazones, featuring a full dance-band outfit with brass instruments, electric guitars, and bass, along with three women singing in unison up front. The band played a short but lively set of covers of old hi-life and rumba hits, but the sparse audience could not match their energy and was largely subdued—although I did notice some of the Bembeya musicians clapping and dancing in a corner behind a speaker.

Jean-Baptiste Williams, a former Touré-era musician and longtime cultural administrator, stepped forward and abruptly cut the band off to call everyone to stand for the prime minister, who had just arrived. Williams then launched into an opening speech that was almost entirely about Sékou Touré, though it also contained references to Telli Diallo (both met with applause from the audience). There was almost no mention of African unity or the OAU itself. The music then proceeded with some of the other acts before Williams suddenly took the microphone again to comment on the recent political violence in Guinea. His statements were somewhat vague, calling for peace in Guinea and conveying his regret for four deaths that week (a number that many commentators and citizens put much higher, including the deaths of two teenagers who had been shot by soldiers in the street just that day). Williams then called for a moment of silence in memory of the dead, and by the time the audience had just about risen to its feet, he abruptly thanked everyone and called on the next act. Yet, despite its rather rushed and ambivalent feel, I was quite surprised that such a public acknowledgment of political turmoil had occurred at all. Official events such as these are usually pure celebration and praise, and regardless of its sincerity, Williams's intervention suggested that even the state recognized that times have changed.

Bembeya Jazz were up next and performed "OUA gagnera," but as is often the case, much of the sound was drowned out by squeaking speakers, and the musicians themselves exhibited little of the spontaneity and joy that characterized their rehearsals. Perhaps it was because the vast hall was only one-third full, or because there was no dancing or tipping, but the song was not quite able to come to life. By this time Williams was also becoming increasingly flustered, clearly concerned that the event had started too late—all the dignitaries were fidgeting to leave. He grabbed the microphone to plead with the prime minister to stay for another ten minutes, then cut the other acts short to introduce the Ballets Africains. Luckily for him, they gave a thunderous performance, after which the prime minister and other VIPs all stood up and filed out the door.

The event at the Palais reflected both familiar continuities and attempts to adapt to new circumstances, politically and musically. Williams feted Sékou Touré and Telli Diallo, but it was only later that I read in a scathing newspaper editorial that Diallo had in fact been imprisoned and tortured at Camp Boiro before eventually starving to death there in 1977.[9] His alleged crime was, of course, plotting to overthrow the Touré government.[10] Naturally, Williams made no concessions to this history. But he did reference the current violence and discontent, a striking departure from the state's usual messaging, and I wondered whose decision this had been. Moreover, musically the regime once again looked to the past to resuscitate revolutionary culture for the present moment. Sékou Bembeya did attempt to introduce his musical innovations, and he and M'ma Condé invested a great deal of attention and care in preparing the pieces for public performance. But sadly, in the end, the concert finished abruptly after the Ballets Africains, and Bembeya and M'ma Condé never got the chance to show off their new material and new sound on stage.

All Together for Peace in Guinea

Like its predecessors, the government of Alpha Condé has continued to look to the past while also seeming to recognize ongoing shifts in public culture. In the context of musical politics, Condé seems torn over how to deal with the practices and expectations of musicians and audiences, as his relationship with praise singing suggests. Musicians themselves are also adjusting, trying to figure out how to operate and make music in this shifting environment.

As they have assessed the situation over the past few years, Guinean musicians have been singing a great deal about peace. I previously mentioned a video that aired frequently on RTG following the 28 September 2009 massacre and featured a number of well-known jelilu and dance-band musicians singing for reconciliation and national unity. Since that time, songs such as "Unity in Guinea," "Guinea United," "Peace in Guinea," and "All Together for Peace in Guinea" have become ubiquitous on the state-run radio, their videos broadcast nightly on state television. Images in these videos show Guinean flags, hands held high, children laughing, and women dancing, while the songs themselves feature musicians from across the musical spectrum, from reggae stars and rappers to traditional instrumentalists and praise singers, all calling for reconciliation, solidarity, and national love. Yet, if one turns the dial away from the state broadcasting station, these calls often quickly disappear.

How do we account for this sudden rush of songs of unity and reconciliation? What are the politics of singing for peace in present-day Guinea, and of the musicians who do so? In his work on Palestinian resistance songs, David A. McDonald describes the songs of Arab unity recorded by cosmopolitan pop stars in Cairo, Beirut, and Paris in response to violence and suffering. As he writes, these songs become "empty commodities" for singing of abstract ideas about unity and place. They do not resonate with Palestinian audiences because of their distance from the realities of Palestinian life (2013, 150–52). In the Guinean case, we can also assess these songs by recalling the ways in which the dynamics of praise singing have further destabilized today. As popular dissent has become more publicly aired in recent years, direct praise of the government is an increasingly fraught practice for musicians, who are expected to represent the people's views rather than those of the president. In the aftermath of the violent CNDD regime in 2009 and 2010, there was heightened public awareness, and wariness, of musical adulation, despite its deep local roots.

The example of Guinea's most popular jeli star today, Sékouba "Bambino" Diabaté, illustrates this point.[11] When the CNDD military regime gave way to the transitional government, Bambino sang in praise of the interim president, General Sékouba Konaté. Konaté was formerly vice president of the CNDD and held the position of interim president until agreeing to step down after democratic elections in 2010. But while Bambino singing in praise of a president may have gone unquestioned in an earlier time, by 2010 the musical and political winds had shifted, and Bambino was called out. In a 2011 interview with the website *GuinéeNews*, for example, Bambino was quickly put on the defensive for the song, titled "Mon général." He countered, "I sang [the name of] General Sékouba because he deserved it for all that he did for the country." Yet it was apparent that this answer no longer sufficed, and Bambino immediately clarified, "I didn't sing [for] the man, but rather the act that he did deserves to be congratulated."[12]

Bambino's words reveal a desire to create distance from the practice of musical naming. Understanding the particular tensions of the moment, Bambino characterized his song as offering praise of actions abstracted from a specific person. Moreover, by citing the good of the country, he sought to figure himself as a popular guide rather than a presidential spokesman.

This is not to say, however, that praise songs to the new government have not continued to circulate. Alpha Condé's election in 2010 was greeted with the usual musical fanfare as many performers hoped for new patronage and support. A number of songs titled "Alpha Condé" appeared in late 2010 and 2011, including releases by the jeli Mory Deen Kouyaté and the popular Guinean-Ivorian singer Aïcha Koné. Moreover, Bambino himself released a song titled "Ankawouly" (Let Us Stand Up) in which he recites the lineage of Guinean presidents, from Sékou Touré and Moussa Dadis Camara of the CNDD to Sékouba Konaté, culminating with Alpha Condé. Through this homage Condé is legitimized as the rightful successor to the Guinean presidency. Similarly, the song "Le retour de Guinée," from the same album, quotes Condé's previously mentioned phrase: "Guinea is back!"

President Condé himself initially sought to dispel musicians' expectations for patronage, however. M'Bady Kouyaté's grandson Demba bitterly complained to me that Condé had not recognized his group, despite the fact that we had all sung in support of him at the pro-RPG rally in 2009. "And we were there when he was a candidate," Demba said with frustration. Demba's view reflected the feeling of disappointment shared by many musicians in Conakry. As with the initial enthusiasm for the CNDD, Condé had represented change and the possibility for new relationships of reciprocity to be formed, but these hopes had not been fulfilled. Revolutionary musicians did play for occasional official events, such as the event at the Palais, just as they had in the past. But as Alya from Étoiles de Boulbinet told me, "The rest of us have been forgotten."

Indeed, Alpha Condé made a pointed statement by refusing to meet Tiken Jah Fakoly during the reggae star's visit to Guinea in 2012. Tiken had previously stated that he had never profited from his song to Condé in 2000 and had never supported a particular politician. Whether or not this is true, Condé certainly wished to dispel the notion of patronage for praise and reportedly rebuffed Tiken's attempts to schedule a meeting with him.[13]

Condé's distancing was in fact perfectly in keeping with that of past new presidents of Guinea. Since Lansana Conté succeeded Sékou Touré in 1984, Guineans presidents have invariably sought to position themselves against the corruption of their predecessors and have begun their various regimes with the claim that they do not desire musical flattery. As noted, even Moussa Dadis Camara had initially presented himself as a reformer, rejecting suggestions of a personality cult before later embracing them. Alpha Condé (like others before him) similarly sought to distinguish himself from the dictatorships of the past, presenting himself in this case as a democratically elected leader who represented a new era of accountability and transparency in Guinea.

At the same time, many musicians wished to avoid controversy in this new moment of uncertainty. Songs of peace and reconciliation have served as useful vehicles for appearing apolitical, addressing seemingly abstract, pacific themes on behalf of the people (Dave 2017). Yet in fact these songs are often thinly disguised and repurposed praise singing. In their lyrics, the musicians follow a well-worn government strategy of discrediting opposition protesters by indirectly blaming them for the current violence. Instead, the singer implicitly exhorts listeners to support the status quo and not demand change. Moreover, the language and underlying ideas are often directly lifted from official speech. For example, in the spring of 2013, in the midst of the violence during the lead-up to legislative elections, the Condé government called for a national day of prayer for "the consolidation of peace, social cohesion and national unity." Similarly, in a speech in late 2012, the Minister of Culture, Tidiane Cissé, explicitly called on artists to "spread messages of peace in order to reconcile Guineans among themselves and preserve our social fabric."[14] Cheeseman suggests that African governments often "obsess" over the concept of unity, seeing disunity as a threat to centralized rule (2015: 26). As he notes, the term echoes language from the nationalist struggle for independence and effectively evokes both the pride and the fears of that moment. In Guinea, the Condé government has deployed the term as an implicit means of recalling the revolution and of looking forward to a democratic future. Figure 14 shows a recent political sculpture by a national fishing company extolling President Condé and calling for national unity.

Singing about reconciliation, unity, and peace thus parrots the official, strategic party line. Lyrics claiming "kɛlɛ mu fan, politiki mu fan" (war is not good, politics is not good), as in DJ Oudy's song "La paix en Guinée," are familiar references for Guinean listeners—standard government rhetoric against the opposition and in support of the incumbent power. By singing

FIGURE 14. Fishing boat installation, Palais du Peuple. Photo by the author.

such texts, musicians suggest loyalty to the government and implicitly censor any critique of it while attempting to position themselves in official favor.

Such songs enable musicians to accommodate both the ruling power, by repeating its rhetoric, and the ever-growing anger and tension on the street, by keeping their themes largely and deliberately vague. Ideas about trustworthiness, betrayal, treachery, and disloyalty are deeply rooted in local understandings, but the state has also mobilized these concepts. Over time the words *peace*, *unity*, and *reconciliation* have become heavily loaded terms in Guinea, carefully chosen by both the government and its musical supporters. On their face, it is difficult to argue with such ideals, yet listeners hear and understand them as strategies for pleasing the state in an uncertain moment. Knowing this, some Guineans—particularly young people—feel that it is now the time for an altogether different tactic.

"Takana Clash"

In early 2013 Takana Zion, Guinea's most popular reggae and dancehall star, shattered many of the long-respected, unspoken rules about local music and politics. With his song "Takana Clash Alpha Condé," the musician released a scathing attack against the newly elected president. While a number of young musicians, particularly in reggae and neotraditional music, have over the past few years sung protest songs, Takana's song was virtually unprecedented within Guinea in its directness, anger, and sting—bitterly naming and shaming the head of state.

"Takana Clash Alpha Condé" begins in its first four seconds with the sound of a gunshot, followed by Takana's voice ringing out, "Eh yo! Alpha Condé!" The confrontation is immediate and direct. Takana evokes the ever-louder sound of street battles between authorities and angry youth in Guinea over the past two decades. Yet what is most startling is not the sounded reference to violence, but the naming of names. Here Alpha Condé is not ensconced in history, heritage, and community; rather, he is shamelessly singled out. Previous protest songs largely avoided naming politicians directly, with references instead to "the president" or more broadly to the general state of affairs in Guinea. "Takana Clash," in contrast, addresses Alpha Condé directly and aggressively, stripping him of all the cultural and political power of his office. He seems to stand alone and exposed before Takana's words.

From this stark beginning Takana launches into a three-and-a-half minute torrent of spoken word. There is almost no melody here apart from a trap-inflected backing track featuring a repeated phrase in D minor on an electronic keyboard and a sparse drum-machine beat. Generically, the song is a departure from Takana's usual upbeat, urban dancehall sound. His voice maintains an even, urgent pitch throughout, broken up by the occasional growl or shout, as a speaker at a political rally might do to energize the audience. The delivery is spoken rather than sung as Takana echoes the harsh, angry voice of street protesters and details in Soso the crimes, lies, and unfulfilled promises of the current regime.

Yo Alpha Conde i 40 ans nan nabaxi	Yo, Alpha Condé, you spent 40 years
I na mangɛya fenfe	searching for power [rule]
Ala bara mɛngɛya fi i ma	God has given you power
I m'a kolon, i sese rabama mangɛya ra, han	You don't know what to do after coming to power
Ka i m'a tɔxi muxu nge to waafe	Or don't you see our mothers crying?
Ka i m'a tɔxi bɔxi to waafe	Or don't you see [our] nation crying?
Ka i m'a tɔxi jeunesse to waafe, han	Or don't you see the youth crying?
. . .	
E a fala nɛ mu be a mangɛya sɔtɔfe a sese m'a ra	They say that obtaining power is not a big deal
Kɔnɔ i nu mangɛya sɔtɔ i naxan nabama a ra	But if you obtain power it's what you do with it

Mixie gbɛgbɛ m'a kolon	Many people don't know
e naxan nabama mangɛya ra	what to do with power
. . .	
Nan na ra i n'a fala mu be a "changement"	That's why if you say "change"
Mu mu noma lade i ra	We cannot believe you
Rasta yo mu noma lade a ra	Rasta cannot believe you

The lyrical and musical attack here is unmistakably pointed, as is the song's angry, inflammatory tone. There is neither humor nor metaphor nor happy melody to detract from the invective. Instead, Alpha Condé stands as an accused before a judge delivering his damning indictment. Condé is named and shamed without the slightest veil of ambiguity.

Yet, despite its antagonism, "Takana Clash" actually does occupy a more ambivalent place than may first appear. A brief discussion of Takana's political history, and in particular his relations with President Condé, illustrates this point.

I first met Takana Zion (fig. 15), whose real name is Mohammed Mouctar Soumah, at a tiny indoor bar in Manquepas that is run by his welcoming and entrepreneurial friend Mounir Conté. My friend Sita set up the meeting, and it had been difficult to arrange. I feared that Takana would be remote and swathed in the trappings of stardom. In person, however, he proved to be immediately friendly, engaging, and unpretentious. He was happy to talk, albeit on subjects of his own choosing.

Takana was born in Conakry in 1986 and has been known in Guinea for some years as a rebellious youth icon. His father was a member of parlia-

FIGURE 15. Takana Zion

ment under Lansana Conté and had been arrested and imprisoned during the revolution. Politics seems to be in his blood, although he told me that he was not always so engaged. In fact, considering his family history, I was surprised to hear a song he had recorded years earlier in praise of Sékou Touré. Takana explained that he knew relatively little about Guinean history until rather recently: he had been living in Bamako and traveling around and was only aware that many Guineans sang about Touré. Today, he added, he is much more critical. In fact, he has become something of a scholar and a voracious reader of local and regional history, with conversational references casually spanning from the origins of the Soso kingdom to the work of the anthropologist Marcel Griaule.

One of my other observations upon first meeting him was that, unlike most Guineans, he speaks fluent English—and in a Jamaican accent. Growing up listening to Jamaican and West African reggae artists such as Peter Tosh, Bob Marley, and Tiken Jah Fakoly, Takana has emulated these performers in musical style and speech. In addition to memorizing beloved reggae albums as a youth, he has also traveled to Jamaica three times and recorded his English-language album, *Rasta Government*, at Marley's Tuff Gong studios in Kingston, where Tiken has also recorded. His earlier music featured a familiar global reggae/dancehall sound of thick bass lines and off-beat accents, with lyrics in Soso and other Guinean languages often adding local references.

With the release of his first album, *Zion Prophet*, in 2007, Takana began to build an enthusiastic fan base in Guinea. Over the next few years his popularity skyrocketed as he also became known for dance-floor beats, slickly produced videos, and a stylish, unruly image. Even in a context in which most young male, and some female, musicians sport dreadlocks, Takana's locks are at least twice as long and thick as anyone else's I have seen in Guinea. Moreover, unlike other reggae stars in Guinea, he is also a practicing Rastafarian and does not adhere to Islam.

In conjunction with this rebellious image, Takana has also cultivated a defiant political stance from early on. *Zion Prophet* featured the song "Crazy Soldiers," which decried army violence during street protests against the regime of Lansana Conté. Nonetheless, like others Takana also remained largely quiet during the violence of the CNDD regime. As noted, he had given a concert at Rogbané beach shortly after the massacre, when the crowd roared out for "Crazy Soldiers," but Takana declined to play it. Accompanying him on kora, Demba had later said to me, "It was too hot," and considering the tension and heavy military presence everywhere at that time, I understood perfectly.

Yet Takana seemed to have regained his voice by the following year, when Guinea entered its preparations for democratic elections. In the 2010 presidential campaign he initially and fervently backed Cellou Dalein Diallo, the UFDG candidate and main opponent of Alpha Condé. Among his displays of support for the candidate were the release of a song titled "Cellou Diallo" and a joint press conference held with Diallo in the southeastern town of N'zérékoré. At this press conference Takana made his position clear: speaking in French in the first-person plural (*nous*), he stated:

> For a long time, we've observed a rather neutral position in relation to political happenings in the country—even if we have lyrics that are socially engaged and that the majority of Guineans see themselves in what I sing. . . . [But] Guineans want a president and for a long time the country's been suffering. . . . So, as a reggae singer, we've decided for the higher interest of the country, for all Guinean children, because their future depends on this election and what's going to come from it, to commit ourselves to the UFDG party. . . . So, if we want a secure future for our children, I ask all those who listen to my music and who trust my merit, who know that Takana Zion has been committed since the beginning, that he's always fought for things he believes in, [you] must come join me with the UFDG party for the good of Guinea.

Takana's statement reveals a degree of ambivalence with respect to political involvement. He begins by saying that he is apolitical, alluding to the commonly invoked local distinction between art and politics, and suggesting that as an artist he has stayed above the fray. Yet he also claims his political and moral authenticity "as a reggae singer" and a longtime crusader for his beliefs. He is also well aware of his popularity and influence—as is Diallo, who sits beside him and welcomes his "great support."

In so doing, Takana unequivocally sided with Diallo and the UFDG in 2010 and publicly broadcast his support. In another instance during the run-up to the election, he stated, "I prefer Cellou Dalein Diallo as president of the Republic. If Alpha Condé wins, I'm leaving Guinea."[15]

Yet Condé did eventually win the elections in November 2010, and nonetheless, after a few months in Mali, Takana returned to his home country. As he told an interviewer shortly after the elections, he was in Mali simply to record his new album, titled *Khamè tokiwouya* (Man of Many Colors). He added that he did not regret having supported Cellou Dalein Diallo and that he wished Alpha Condé good luck, remarking, "I didn't battle against a man, but against the negative spiritual powers that work between the earth and sky."[16]

From this position Takana fully recanted his earlier stance and within
a year held a highly public reconciliation with Condé. In early November
2011 Condé received Takana at the presidential palace in Conakry. Television
footage of the meeting shows the musician in a crisp white suit striding into
the palace and bowing and shaking hands with the seated president. Following the meeting, a clearly excited Takana delivered a televised statement of
support:

> Frankly I'm very moved and honored to be received by the president of the
> republic, so we've come to show our good faith in the program he's leading
> in Guinea. . . . We're at the government's disposal concerning everything with
> unity and peace and reconciliation between Guineans, so that we may know
> that we're all the same family, that a house divided between itself can never
> stand. . . . So, we've come to give this message to the president of the republic.
> We're very, very happy. It's a blessing.[17]

Perhaps not uncoincidentally, just over a week later Takana accompanied
Alpha Condé on a diplomatic visit to Brazil. During the visit the musician
gave a concert in which he waved a white handkerchief, the still-resonant
Touré-era symbol of Guinean unity and presidential support. Video footage of the event showed Alpha Condé seated in the front row during the
performance and rising at the end to shake hands and have his picture taken
with Takana, who once again bowed deeply before him, saying, "Thank you,
Mr. President." Takana then resumed the stage, declaring, "He is our professor. He is our father as well. He's the father of all the Guinean nation. Long
live the unity of the people! Long live Guinea!"[18]

This story is one of changing allegiances in which Takana deployed his
public role in support of the main two opposing political figures in Guinea,
and at a time of bitter political and ethnic rivalry. Such a role for musicians
is obviously not without precedent in Guinea. Yet what distinguishes the case
of Takana Zion is his outspoken musical and political stance as a reggae star
and a rebel. A number of journalists and Internet commentators claimed
that Takana was behaving not like a reggae man but like a jeli, with one disappointed fan commenting of Takana's Brazil performance that "this role
isn't worthy of a Rasta."[19] Rumors circulated regarding the amounts he had
been paid by Diallo and Condé, with claims of his having received more than
GNF 300 million (around US$45,000) from each. Popular opinion suggested
that the prospect of more money and overseas travel had been enough to tip
the scale in favor of President Condé.

Yet despite his words of praise, Takana soon came to regret his glowing endorsement of Alpha Condé in 2011, and within a year and a half he released "Takana Clash." It is not entirely clear what tipped the scale once again, but the song added a lot of fuel to the fires of the Conakry rumor mill, with questions circulating about Takana's domicile, the funding of his trip to Brazil, and the nature of his true political leanings. One rumor held that soldiers had destroyed a restaurant he owned on Rogbané beach and Takana had subsequently fled to Mali. For a couple of years after the song's release, and in contrast to his many press conferences and public statements in the preceding years, Takana remained largely silent on the subject of politics, distinctly avoiding speaking about "Takana Clash" and maintaining a low profile overall.[20] As he told me in 2016, "I cannot talk too much publicly [about it]," and indeed, when I brought the song up, he dropped his voice to a whisper, despite the fact that we were at a friend's place with only a couple of his close companions present and a loud TV blaring in the background.[21] On the one hand, he remains proud of the song, claiming defiantly—and rightly—that no other Guinean musician has done what he did in so addressing the president. "It's very different. It's different from all other songs," he said to me, before launching into the first few lines and finishing with a hearty laugh. On the other hand, he at times declines to embrace it publicly (or perhaps even privately) and, as journalists who have interviewed him also attest, can demur when the subject is raised. When I attempted to ask about the song later, he deflected, saying without irony, "Politicians don't want to speak to us directly. They use words that make no sense to us. It's a way of not speaking."

Yet despite these evasions, the lyrics and delivery of his "Clash" are unequivocal and available for anyone to hear, and they represent an incontestable rupture with Condé. Takana's reluctance to discuss the song must be understood within this context of knowing when, and when not, to name. Like most other Guinean musicians I know, he is an artist with intelligence and ideals, as well as a savvy pragmatist. While it remains unclear whether he suffered any material or physical harm from the Condé government—and I was not able to find out—Takana has incontrovertibly broken the codes of silence and discretion in Guinea and now finds himself on precarious ground. In fact, he finds himself—in the eyes of many fellow musicians, government officials, and ordinary citizens—the very symbol of this uncertain moment. As a result, he has taken an understandably more guarded stance in talking about politics and his song—a stance that of course has a long history of precedence and firm place in Guinea.

Whatever steps they may or may have not taken, it is clear that the regime was incensed, feeling betrayed by the song's release. RTG retaliated over the following weeks by repeatedly airing footage of Takana's praise to Condé in Brazil. Moreover, at the March 2013 public meeting that I mentioned in the introduction of this chapter, the Ministry of Culture was an active and vocal participant.

The meeting at La Paillote was convened by a group of Touré-era musicians, artists, and cultural promoters, who invited the Ministry of Culture to participate in a discussion about how to respond to this perceived crisis. More than two hundred participants were in attendance in a packed courtyard, with cameramen and reporters jostling to cover the event for the national broadcasting station. While neither Takana nor his song was directly mentioned, the meeting's target was unmistakable. Over the course of the event, a succession of musicians and government officials took to the microphone to heatedly denounce any song or musician that would "insult" the president.

The views of one speaker reveal the shock waves that Takana's song created in Guinea, particularly among those who still hold to the earlier model of cultural politics:

> Concerning the political problems in our country, it's regrettable that certain artists and certain of our brothers allow themselves to insult the head of state. . . . We've never known that in our country. The artist makes his art. He sings in parables. But he cannot name someone, as is happening now. Someone was named and addressed in abnormal conditions. . . . We've had national bands here, national ensembles, but no one ever insulted a politician, no matter what his level, and certainly not a head of state. It's deplorable.[22]

The central aim of this speech, and of the meeting in general, was to reassure the government that it had not lost the support of other artists. Takana's action is clearly positioned outside the norm, as an aberration, while the vast majority of artists are presented as discreet and, most important, loyal. In Guinea, of course, musical loyalty calls for material reciprocity. Thus, the speaker asked for artists and the government "to see what we can do together in this crisis, because . . . everyone is singing for peace, everyone is touring, but we need a strategy. This strategy rests with the Ministry of Culture. That's why we want to know how the Guinean artist can be involved in this process."

The next speaker made this request more explicit, declaring that art is a source of peace but that artists need subsidies from the government to survive.

These remarks were followed by a particularly agitated and indignant address from Riad Challoub, a long-serving ministerial official and former Touré-era musician. Challoub made the government's position clear. Speaking on behalf of the culture minister, he expressed his incredulity at the cur-

rent turn of events. Challoub began his speech with a manifesto on the role
of the artist that echoed the revolutionary past and the familiar language
of Touré.

> The artist only has worth because he serves a society, a nation. The artist only
> has worth because he contributes . . . to prosperity, national agreement, na-
> tional solidarity. An artist has to say what others cannot, but in the correct
> manner. He has to say things that unite, and not that anger and divide. An
> artist has to contribute to the spread of national virtues. *There are no protest
> artists in the real sense of the word "artist."* (Emphasis added)[23]

Challoub then continued by evoking the local trinity of authority as envi-
sioned in the official imagination: Mande culture, Sékou Touré, and God.
Building from one to the next, Challoub concluded that artists have neither
the historical and cultural precedent nor the moral right to disrupt the nation's peace. Their sole purpose is to serve society: "We cannot sing of just
anything at all. . . . I tell you that the question is resolved."

Challoub's aim here is in full accord with that of the organizers: to distinguish between true artists, who represent the majority and respect their
traditions and culture, and the one or two nonconformists, who have forgotten their history, religion, and moral values. Challoub's use of language and
imagery is carefully chosen to discredit these dissenting outliers within local
understandings of art, music, and society. By alluding to much-loved traditions of praise, in both the pre- and postcolonial past, the speaker sought
to exclude Takana from the very definition of Art, and thus from Guinean
culture itself.

Moreover, through their statements, both the musicians present at the
meeting and the representatives of the state sought to reaffirm their mutual
relations and interdependence. Artists called on the state to provide moral
and monetary support and subsidies, while the state renewed its evanes-
cent promises of revitalized cultural activities and sponsorship, much as the
CNDD had previously done. As Riad Challoub declared emotionally at the
end of his speech, in an almost-shouted crescendo of zeal, "We are going
to relaunch the National Festival . . . this year! Better than all the previous
years!"—an announcement met by the crowd with scattered applause, if not
entirely with confidence.

Displeasures

Alongside these statements of official censure and unease, many Guinean
musicians and ordinary citizens have also expressed discomfort and anxiety

at the emergence of musical protest. The shock of "Takana Clash" reverberated in Conakry for months, with radio stations and websites inviting and broadcasting the ensuing heated discussions. As the singer at the meeting at La Paillote declared, "We have never known this in our country"—and to a considerable degree this was true. Despite his ambivalence and guardedness, Takana had charted new musical territory in directly and angrily naming and denouncing the president.

The official media carefully avoided directly referencing either the song or the artist, but the private media waded eagerly into the fray. The influential website *GuinéeNews*, for example, interviewed private citizens on the streets of Conakry to assess the public mood, and while opinion was somewhat divided, everyone had strong views. One of those interviewed argued that Takana should have delivered his critiques through proverbs or anecdotes, rather than by directly naming the president. Another cited Takana's ambivalent political history and suggested that the artist was angry because Alpha Condé had not fulfilled his financial promises to him. Yet others defended Takana: one student declared him "the spokesperson of the youth," while another argued that although everything Takana had sung was true, Guineans do not like to hear the truth.[24]

My own conversations with musicians and other friends and acquaintances reflected a similar mix of views. "Takana Clash" was a favorite topic of conversation among the residents of Conakry in 2013, bringing together sticky questions of music, money, power, ethics, ethnicity, culture, and of course, the elections. Even among those who agreed with the song, many still questioned the musician's history, motives, and methods. In particular, the directness of his attack was viewed as a problem. As the singer Robert Kamano said to me, "Even if your father is a liar, you can't directly call him a liar." There was a strong sense that age and authority are owed a certain level of respect, which Takana had violated. As an otherwise sympathetic commentator wrote, Takana may have a right to criticize the president, but the bitter, angry tone of his song resulted in "banalizing" the office itself.[25]

Moreover, many felt that Takana's attack, like other recent examples of musical protest, was somewhat reactionary and self-serving and did not promote any real solutions. Cédy, the former culture ministry official, who is unusually frank in his criticisms of the government, described Takana and others like him as politically directionless. In our conversations Cédy spoke with admiration of the emergence of protest music, yet he suggested that artists such as Takana were primarily engaged in a generational conflict rather than a political one. Their struggle was against their elders, but they lacked both a clear ideology and a political objective. This viewpoint reflected the feelings of many former *militants*: that Guinea today is divided and its youth apathetic because it has lost the focus and zeal of the revolution.

In addition to these criticisms, in 2013 a number of musicians released their own musical replies to "Takana Clash." The hip-hop duo Jumeaux Damaro angrily "clashed" Takana back, denouncing the reggae star for dividing the nation and threatening national reconciliation, and for his hypocrisy in having supported Alpha Condé in the past. The song keeps Takana closely in sight as its target, accusing him of being a fraud and a false reggae man. The musicians denounce him for drinking alcohol and eating meat—contrary to the prescriptions of Rastafarianism—and even question whether his dreadlocks are real. They conclude the song by issuing a call to the country's political class, including to the "Father of the Nation," and affirming that they want "peace . . . [and] a united and prosperous Guinea. Long Live Guinea!" Others also jumped into the debate. One artist anonymously posted a song on YouTube, "I fassy wolè," denouncing Takana as a liar. Another, Caporol Dônkôdi, issued a clash back at the Jumeaux Damaro, defending Takana and laughing at the hip-hop duo's claim of supporting national unity.[26]

The story of this Clash and its many reverberations reveals the anxieties felt by many musicians, including Takana himself, about recent political and aesthetic shifts in Guinea. Many were wary, if not angry, about the emergence of protest, both musical and otherwise, for a number of reasons. For one, protests and violence disrupt much-needed opportunities for musicians to perform and earn money. Insecurity and violence keep people indoors, and many ceremonies have been curtailed or canceled in the prolonged uncertainty of the current environment. For most musicians, it is the opposition that is clearly to blame, and as Alya, Demba, and others often said to me, "The protesters are ruining things for everyone."

Among musicians and audiences alike, the discomfort over Takana's action stems in part from anxieties about the loss of popular pleasure in Guinea today. Political tension and protests mean that musicians have fewer opportunities to perform because people avoid public celebrations and ceremonies when the streets are too hot—choosing instead to keep quiet and maintain a low profile. A number of my friends canceled or postponed weddings and baptisms while street battles or tension between protesters and the authorities raged in their neighborhoods. Moreover, the heated and highly partisan atmosphere has led to another loss of public pleasure, as the pleasures and pride of praise singing have become further destabilized. Praise singing, whether through jeliya or through other forms, has always been subject to anxious talk and social regulation. But as political battles spill out into the open in new, increasingly vocal ways, criticisms of praise singing are elevated to new levels. Musicians are attacked and attack each other for offering public praise, and praise songs often give way either to the more general, generic songs of peace, reconciliation, and national unity, or to songs of irrefutable dissent and rupture like "Takana Clash."

Crucially, however, these other forms lack key features that have long generated excitement and moved audiences in Guinea. Both songs of peace and songs of protest depart from older practices of naming and are unable to capture and evoke the sentiments and pleasures that naming has long created. As we have seen, the potency of praise performance lies in the naming of names, exceeding the direct referential meaning of the words to convey collectivity, memory, place, and pride. The words and names activate and make possible an evocation of a rich, shared past, bringing it alive through the senses for a present, living moment.

Moreover, by shifting away from naming, such songs depart significantly from the dynamics and meaning of live performance. The naming of names represents the climactic moment of much performance—the site of its spectacular intensity and immediacy—whether in jeliya or other genres. And as discussed earlier, praise recordings often have short-lived value, while the potency of the form lies in its live performance. By contrast, protest songs are often less oriented to live performance. In many cases these songs circulate primarily through recordings and are intended to be heard in smaller, less public spaces. In some cases, such as at Takana's 2009 concert, rebellious young musicians even refuse to protest live. Protest's detractors fear that, rather than creating a powerful political-affective space of cultural continuity and collectivity, musical protest threatens to destroy it.

Yet, although certain forms of sensual and social pleasure may appear to have been lost, other new ones have sprung up. Protest songs do not, perhaps, evoke memories of the Mande empire or the sense of national unity and optimism that revolutionary songs sought to convey. Yet, for these musicians and their listeners, protest offers new forms of pleasure that are explicitly premised on rejecting the old in favor of the new, on subversion, on being young at this particular moment and in this particular place—even while building on oft-quoted older ideals of singing truth to the king. Since the release of "Takana Clash," more young musicians in Guinea have been emboldened to directly name and shame the president, with songs that are not afraid to smack down elites to the sounds of auto-tune and charged-up drum machines. The hip-hop artist Djanii Alfa, for example, has electrified fans with his song "Gnakidin" (Mosquitoes) and its visceral, beats-driven anger against Guinean security forces for killing protesters.[27] In part, the pleasures here are of night life, of listening and dancing to new beats and new sounds, of being in clubs and at parties. But these sounds increasingly ring out on the street and capture public space. In protests or on the corner, through cranked-up car stereos or speakers, protest and socially conscious songs play out alongside R&B and electronic beats, the pleasures of anger and demands for change melding with the pleasures of being young. Listeners—in particular young people—revel in this musical and political innovation and the angry protest that it entails, and they are calling for much more. Through this music they claim solidarity with others caught up in a similar struggle for a new future, while also claiming the pleasures of dance floors, fashion, sex, and sociability.

In this way, these pleasures are perhaps not so different from the musical pleasures of the revolution. In this case, however, the revolution is not state sponsored—what is being challenged is not imperialism and foreign intervention, but rather the state itself. Protest songs are linked to new forms of recognition as young Guineans seek to claim space over the airwaves and in the streets to claim a twenty-first-century modernity that openly challenges state authority and looks beyond it to new possible ways of being. But like Takana Zion, artists, listeners, and fans are also ambivalent—living within state politics but also beyond it, making fierce claims for the future at times, but, like all young people everywhere, wanting to enjoy their lives and have fun.

The anxieties around protest music today reflect the similar long-standing anxieties around jeliya that I discussed earlier. In both cases audiences and musicians express a "structural nostalgia"—a longing for a return to an imagined moment when social ideals were respected (Herzfeld 1997: 109–10). Takana Zion references the deep history of Soumaoro Kanté, the former Soso king, as a lesson for politics and ethics today. But at the same time that he and others continue to look to the past, they also look ahead. Hoffman notes that this dynamic has always been the case in jeliya, that "the ways of the past always serve as both guideline for present action and jumping-off point for the creation of new ways of behaving" (2000: 164). Historical precedent does not ensure that the process is easy, however. In her work on postsocialist dance in Conakry, Cohen notes that changing practices involve an "active struggle with loss" as dancers struggle with the ethics and aesthetics of generational shifts (2016: 654). Dancers, like musicians, do this by adding and innovating, but within parameters of acknowledgment and respect for the past. They are reluctant to turn their backs entirely on older practices and values, but they also recognize that such forms "no longer capture what it means to be young and resourceful in Guinea" today (ibid.: 655).

Conclusion

As in other postsocialist, postauthoritarian contexts, Guinea presents a case of "democratic schizophrenia" (Boym 2001: 608), in which the promise of democracy has created anxiety and fear. Today large parts of Conakry seem to exist under clouds of tear gas—no sooner have the fumes died down than the police and opposition clash once again, and neighborhoods are engulfed in violence. In some ways this story is not new: volatility has long been a feature of the country's history. Yet the difference today is that the crisis no longer has a name to it; no wonder people are ambivalent about democracy. While donors may maintain a "naïve faith in the power of elections" (Cheeseman 2015: 117), ordinary citizens realize that elections are not an end point in themselves. Where does authoritarianism end and democracy begin? Has it happened yet? Is this it?

Alongside criticisms of Takana Zion and his musical dissent, many Guineans have denounced the private media and the protesters, who they feel are "ruining things for everyone." Others express a sense that Guinea is not yet ready for democracy, that perhaps military rule is preferable if it means that order is maintained. And unease about all this open, public protest reflects a sense that there is too much change happening too fast.

These feelings reflect not just postsocialist disorientation, but a longer-term destabilization, as reference points become murky and it is at times hard to find a focus for public pleasure. While the sensual effervescence of much Guinean music rests on naming, self-recognition, and the evocation of collectivity, history, place, and pride, many feel that musical dissent leads toward uncertainty, anger, and a loss of knowing oneself. Even musicians who engage in this form are not entirely comfortable with it—as we see in the example of Takana Zion and his ambivalent stance toward the current regime.

Protest—like jeliya—generates both anxiety and excitement, and often from the same people. The genres that I have discussed here and throughout this book do not inhabit discrete, isolatable spaces, but are overlapping practices and political-aesthetic forms that build on shared histories, concerns, and feelings. Musicians perform and audiences listen across spectrums of praise and protest, pleasure and anger, collectivity and the drawing of identity borders. Musicians such as Takana Zion may sing in praise one day and protest the next, may call for peace and reconciliation and mean quite different things by that phrase from one moment to another. Their skill is in finding a balance between innovation and accommodation—a skill that may not succeed in ending authoritarianism, but that acknowledges the affective sensibilities that underlie public life. The ongoing turn toward democracy has challenged well-established aesthetic practices in Guinea, and musicians, like everyone else, are attempting to mediate the shift: seeking to evolve old forms of pleasure and searching, hoping, for new ones.

6

Blue Zones

The CNDD regime feels at times like a short-lived blip in Guinea's post-colonial history, but *l'armée guinéenne* is still a common sight on Conakry's streets, while the current stage of Guinea's political project remains a vexed question. In late 2017 government crackdowns on the independent press and on a strike by the teachers' union led to angry comparisons between President Condé and Sékou Touré.[1] Around the same time, the deputy of the ruling RPG party stated that the top priority facing the country was neither good roads nor electricity nor even water, but rather an assertion of the state's authority, adding, "Even if we must massacre, let's accept [it]."[2] Moreover, Condé himself speaks increasingly about amending the constitution so that he can run for a third five-year term, a move that the Russian ambassador to Guinea has recently supported. The lines between authoritarianism and democracy evidently remain blurred. In this space, new actors and new forces jostle alongside familiar practices and feelings as Guineans continue to work out questions of self-recognition, of who they are, where they have been, and where they are heading.

The Ebola Bye-Bye Show

In 2014 and 2015 Guinea and its neighbors Liberia and Sierra Leone suffered the worst outbreak in history of the Ebola virus.[3] The epidemic ravaged parts of the forest region and upper coast in Guinea, but its effects reverberated throughout the country and well beyond its borders (Morfold 2017). Cases in Europe and the United States generated an enormous amount of news coverage in the Western media, which in turn created concerns about representation in West Africa (Monson 2017). "Things are fine here," insisted the

Bembeya singer Mamadi Diabaté to me over the phone in 2015. "It's not like what they're saying overseas."

Nonetheless, upon my return to Guinea in 2016 shortly before the epidemic was officially declared over, I noticed its impact everywhere in Conakry. From mandatory temperature checks at the airport, to plastic buckets of chlorine hand-washing solution around town, to the conversations of friends and strangers, the specter of Ebola was unavoidable. Friends told me of their fears about keeping themselves and their family members safe, or of the difficulties in finding health care for other urgent conditions such as malaria and typhoid, while clinics were entirely focused on Ebola. Artists also responded to the tragedy. A number of local and regional pop stars recorded the single "Africa Stop Ebola" in late 2014, spreading messages about sanitation and health care.[4] The theater director Fifi Tamsir Niane also featured a scene in her new play, *N'ko farafina, J'ai dit l'humain*, in which actors dressed in full-body protective clothing and danced zombielike to Michael Jackson's "Thriller." At the performance I attended, the audience roared its approval of this scene, both mocking and making sense of the ubiquitous medical gear.

In this climate I spent an afternoon catching up with Mathieu Fribault, an anthropologist I had first met in 2009, and his colleagues Ramatoulaye Diallo and Mohamed Diaby. The three had spent several months conducting research on the epidemic's impact in villages in the forest and coastal regions as well as in Conakry. Their observations detailed not just the health but the social costs of the disease as fear, suspicion, conspiracy theories, and rumors tore at the fabric of communities. Anxieties abounded about Ebola's origins, about why it had spread, who was behind it, why some had died but others had survived, who could be trusted, who could not.[5] The sudden, violent intrusion of this virulent illness into the lives of many Guineans evoked old fears and memories, including ones of state-sponsored violence in the Touré era, particularly for people in the forest and coastal regions. At the same time, rumors proliferated about Ebola as a means for President Condé to consolidate his political and financial power: some of the ethnic groups that do not support him were hit the worst by the disease, and foreign aid had flooded in to support the government.

Regardless of these rumors, Condé certainly recognized the political capital of the epidemic's end. Music and musicians were called upon to mark the occasion, and two large-scale concerts were held in the grounds of the Palais du Peuple at the end of 2015.[6] Both featured a line-up of big names in Guinean and West African music. In September the Ebola: All Together for Victory concert included the hip-hop duo Banlieuz'art and the singer Sia Tolno, as well as the Afrobeatz star Wizkid and the Senegalese rapper Didier

Awadi. Thousands attended the free concert, which had only been officially announced earlier that day. As a follow-up, the president announced a second concert two months later. The Ebola Bye-Bye Show featured an even bigger line-up, including Awadi as well as his compatriot superstar, Youssou N'Dour, alongside Guinean stars such as Sékouba "Bambino" Diabaté, Mory Kanté, and many younger acts such as Banlieuz'art and Kandia Kora. President Condé himself appeared at both of these events, and video footage shows effusive cheers and applause from the audience, who called out "Presi! Presi!" Many of the artists lavished praise on him throughout their performances, thanking him for his support. Moreover, in the run-up to the Ebola Bye-Bye Show, fliers and social media posts advertising the event prominently gave thanks to "the leadership of the president of the republic, Professor Alpha Condé."

Speaking to people in Conakry a few months later, I found that the Ebola concerts seemed for the most part enthusiastically received, as was Condé's role in them. Many people felt that the concerts celebrated a good cause and provided the city with some much-needed relief and enjoyment. Others were more skeptical. One Guinean friend remarked to me that the September concert was held just two weeks before presidential elections that year. Moreover, the concert was sponsored by the French media conglomerate Vivendi, whose CEO, Vincent Bolloré, is a longtime associate of Condé's.[7] Around the same time as the September Ebola concert, the Bolloré Group—Bolloré's transportation, telecoms, and logistics company—also opened a "Blue Zone" in central Conakry, a vast arts, sports, and technology complex featuring manicured lawns and curated graffiti murals.[8] For a subscription of GNF 10,000 per month (roughly US$1), users have access to sports and cultural facilities, Internet, a café, and meeting spaces, not to mention electricity and clean drinking water.[9] Blue Zones have also been constructed in other Conakry neighborhoods, and the government announced plans for similar sites across the country.

The fact that these projects were launched around the same time that Bolloré was granted total rights over Guinea's main port has not gone unnoticed.[10] Questions have been raised about Condé's relationship with Bolloré, the circumstances of the port concession, and the timing of Bolloré's investments in cultural projects in Guinea. These projects are notably geared toward young people, and Blue Zones are designed specifically as youth art, sports, and technology spaces. Similarly, Condé explicitly billed the Ebola Bye-Bye Show as a concert for Guinean youths celebrating the end of the epidemic. The Touré-era dance bands were notably absent from both Ebola concerts' line-ups, in contrast to their usual deployment in service of the state. Youssou N'Dour did reference Bembeya's song "Doni doni" a few times in his performance, but for the most part, the concerts showcased younger Guinean vedettes, including hip-hop and R&B stars of today alongside je-limusos and big names from the 1980s and 1990s. The concert and related events, including the opening of the Blue Zone and the announcement of a new performance venue, are direct overtures to young people, who are of course vital to Condé's power base in Guinea today.

Look to the Future and the Past

The Ebola concerts and surrounding initiatives highlight some familiar tendencies in musical politics in Guinea, as well as some newer ones. At the ceremony announcing the new concert hall, the Guinean culture minister Amirou Conté echoed a familiar line when he referenced Guinea's "rich and stirring cultural past" and described Bolloré's artistic initiatives as representing "the revival of culture in Guinea."[11] Like the CNDD regime before it, Condé's government was referencing bygone artistic glories and looking to music and culture to bolster its legitimacy. Yet in direct contrast to the half-hearted attempts of 2009, the current regime has real money and technical expertise from powerful allies behind it. Bolloré was allegedly able to gain lucrative contracts in Guinea, while Condé could claim something concrete for Guinean youth. The private sector has a new, public role in this mix, which creates exciting possibilities around new technologies and spaces (for those who can afford entry)—as well as heightened concerns about neoliberalism, increased inequality, and the workings of power.

The signals to youth and youth music suggest that the state is looking anew to the future. But older artists have not been entirely forgotten; nor has the era that they represent. Condé's government recently organized two national arts festivals, for instance, in 2015 and 2017, although times have obviously changed, and the festivals were much smaller than their revolutionary counterparts—and indeed, many people I spoke to seemed unaware that they had even taken place. Bembeya Jazz and the Amazones de Guinée are also still called on to perform for official events, although the other revolutionary dance bands are largely inactive today.

As for this generation of artists themselves, despite their increasing marginality, they are still musicians, and music still matters to them. A couple of years ago, for instance, I attended a concert at La Paillote in which Sékou Bembeya performed as one of the last acts of the night. In an unusual move, he began his set by asking the audience to remain in their chairs and not climb up onto the stage to dance or tip. This flouting of conventions meant that the beloved guitarist relinquished the chance to make extra money or be honored by his fans, although a few older women did disobey his order and got up on the stage nonetheless. But even more striking, as he launched into his eponymous instrumental piece "Petit Sékou," he turned his back not only on the VIP section, but on the entire audience as a whole. Instead, he came and played in front of all the other musicians in attendance, who were sitting to one side of the stage. I happened to be sitting in that section and could feel a swell of emotion and pride around me as his fellow artists exulted in this performance. As the piece came to an end, they leapt up to embrace Sékou onstage, holding one another and swaying back and forth as they all rocked with laughter and wiped their eyes. The musicians seemed to forget the audience, instead celebrating their own intimate musical community. It was a moment less about the public and more about personal pleasure that was all for and about them.

The revolution lives on vividly in these musicians' memories. But beyond them, it also continues to echo in varied ways in Guinean public life, even as practices related to it evolve. Popular music still offers a site where public pleasure and authority are entangled, while practices of musical praise and patronage still matter. As the Ebola concerts illustrate, these questions of authority and control today involve the private sector in new ways, as foreign companies invest in music and performance and mobilize pleasure in support of the state. But despite this new source of patronage, most musicians continue to look to the state, just as, in turn, the state looks to them. This relationship is based in part on the history of practice and material possibility in postcolonial Guinea, which memories of artistic fortnights, presidential medals, and monthly salaries for artists still influence. But as I have described in this book, these entanglements also derive meaning from their evocations of a deeper history and deeper currents of feeling that have not been extinguished. Jeliya and its variants matter to people because of these evocations and because of what they name and recognize within local listeners, and while continually debated and reimagined, they still exert an intimate draw. As Sita Camara once said to me, "Jeliya will not end, and singing praise will not end. These practices are things that will never finish."

224

In a 2014 essay Michael Ignatieff asked the question, "Are the Authoritarians Winning?"[12] Years before the Central European University (of which Ignatieff is president and rector) was effectively forced to leave Viktor Orbán's Hungary, Ignatieff warned of the emergence of a new authoritarianism throughout the world. From Armenia to Zimbabwe, this authoritarianism is characterized by new alliances amongst autocratic leaders and renewed forms of nationalism. Moreover, as he notes with prescience, liberal democracies such as the United States and European nations are increasingly isolationist, politically paralyzed, and weak.

In this global context, it is important to understand that authoritarianism is not only a top-down form of governance, but a system of power that ordinary people at times invest with meaning and feeling. The example of Guinea shows how authoritarianism and its legacies live on in part because of complex understandings of history, identity, and national pride. From my earliest conversations about Guinean music and politics in Bob's Bar in the early 2000s, Guinean friends and acquaintances complicated the simple narrative I wished to construct between oppression and freedom. Public praise for dictatorial leaders, discomfort with a noisy free press, and muted expressions of dissent are all hallmarks of authoritarianism, yet they continue to resonate in Guinea—not just because of state or military action, but to some extent because of the pleasures of knowing oneself and one's history.

Yet, change is happening in Guinea. Activists are demanding democratic reforms, and (some) musicians are beginning to echo their calls. How, then, might pleasure and aesthetics create and sustain a different kind of politics than the country has known so far? What if any role might music play in proposing a new name and a new sense of self-recognition for Guineans in the twenty-first century?

Jeliya itself—or at least its idealized past—offers some answers to these questions. As noted, the possibility of social change, advice to the leader, and even protest is held to exist within the form itself, even if its practice most often emphasizes praise over counsel. Such idealized talk about music sometimes seems to back musicians into corners, while at other times the historical reference point it represents is further destabilized and buried underneath political conflict. Yet jeliya also provides an example of a form that has been able to evolve and change due to its emotional pull: even if naming is shrouded in debates about ethics, the emotions it produces are real. Young artists such as Espoirs de Coronthie and Takana Zion are not hereditary jelilu, yet they proudly claim their heritage as descendants of the broader historical and aesthetic landscape. Tradition, *naamunyi*, matters to these artists, despite their dreadlocks and DJ booths, and it is this cultural allegiance that disapproving elders ignore when they attempt to exclude them from tightly circumscribed notions of local culture. Such lines have long been drawn and redrawn, from Touré-era distinctions between artists and jelilu to ongoing debates about who has the right to sing praise. Yet without claiming to be jelilu, many young artists proudly claim the practice of naming as a mark of their rootedness, their Guinean-ness. Sanso, the leader singer of the Espoirs, was glowing with pleasure as he bounded offstage at a recent concert in Conakry, for instance. Alongside singing of suffering and justice, he had sung names, and as he said to me, "That's our tradition!" While Mande social organization delineates distinct roles and responsibilities for different groups, many non-jeli musicians claim the underlying model and the feelings that it generates as "our tradition."

For Sanso, Takana, and other musicians, acts of praise, naming, and guardedness exist fluidly within the spectrum of local music making alongside acts of witness and, at times, protest.[13] These vacillations are not simply political expediency, but knowing acknowledgments of the dynamic interplay between voice, silence, pleasure, protest, and authority in Guinea. Musicians push and pull, back away, check the local temperature, consider their positions and possibilities, and revel in their artistic forms—all while keenly aware of what others imagine in music, what they want from it, how it moves them, and how it could continue to do so in a changing terrain.

Solidarity, love of country, history, and pride are forces that propel musicians to sing the state, just as they occasionally—perhaps increasingly—lead them to sing against it. Young artists wave Guinean flags and give shout-outs to 224 (the country's international dialing code) at the same time that they may sing of the sheer hardships of living in Guinea or even call out abusive leaders. In referencing and naming Guinea in songs such as these, in naming "the youth" as they frequently do, they suggest that the pleasures of recognition and collectivity may exist across an array of aspirations and sensibilities. Activists are opening up new spaces to challenge authoritarianism in Guinea today, spaces in which a few musicians are experimenting. Without insisting on any direction these artists take, we can watch and listen, as they continue to draw from the past while possibly allowing for new futures further ahead.

Notes

Introduction

1. For Freud, pleasure exists within a dynamic struggle against repressed anxieties and desires, destructive impulses, and even death wishes. Freudian psychoanalysis does hold that pleasure matters as a motivating force behind human action that seeks to reduce pain. Nonetheless, as children progress to adulthood, this "pleasure principle" is increasingly dominated by an instinctive need to "return to the peace of the inorganic world"—in other words, to death (1920: 81). Pleasure is not just unreasonable and a mark of immaturity, but also ultimately fragile.

2. For Horkeimer and Adorno, "pleasure always means not to think about anything, to forget suffering even where it is shown" (1969: 144). These theorists have achieved a certain notoriety for their views on popular culture and music, but their critiques were not limited to these forms. In his essay "Commitment," Adorno warns that even an avant-garde composition such as Schoenberg's *Survivor of Warsaw* is dangerous: it turns the suffering of the victims of war into an object of aesthetic enjoyment (2007: 189).

3. In his book *What Art Is*, the philosopher and critic Arthur C. Danto argues that aesthetics—aesthetic pleasure—is not the main point of art and never has been. Aesthetics and the giving of aesthetic pleasure is of course *part* of a great deal of art, both traditional and contemporary, but the aim of giving pleasure is not its primary purpose. Rather, as he describes it, art's primary aim and fundamental characteristic is to embody meanings (2013: 149–50).

4. Reflecting long-standing ideas about what music scholars should and should not discuss, Susan McClary has recently confided that the pleasure she found in seventeenth-century music long remained "the big unstated motivation behind all my theoretical formulations" (2012: 3).

5. Keita and his former-group, Les Ambassadeurs du Motel, were invited to perform at Guinea's 1977 national arts festival. Although Keita is from a noble family, he often performs in the tradition of hereditary praise-singers, with "Mandjou" as the most iconic example (Keita 2011). The song identifies Touré as the grandson of the Almamy Samory Touré. Moreover, the song traces Touré's genealogy to the first *mori* or Islamic holy men in West Africa (Charry 2000: 38). Keita based his song on a 1971 recording, "Wajan," by the Malian jelimuso Ami Koita, a song created in honor of her uncle, the jeli Wa Kammisoko (Durán 2015).

6. Although he praises the artistry of the song, Cheick M. Chérif Keita describes it as part of "a grotesque manipulation of history to give legitimacy to corrupt leaders" (2011: 81). In addition, Ryan Skinner writes that Salif Keita's performance attracted criticism from two groups:

Malians opposed to Sékou Touré and Keita's own bandmates, who felt that their role had gone unacknowledged (2012: 528–29).

7. Mamadou "Le Maître" Barry, personal communication, 24 September 2009.

8. "The huge spiritual world that music produces in itself . . . ends up overcoming material poverty. From the minute a child is taught how to play an instrument, he's no longer poor." "The El Sistema Music Revolution," *TED2009*, February 2009, https://www.ted.com/talks/jose_abreu_on_kids_transformed_by_music?language=en, accessed December 2017.

9. It should be noted that this emphasis on autonomy has often been mischaracterized. Adorno's intent is precisely for art to be engaged in meaningful ways with the real world, but for him, this happens through autonomous form rather than through art that has explicit political meanings. Thus, "an emphasis on autonomous works is itself socio-political in nature" (Adorno, Benjamin, Bloch, Brecht, and Lukács 2007: 194). His passage on the work of Kafka and Beckett is a forceful illustration of why he upholds and champions such art (ibid.: 191).

10. I adapt this question from Berys Gaut's insightful discussion of art and ethics (2002: 342).

11. I am grateful to Brian Larkin for drawing my attention to Groys's work.

12. As Charry notes, the Mande "core" constitutes Maninka-, Mandinka-, and Bamana-speakers, while Soso speakers constitute a neighboring but closely related group (2000: 19).

13. The writers Amadou Diallo (1983), Ousmane Ardo Ba (1986), and Alpha Abdoulaye Diallo (1985), for instance, have all written about state-sponsored violence and detention in Touré's Guinea. Research on Fulbe music in Guinea has been undertaken by Katharina Lobeck (2003), while D. W. Arnott conducted research on Fulbe music and language across the region (2001). William Derman published an ethnographic account of Fulbe economic and political life in rural Guinea during the Touré era (1973). In *Fiddling in West Africa* (2008), Jacqeline Cogdell DjeDje addresses many aspects of Fulbe music, performance, history, and culture in her extensive study of Fulbe fiddle-playing in Senegal and Gambia.

14. Ardener stresses that "mutedness" in his sense refers not simply to linguistic silence, but more broadly to the structural role of subordinate groups in relation to the dominant. As he argues, the structures of the dominant "regularly assign contending viewpoints to a non-real status; making them 'overlooked,' 'muted,' 'invisible': mere black holes in someone else's universe" (1975b: 25).

15. Ian Birrell, "Music Is Vital to Political Struggle in Africa—Not Just in Mali," *Guardian*, 27 January 2013.

16. Chika Okeke-Agulu, "Modern African Art Is Being Gentrified," *New York Times*, 20 May 2017.

Chapter One

1. Ryan Skinner describes in detail the history and implications of the word *ambiance* in Mali and the ways in which it conveys a sense of the pleasures of postcolonial modernity (2015: 58–61).

2. Lansana Condé, personal communication, 23 August 2009.

3. The ensemble was originally named L'Ensemble Instrumental Africain de la Radiodiffusion Nationale.

4. Hamidou Bangoura, personal communication, 11 August 2009.

5. Because of its earlier history, the Ballets Africains maintained a semiautonomous status even after independence and was allowed to travel and perform more or less freely overseas. From 1959 to 1974 some of its performance revenues went into the state coffers, while the rest

were used to fund the group privately. In 1975, however, Touré fully nationalized the Ballets Africains: its members were paid government salaries, and all its revenue was directed to the state.

6. Belafonte's exact role in Ballet Djoliba is unclear. In his memoirs he writes that he founded Ballet Djoliba as part of a larger plan to support Guinean art and establish cultural exchanges between Guinea and the United States (2012: 293–94). In my conversations with Guinean artists, I was told varyingly that his role lay in supporting either Djoliba or the Ballets Africains in their overseas tours. He is not directly mentioned in *Horoya* or other government documents I have reviewed from the 1960s, although very few other dignitaries are, as Touré wished for the spotlight to remain firmly on himself.

7. Ballet Djoliba's mandate was more explicitly ideological than that of the Ballets Africains, and the troupe performed mainly at festivals and competitions in socialist countries throughout the Touré era.

8. Mohamed Saliou Camara writes that from 1961 to 1970 the national radio broadcasting station had a daily program of "Latin American/Middle Eastern/Black American Music," while other programs involved "Traditional Music of Guinea and Africa," "Songs of Laginè Ginè [Guinean women]," and "Party Folk Songs" (2005: 104).

9. Personal communication, 2 June 2009.

10. André Lewin, Touré's biographer and a former French ambassador to Guinea, notes that the president's family is of Soninké ethnicity, a northern Mande language group (2009: 22).

11. Eric Charry has written extensively of the guitar's role in bridging traditional jeli and modern dance music in Guinea. Since at least the 1920s musicians from jeli families had been transposing bala melodies to acoustic guitar, developing a distinctive finger-picking style in which the index finger played the bala patterns of one hand while the thumb played the patterns of the other (2000: 295). As Charry notes, the guitar opened the door to musical innovation by adapting jeli music to a new format.

12. For instance, the band Syli Authentique sang "Andrée" to the president's wife, Andrée Touré; while the Orchestre Fédéral de Macenta recorded "Le complot ne passera pas."

13. The musicologist Graeme Counsel has conducted extensive research on the RTG archives and has painstakingly digitized the entire Syliphone catalog. This collection is now available through the British Library Sound Archive. As Counsel notes, a large part of this catalog was destroyed by fire at the RTG headquarters in 1985 during an attempted coup d'état (2015: 549).

14. These records were compiled by the American broadcaster and sound engineer Leo Sarkisian, who befriended Touré while working in West Africa and was later employed as a civil servant to teach sound-recording techniques in Guinea. Ten discs from the *Sons nouveaux d'une nation nouvelle* series were released between 1961 and 1963 by the Tempo International label (Counsel 2015: 552).

15. *Horoya* was the successor to the pre-independence newspaper *La liberté*, of the Guinean nationalist party Rassemblement Démocratique Africaine (RDA). Following independence, the PDG retained the name *La liberté* until 1961, when it adopted the Maninka word (Camara 2005: 86).

16. "Chronique littéraire: Hommage à la danse," *Horoya*, 4 July 1961, 3.

17. "Discours du responsable suprême de la Révolution aux cadres de l'information, du cinéma et de l'INRDG, le 18 avril 1968," reprinted in *Horoya*, 16–17 June 1968, 1–4.

18. I. K. Diaré, "A l'occasion des 22 ans du PDG: Des concerts à la gloire du PDG," *Horoya hebdo*, 24–30 March 1969, 49–50. Bembeya Jazz's lead guitarist, Sékou Diabaté, is not to be confused with the older Guinean guitarist, Sékou 'Le docteur' Diabaté.

19. "L'art africaine," *Horoya*, 8–14 February 1969, 3–10.

20. Personal communication, 26 May 2013.

21. Angus Maddisson, "Confessions of a Chiffrephile," in *World Economic Performance: Past, Present and Future*, ed. D. S. Prassada Rao and Bart van Ark (Cheltenham, UK, and Northhampton, MA: Edward Elgar, 2013), 380.

22. The historian and writer D. T. Niane was among those arrested and imprisoned for involvement in this strike.

23. "L'ensemble instrumental africain de la radiodiffusion nationale," *Revue de l'éducation nationale, de la jeunesse et de la culture* (2 October 1963): 25.

24. Touré's speech to the Third Session of PDG Central Committee, Kankan, 29 July 1968.

25. Ibid.

26. Indeed, Touré's most famous phrase—"We prefer freedom in poverty to slavery in opulence"—from his 1958 speech in front of de Gaulle and declaring Guinea's intention to choose independence, was adapted from the classical Greek philosopher Democritus, who stated that "poverty in a democracy is preferable to prosperity in a tyranny."

27. In their essay on the Mande hero, Charles S. Bird and Martha Kendall note that a Mande hero is willing to risk everything for a praise song, because a great song ensures his immortality (1980: 21).

28. Bureau Politique National, "Rapport sur le complot militaire de février 1969," *Horoya*, 9 May 1969, 3–13.

29. Touré, "Speech to the Third Session of the PDG Central Committee, Kankan, July 1968," reprinted in *Horoya*, 31 July 1968, 1–3.

30. The writer Michel Roger Emvana cites a rumor that those in private audience with Touré would never look directly at his handkerchief for fear of being hyponotized by it (2005: 168). On the other hand, in his somewhat favorable account of the Touré years, Mohamed Camara dismisses these rumors as "mere speculation" (2005: 111).

31. Schmidt (2005b) writes that women activists in the pre-independence RDA party first started using white for their party uniforms, because that was the color of percale, the most widely available and inexpensive fabric. Male party members took up the color, which became indistinguishable from the RDA and the nationalist movement.

32. Telivel Diallo, personal communication, 22 August 2009. The local broadcasting station was initially known as Radio-Conakry, built by the French in 1952, but was renamed Voix de la Révolution (Voice of the Revolution) in the 1960s (Camara 2005: 89). Following the introduction of television to the country in 1977, the national TV and radio outlets were combined into Radio Télévision Guinée (Camara, O'Toole, and Baker 2014: 251).

33. "Appels au peuple: La révolution n'est jamais isolée," broadcast on Voix de la Révolution. This recording is accessible online via the British Library Syliphone archive, https://sounds.bl .uk/world-and-traditional-music/Syliphone-record-label-collection/025M-C1583X1X029X -0001V0, accessed 9 May 2015.

34. Hoffman also notes that nobles are supposed to be reticent rather than verbose (2000: 93)—a norm Touré was happy to flout.

35. Mohamed Saliou Camara also notes that Touré insisted on revising his speeches after their delivery so that the most enthusiastically applauded passages could be elaborated and the less well received parts minimized for the final, written version. As Camara notes, the written version sometimes bore no resemblance to the original, oral version (2005: 122–23).

36. "Réunion des orchestres de Conakry sous la présidence du Comité National de la JRDA," *Horoya*, 31 August 1968, 4.

37. "Discours de clôture du 1er Festival Culturel National," *Horoya*, 4–10 April 1970, 4.

38. In 1962, for instance, the Ministry of Youth, Art, and Sport called for two musicians from each administrative region to be selected to participate in a training course on European music theory and *solfège*. Similarly, in August 1968 the regime called for officials to attend and oversee music rehearsals. But because Touré was reluctant to explicitly delegate authority, and because decisions were pursued inconsistently, weekly performances before party leaders soon ceased.

39. Musicians were also expected to sing in Maninka if they wished to be successful. Counsel notes that many Fulbe bands from the Fouta Djallon highlands thus sang in Maninka. Personal communication, 3 June 2017.

40. Ismael Touré, "Aperçu sur le sabotage culturel en République de Guinée," *Horoya*, 5 March 1972, 2–3.

41. Ibrahima Khalil Diaré, "Quinzaine Artistique Nationale 1968: Ensembles de musique et danse," *Horoya*, 28–30 September 1968, 3–4.

42. For example, *Horoya* reported of a 1968 visit by the American blues artist, Junior Wells. "L'arrivée de l'orchestre de Wells en Guinée," *Horoya*, 6 January 1968, 3.

43. "Réunion des orchestres de Conakry sous la présidence du Comité National de la JRDA," *Horoya*, 31 August 1968, 4.

44. "Quinzaine Artistique Nationale," *Horoya*, 6–7 October 1968, 1–2.

45. Historians have noted the ways in which the Guinean nationalist movement actively elevated precolonial political leaders from different ethnic groups and regions as resistance heroes for the new nation to rally around. Samory Touré, a Maninka leader, and Alfa Yaya Diallo, a Fulbe leader, were two key figures in this narrative (Goerg 2011; Schmidt 2005a).

46. Interview with Sékou "Bembeya" Diabaté, http://www.afropop.org/multi/interview/ID/47/Sékou%20Bembeya%20Diabate-2002, accessed 10 December 2010.

47. Personal communication, 23 September 2009.

48. Lewin presents competing accounts of Touré's ties with Samory, as well as Touré's own claims of affiliation (2009: 23–24). The song "Touré barika," as originally sung by Jeli Kaba, traces Sékou Touré's lineage back sixteen generations and includes Samory Touré prominently in this genealogy (Camara 1992: 280–81).

49. A follow-up performance featured "Chemin du PDG," which constitutes the third and final part of the RSLP album in which Touré is upheld as the leader and future. Dedicated to the Guinean struggle from colonialism to independence, "Chemin du PDG" featured instrumental music, song, speech, and movement and was praised by one journalist as a Guinean "opera"; *Horoya*, 24–30 March 1969, 50. Owing to these successes, "Regard sur le passé" was quickly emulated. At a November 1970 concert in honor of the Guinean army, for example, the band Balla et ses Balladins performed a twenty-minute praise piece to Sékou Touré entitled "L'homme d'Afrique" (The Man of Africa). The piece included the jeli instrument *kora* (harp) alongside guitar, trumpet, and saxophone. Like those of "Regard sur le passé," the lyrics were divided into sung and spoken passages, which the audience listened to in "attentive silence." At the same concert, Bembeya Jazz followed up on their earlier successes with a new piece entitled "Echos des anciens" (Echoes of the Ancestors). The main melodic theme of "Echos des anciens" was played on bala and based on the jeli pieces "Boloba" and "Duga," praise songs respectively to the thirteenth-century Soso king Soumaoro Kanté and to the courage of warriors. The performance also included a recitative section by Sékou "Le Growl" Camara praising the Guinean army.

50. As part of this effort, the state even had a new headquarters, the Palais des Nations, built for the OAU, as well as a complex of villas for its ambassadors.

51. "Pan-African Cultural Manifesto," Organization of African Unity: First All Africa Cultural Festival, July–August 1969.

52. Touré's argument with Senghor was not just ideological, but also political, based on Senegal's perceived support for anti-Guinean actors. Senegal was home to many Guineans who fled their country through the 1960s, while Touré later suspected Senghor of supporting the 1970 attempted Portuguese invasion of Guinea (Camara 2005: 106–7).

53. Gehrard Kubik, "Letter to Hugh Tracey on the Pan-African Cultural Festival," 28 July 1969. Unpublished document, International Library of African Music Archive.

54. "Vie culturelle: La jeunesse de la Révolution Démocratique Africaine au rendez-vous d'Alger," *Horoya*, 19–25 July 1969, 26–33.

55. Personal communication, 17 May 2013.

56. "Vie culturelle: La jeunesse de la Révolution Démocratique Africaine au rendez-vous d'Alger," *Horoya*, 19–25 July 1969, 26–33.

57. N'Famara Keita, "La jeunesse doit bénéficier d'une éducation révolutionnaire rigoureuse," *Horoya*, 10–16 January 1970, 34.

58. Personal communication, Amirou Conté, 12 May 2009. Counsel notes that Fodé Conté's song "Bamba toumani," which describes a caterpillar whose head eats everything, was banned by state censors; the artist subsequently fled the country (2015: 564).

59. Mohamed Saliou Camara writes that the Bembeya Jazz song "Doni doni" was a subtle critique by the lead singer, Demba Camara, of the regime's actions preventing Guineans from building better lives elsewhere (2005: 164–65; see also Counsel 2015: 564). Camara also notes the many rumors suggesting state involvement in Demba's death and links these rumors with the song's lyrics. In some accounts I heard, in contrast, "Doni doni" was interpreted as a patriotic song warning against leaving one's country, while Touré's possible links to Demba's death were attributed to his jealousy of Demba's popularity. Telivel Diallo, personal communication, 22 August 2009; Mamadi Diabaté, personal communication, 4 September 2009.

60. Moorman notes that while nightclubs were not socially acceptable places for most Angolan young women to frequent, radio and recordings permitted music to spread beyond bars and clubs (2008: 87). This dynamic holds true in Guinea, where radio broadcasts made revolutionary music accessible to those who could not afford entry to or did not wish to frequent nightclubs.

61. Interview with Salifou Kaba, http://www.afropop.org/multi/interview/ID/48/Salifou %20Kaba,%20of%20Bembeya%20Jazz-2002, accessed 3 March 2011.

Chapter Two

1. Mamadou "Le Maître" Barry, personal communication, 24 September 2009.

2. Bembeya Jazz and other bands were invited to headline Guinea's fortieth-anniversary celebrations in 1998, for example. Lanciné Camara, "An 40 de l'indépendance: Une mémorable soirée de gala," *Horoya*, 7 October 1998, 8.

3. Personal communication, 22 September 2009.

4. Many Guineans had long been discussing this possibility. The International Crisis Group noted in a 2006 report that the "probability is now high that President Conté's term will end in a military takeover." "Guinea in Transition," Policy Briefing 37, 11 April 2006.

5. *Kumbengo* and *birimintengo* are the two patterns of playing that together constitute *kora foli* (kora playing), the first involving cyclical accompaniment patterns that form the basic melodic structure of a piece, the latter involving fast, ornamented melodies that often descend

stepwise. Charry translates *birimintengo* in *kora* playing as "rolling" (2000: 168). He notes that the same style of playing on the bala is referred to as *bala wora*.

6. Graeme Counsel reports that the song may not have first been recorded by Bembeya Jazz: an earlier recording appears to have been made by the National RTG Ensemble in 1964 (2010: 99).

7. Bird and Kendall write that the song tells the story of two precolonial warriors who fought each other, Duga Koro and Da Monson Jara. The vanquisher, Da Monson, king of the Segou empire, claimed the song of his enemy, Duga Koro, for himself (1980: 21); see also Durán 2007: 592–93 for further analysis of the song's narrative.

8. "L'éspace culturelle," RTG Radio, 29 May 2009.

9. While the minister did not make any explicit promises of patronage to the band, he did announce gifts to Bembeya from the Embassy of Mali and the telecommunications company Areeba, for one million and ten million GNF respectively.

10. Personal communication, Camille Quénard, 15 June 2009.

11. At the time of the festival, Algeria presided over the AU's culture ministries conference, which perhaps explains why it once again was the host.

12. "L'éspace culturel," RTG Radio, 29 May 2009.

13. Guinea's national representation to Algiers in 2009 also included a replica of the Sosso bala, the original bala created by Sunjata Keita's rival, Soumaoro Kanté, in the thirteenth century. The Sosso bala has been guarded for centuries by the same Kouyaté family in Niagassola, Guinea, and in 2001 UNESCO declared it one of the nineteen Masterpieces of the Oral and Intangible Heritage of Humanity. The Sosso bala is considered the original bala; all others are copies of it. It is the only bala that has twenty keys; most have twenty-one or twenty-two, while a recently created chromatic bala has twenty-five keys.

14. Personal communication, 28 August 2009; The ministry did announce plans for a local rap festival in 2009, but like so many other initiatives, this one was never realized.

15. Personal communication, Sékou Diabaté, 22 June 2009.

16. The Trio Bazooka consisted of Salifou Kaba, Moussa Touré, and Mory Kouyaté. This formation stayed in place until 1979, when Sékouba "Bambino" Diabaté joined Bembeya Jazz as the band's lead singer.

17. Counsel has digitized a number of these videos through his extensive work in the RTG sound archives (2015).

18. See http://www.guineenews.org/articles/detail.asp?num=201141413052, accessed 16 April 2011; my translation.

19. Banning Eyre, "Oh Bembeya!" *fRoots* 233 (2002); Chris Nickson, "Diamond Rich," *Seattle Weekly*, 9 October 2006, http://www.rockpaperscissors.biz/index.cfm/fuseaction/current .articles_detail/project_id/102/article_id/1050.cfm, accessed 19 November 2009.

20. Personal communication, 24 September 2009. Unlike many other dance-band musicians, Barry has changed his style over the past few decades, experimenting with soul music and collaborating with younger Guinean neotraditional groups rather than recreating his music from the 1960s and 1970s. This is due in part to his success in gaining new audiences, both at the French cultural center in Conakry and on tours in Europe. Barry is thus less dependent on state patronage than are many of his contemporaries in Conakry.

21. Personal communication, 15 September 2009.

22. Cécé Paul Kolié, personal communication, 2 September 2009.

23. Musically, *forestier* and Fulbe traditions differ from Mande traditions. Kpelle music, for example, is particularly distinctive for its vocal and instrumental polyphony (Stone 2005:

26–27). Thus, Woï Loiny's performance at the Cases de Bellevue featured horn ensembles using short, interlocking motifs to produce hocketing patterns. Fulbe music is more closely related to Mande traditions, centering on solo vocal performance by hereditary court musicians who are believed to have been absorbed from neighboring Mande groups. Song texts, however, deal with the Fulbe rather than the Mande past (Arnott 2001).

24. Charter for African Cultural Renaissance, Article 13, adopted at the Sixth Ordinary Session of the African Union, 23–24 January 2006.

25. *Bembeya Jazz National—The Syliphone Years*, Sterns 3029–30 (2004), 2 compact discs; *Kélétigui et ses Tambourinis—The Syliphone Years*, Sterns 3031–32 (2009), 2 compact discs; and *Balla et ses Balladins—The Syliphone Years*, Sterns 3035–36 (2008), 2 compact discs.

26. In her study of a South African recording studio, Louise Meintjes writes about the ways in which "overseas" is imagined in local music making. For South African musicians, the 1990s exploded with new opportunities for touring and performing internationally. At the same time, such opportunities come with demands. Meintjes notes that in seeking out international audiences, South African musicians "face a pressure to metaculturally mark their global participation as ethnically specific and emplaced" (2003: 220). Audiences in the global north who seek an authentic and culturally particular experience from the music of elsewhere thereby categorize and confine musicians, both by place and time.

27. "Oh Bembeya!" *fRoots* 233 (2002).

28. See, e.g., Banning Eyre, "Interview: Eric Charry on Bembeya Jazz," *Afropop Worldwide: Afropop Closeup, Season Three* (8 November 2012), afropop.org/articles/5957, accessed 19 April 2012; and Chris Nickson, "Diamond Rich," *Seattle Weekly*, 9 October 2006, http://www.rockpaperscissors.biz/index.cfm/fuseaction/current.articles_detail/project_id/102/article_id/1050.cfm, accessed 19 April 2012.

29. *Kélétigui et ses Tambourinis—The Syliphone Years*, Sterns 3031–32 (2009); *Balla et ses Balladins—The Syliphone Years*, Sterns 3035–36 (2008). Thomas Turino writes that similar imagery was commonly used in South African jazz releases in the 1940s and 1950s. He notes that it is derived from Tin Pan Alley representations in the early twentieth century (2000: 142).

30. The Kélétigui cover was originally featured on the single "Famadenke—Cigarettes allumettes," SYL502 (1969), while the Balla cover was featured on the singles "Diaraby," SYL505 (1968) and "Soumouyaya," SYL507 (1968). Graeme Counsel notes that political cartoons were also used as album covers, as was the case for three albums released after Guinea defeated Portuguese troops in an abortive mission to overthrow Touré in 1971 (2006: 112).

31. Personal communication, 2 March 2009.

32. http://www.bbc.co.uk/radio3/world/awards2003/profile_jazz.shtml, accessed 15 May 2011.

33. Chris Nickson, "Diamond Rich," *Seattle Weekly*, 9 October 2006, http://www.rockpaperscissors.biz/index.cfm/fuseaction/current.articles_detail/project_id/102/article_id/1050.cfm, accessed 19 November 2009; Andrew Morgan, "Biography of Bembeya Jazz," 2003, http://womad.org/artists/bembeya-jazz, accessed 24 May 2011.

34. This story can be linked to Touré's own writing and legislation regarding agricultural duties. In *Islam at the People's Service*, Touré writes of the Muslim duty to plant trees, a practice that traditionally took place in Guinea to celebrate the birth of a child. Here, however, Touré's particular aim is to contextualize the *loi Fria*, a law adopted by his party that mandated the planting of fruit trees to celebrate not just marriage and the birth of a child, but also the anniversary of the PDG's founding and the birthday of the prophet Mohammed (Touré 1977: 75–76). Interestingly, in his biography of Touré, André Lewin notes that as a representative in the French

West African territorial assembly in the 1950s, Touré had opposed colonial attempts to make the customary planting of trees a legal obligation (2009: 188).

35. Personal communication, 23 August 2009.

36. Personal communication, 11 October 2009.

37. Personal communication, 11 September 2009.

38. Demba is the son of M'Bady's late daughter, who married a Fulbe man by the name of Diallo. Because Diallo is immediately known to Guineans as a Fulbe—and therefore non-jeli—name, Demba sometimes uses the name Kouyaté when he needs to assert his lineage.

39. Personal communication, 16 September 2009.

40. André Lewin, the former French ambassador to Guinea, spoke in a similar vein in Conakry in April 2011 about his biography of Touré. One journalist in attendance later wrote of the speaker as a "friend of Sékou Touré, but not of Guinea"; http://konakryexpress.wordpress.com/2011/04/25/guinee-m-andre-lewin-ami-de-sekou-toure-mais-non-de-la-guinee/, accessed 17 April 2012.

41. Festi-Kaloum is a private cultural agency founded by Amirou Conté, a former member of the Touré-era national theater troupe, the National Director of Arts and Leisure from 1994 to 2004, and most recently the Minister of Culture in the government of Alpha Condé following the death of the previous minister in 2010. The aims of the agency are to promote Guinean culture and to organize performances and other culture-related events in Conakry, Kaloum being the name of one of the five precincts of the city.

42. Cissé later become Minister of Culture in 2010 under the presidency of Alpha Condé.

43. Souleymane Diallo reprinted the first version of Niane's poem in his doctoral thesis, "Le thème de la peur à travers les romans de Peter Abrahams" (Ph.D. diss., Université de Nice, 1985), 12. I am grateful to him for providing me with more information about it. The later version of the poem has been published in Goerg, Pauthier, and Diallo (2010).

Chapter Three

1. As Mandinka-speakers, M'Bady and his wife Diaryatou use the Mandinka term *jalolu*, but I use the Maninka *jelilu* here for consistency.

2. Personal communication, Soundjoulou Cissoko, 13 September 2009.

3. Personal communication, Mama Kouyaté, 4 October 2009.

4. Reprinted in *Horoya*, 4–10 April 1970, 18.

5. *Résolution adopté au 5ᵉ Congrès National de la JRDA*: "Décidé . . . 2.b. Pour mettre fin au 'griotisme,' le président ou un membre du comité de base, devra seul et sans l'aide du 'griot, répétiteur' procéder effectivement à toutes les formalités coutumières qu'exigent ces différentes cérémonies. (c) En cas de non respect de ses mesures ci-dessus énoncées la JRDA est autorisée à arrêter les manifestations et à confisquer tous les biens matériels réunis pour la circonstance." *Horoya*, 8 March 1968, 1–3.

6. Quoted in "Bakary Cissoko, un artiste populaire, un messager de la culture africaine," *Horoya*, 21–22 January 1968, 2.

7. "Discours du chef d'état," reprinted in *Horoya*, 1 March 1972, 4–5; also, Touré writes about the need to de-caste Guinean society ("Art africain," *Horoya hebdo*, 8–14 February 1969, 4).

8. As Cohen (2018) notes, in the absence of state sponsorship performers turn increasingly to *saabui*, patronage or individual mediation, to find support for their art . Such support can entail helping to secure performance contracts and visas for overseas travel.

9. McNaughton (1988) discusses *ŋama* in detail, arguing that this power and force is at the root of Mande sociality, because groups interact in such a way as to maintain social balance.

10. Durán (2015) notes that "Soliyo" is a key song in the repertoire of Mande jeliya. Although it is often used formulaically as a vehicle for praise, at its best it can be exhilarating and powerful. She writes that it can be as short as thirty seconds and is often embedded within other songs. As Durán observes, and as in most versions I heard in Guinea, it also frequently invokes the name of Silamkanba Koita, a horseback warrior and the ruler of the ancient city of Soro.

11. Durán notes that jelimuso concerts are modeled on weddings and street parties, in which women dominate as both audiences and singers. These settings allow women to reverse gender norms. Personal communication, 21 September 2017. Hélène Neveu Kringelbach has documented the ways in which Senegalese women dance and at times even remove their clothing in playful, erotic displays at *sabar* dance parties (2013: 89). Sabars have also become popular female-dominated street parties in Guinea, where women engage in similar acts.

12. Newell writes that the display is valorized by others: the giver is differentiated by others through his ability to waste, but at the same time the entire act brings the collective together (2012: 110). He also notes that the relationships created in this process are central to urban economic life, as money circulates and is redistributed (ibid.: 141).

13. This video was in fact produced by Jean-Baptiste Williams, who was soon thereafter appointed the National Director for Culture.

14. *Mamaya* is a Maninka group dance originating from the savannah region in northern Guinea. The term is now often used, sometimes derisively, as shorthand in Conakry for jeliya and praise singing.

15. *Yamaru O* is used here as shorthand for praise. More precisely, however, it is a common phrase in jeliya used to call out the object of praise, and translates as "I call you, my master." Lansana Condé explained to me that the phrase derives from the word *mory*, or Muslim leader and master. Personal communication, 23 March 2009. See Johnson 1999: 14 for a discussion of mory roles.

16. Personal communication, 5 September 2009.

17. Djessou Mory Kanté, personal communication, 8 September 2009; Soundjoulou Cissoko. personal communication, 13 September 2009.

18. The Kurakan Fuga is believed to have been created in the fourteenth century and was fully compiled and recorded in writing during a meeting of jelilu, historians, and other scholars in Kankan, Guinea, in 1998. The authenticity of the charter is debated, however (see Diakité 2009). I am grateful to Joseph Hellweg for drawing my attention to this clause.

19. Kurakan Fuga Charter: 8, accessed 25 July 2011, http://www.wildaf-ao.org/eng/IMG/pdf/THE_CHARTER_OF_KURAKAN_FUGA_Anglais_1.pdf.

20. In music, vocal clarity has become more important as texts and melodies need to be understood in order to be passed down across time—but even here the meaning of the words may often be obscure and incomprehensible, allowing for flexibility of interpretation (Durán 2015).

21. In 2009, for example, televised broadcasts of President Dadis interrogating Guinean citizens accused of corruption and drug crimes became known as the "Dadis Show" and were a source of popular fascination and amusement, in large part because of the president's screaming fits and tirades.

Chapter Four

1. Soso culture also recognizes the categories of male and female jelis: *jelixamè* and *jeliguinè*. As with musical genres, ethnic categories are not rigid dividers and should not mask the many features that the various groups in Guinea share.

2. Other groups include Linké Stars de Coléah, Bongo Stars de Yimbaya, Tempo Stars de Dixinn, Messagers de Boullbinet, all from Conakry and identified by their neighborhood, as well as Bombay Stars de Kindia, from a nearby town. This practice of naming a group according to locale is one that derives from the Touré era, when each district and region had its own dance band and ballet.

3. "Fougou fougou faga faga" is an onomatopeic phrase describing the sound of a bird's wings. The Espoirs also have an album and song by the same name.

4. While the bala is often played by jelilu and closely associated with jeliya, its origins are actually in Soso culture, where, according to the *Sunjata* epic, it was originally created by the Soso king Soumaoro Kanté.

5. The local name for this Kpelle slit-drum from the forest region, made from either bamboo or wood, is *kono*. However, *krin* is the name in more general use, having been adopted by musicians from other parts of Guinea. Cécé Paul Kolié, personal communication, 2 September 2009. Unlike Mande drum ensembles, Soso neotraditional groups usually do not feature *dundun* or *sangban*, the large and medium-sized stick drums that accompany jembe in Mande drumming.

6. Personal communication, 18 September 2009; tragically, Branco died in February 2017 at a relatively young age.

7. Lucy Durán makes a similar point in a discussion about the Malian singer Oumou Sangaré. As she notes, Sangaré is rarely explicitly confrontational in her songs, but Mande audiences understand the implied subtexts (2000: 143).

8. "Report of the International Commission of Inquiry Mandated to Establish the Facts and Circumstances of the Events of 28 September 2009 in Guinea," United Nations Security Council document S/2009/693. The Commission concluded that the events constituted a crime against humanity; see also "Bloody Monday: The September 28 Massacre and Rapes by Security Forces in Guinea," Human Rights Watch, 17 December 2009, https://www.hrw.org/report/2009/12/17/bloody-monday/september-28-massacre-and-rapes-security-forces-guinea, accessed 8 August 2014.

9. McGovern (2017) writes that the labor unions had originally called for Conté to step down, but eventually settled on reforms in order to maintain stability in the country.

10. There is a historical precedent for such recruitment. During his regime, the former president Lansana Conté recruited ex−rebel fighters from Liberia to quash the Guinean antigovernment demonstrations of 2006 and 2007 (McGovern 2017).

11. I have written in more detail about sexual violence in Guinea, including the 28 September massacre and debates around it, in Dave (2019).

12. It should be noted that since 2009, survivors and families of victims have worked with advocates to seek justice. The government of Alpha Condé put in place a National Commission to investigate the massacre, but their conclusions greatly minimized the number of deaths and rapes, in contrast to the investigations of local and national human rights monitors. A number of high level CNDD officials, including Dadis, have been indicted, but as of the date of this writing no trial has been held. Alsény Sall, personal communication, 8 January 2019. See also [FIDH] (2018): 288−99.

13. There had also been rumors in Conakry surrounding a concert given by the Étoiles at Sonfonia University in Conakry in honor of President Dadis. Gossip circulated that Dadis had given one of the singers a car in return for the performance, a rumor the singer denied, saying that the car was a gift from another patron for whom he had sung.

14. Quoted in Hamidou Sow, "La fermeture du Centre Culturel Franco-Guinéen: Les

hommes de culture désapprouvent la décision du Quai d'Orsay," http://www.guineenews.org/
articles/article_tempo.asp?num=200912394559, accessed 3 December 2009.

15. Personal communication, 17 October 2009.

16. Personal communication, 5 October 2009.

17. In an interview with the news magazine *Jeune Afrique* in November 2017, the Malian
superstar Salif Keita even publicly supported President Dadis after the massacre. Keita stated
that the massacre was a "plot against Dadis" and added, "I don't know Dadis, but I respect
him." http://www.jeuneafrique.com/200057/culture/l-autre-salif-keita/, accessed January 2018.

18. I borrow this notion of accommodation from Aaron Fox's discussion of the competing
attitudes among working-class Texans toward economic and political marginalization and social change since the 1970s. As Fox (2004) writes, the voices of working-class Texans reflect both
resistance and accommodation.

19. Johanne Burgell, "Les Espoirs de Coronthie, de la Guinée à Laval," 26 September 2013,
https://www.ouest-france.fr/les-espoirs-de-coronthie-de-la-guinee-laval-31307, accessed December 2016; Squaaly, "L'envol des Espoirs de Coronthie," 30 September 2013, http://www.rfi
.fr/mfi/20131008-musique-envol-espoirs-coronthie, accessed December 2016; Elisabeth Stoud-
mann. "Les Espoirs de Coronthie," 9 October 2013, https://www.newmorning.com/20131009
-2811-les-espoirs-de-coronthie.html, accessed December 2016.

20. See http://www.myspace.com/espoirscoronthie, accessed 12 February 2010.

21. Wess's 2004 album *Koutou koutou* was censored by the government for its criticisms of
then-President Conté. The regime was also reported to have made attempts on Wess's life, and
in 2004 he fled the country and sought refuge in France. His album was later retitled *Le choc des
cultures* (released on the label Makasound).

22. Lila Abu-Lughod first described the "romance of resistance" in her 1990 article on scholarly interest in resilience and creativity in the face of power and domination.

23. Alpha Wess also later released the song "Manguè Salamalékoun" as a mark of respect
to the current president, Alpha Condé. "Alpha Wess: J'appelle les guinéens à l'unité," http://
lexpressguinee.com/fichiers/videos5.php?langue=fr&idc=fr_Alpha_Wess__artiste__musicien
_et_juriste____J__appelle_les_Gu, accessed 22 February 2019.

24. "Musique métisses aux couleurs de la Guinée!" RFI Musique, 1 June 2009, http://musique
.rfi.fr/musique/20090601-musiques-metisses-couleurs-guinee, accessed 25 October 2010.

Chapter Five

1. Lansana Conté opened the way for multiparty elections in the early 1990s, but the fairness
of this contest was hotly disputed, and Conté presided over a quasi-military dictatorship until
his death in 2008.

2. Joseph notes, for example, that while many development economists support the "authoritarian modernization" approach of Paul Kagame's Rwanda, research shows that people all
across the continent desire accountability from their leaders; they are not satisfied with strong
economic growth at all costs (2014: 64). As he argues, countries such as Nigeria present a paradox of long-standing civilian rule with serious regional divisions, security threats, and inequality—a paradox that must be understood on its own terms rather than through older paradigms
focusing on good governance or economic performance.

3. Condé introduced this slogan at his inauguration speech in 2010, and it has since become
a common phrase among the country's political class.

4. During the 2010 campaign, violence erupted between Fulbe and Maninka people in a

number of towns in Guinea. In particular, the northern town of Siguiri saw intense fighting between 22 and 23 October, and state security forces were accused of turning a blind eye to the killing and targeting of Fulbe people ([FIDH] 2018: 273–74).

5. The International Crisis Group reported in a 2006 briefing that Cello Dalein Diallo was removed from his post as prime minister in the government of Lansana Conté after allegations were made that he forged a presidential decree in order to consolidate his own power. "Guinea in Transition," Policy Briefing no. 37, 11 April 2006.

6. The satirical newspaper Le Lynx often refers to Alpha Condé by this name.

7. Guinean news outlets reported an assassination attempt against the president in July 2011. According to the official version, the attempt was carried out by members of the military who retained loyalty to the CNDD military regime.

8. These choral songs were performed by the choir of Pita and the choir of Conakry.

9. The editorial, published in Le Lynx (20 May 2013), was in fact written by Diallo's son, who has been living in exile Senegal since his father's death.

10. In a biography of Diallo, André Lewin writes that Sékou Touré invited Diallo to dine with him at the presidential palace just a few hours before his arrest, when soldiers arrived unannounced at his house in the middle of the night (1990: 193). Diallo spent several months in Camp Boiro before his death there on 1 March 1977.

11. Sékouba "Bambino" Diabaté is not related to Sékou "Bembeya" Diabaté, although they are of the same broader lineage.

12. "Arts et culture: Sékouba Bambino Diabaté; J'ai chanté le général Sékouba parce qu'il mérite d'être chanté." GuinéeNews, 1 February 2011.

13. Tiken requested a meeting with Condé on his trip to Conakry to promote his project of building a school in the Guinean prefecture of Dalaba. Told that it would not be possible to meet, Tiken was said to have left Guinea frustrated and to have renounced his project.

14. "Arts & Culture: L'Agence Guinéenne de Spectacles rénove son siège à Conakry," http://www.guineenews.org/detail_article.asp?num=201352931250, accessed 1 June 2013.

15. This statement was delivered at a concert for peace and reconciliation in Conakry with Tiken and DJ Awadi. GuinéeNews, 18 November 2011.

16. Quoted in Guinéeinter.com, http://www.guineeinter.com/fichiers/videos5.php?langue=fr&idc=fr__Interview_de_Takana_Zion__reggeaman_guin_en____Je_ne_regrett, accessed April 2016.

17. See https://www.youtube.com/watch?v=8WfSH-jVlhk&t=33s, accessed 12 May 2013.

18. See https://www.youtube.com/watch?v=OqsvT1EWSic, accessed 10 October 2013. A number of other Guinean artists were also present at this concert, including Sekouba Kandia Kouyaté, Aicha Koné, and the Groupe Standard de Petit Conde, although, as a popular reggae man, Takana received the most attention and commentary.

19. Ibid., comments.

20. "Clash Takana Zion—Alpha Condé: Des citoyens réagissent . . . ," GuinéeNews, 24 March 2013, http://www.guineenews.org/detail_article.asp?num=20133245524, accessed 29 March 2013.

21. Personal communication, 17 May 2016.

22. See https://www.youtube.com/watch?v=mpccoS3NG6c, accessed 12 May 2013.

23. Ibid.

24. "Clash Takana Zion—Alpha Condé: Des citoyens réagissent . . . ," GuinéeNews, 24 March 2013, http://www.guineenews.org/detail_article.asp?num=20133245524, accessed 29 March 2013.

25. Boubacar Sanso Barry, "Reflexion: Takana Zion, Alpha Condé et la banalisation de la function présidentielle,'" http://www.guineeconakry.info/article/detail/reflexion-takana-zion -alpha-conde-et-la-banalisation-de-la-fonction-presidentielle/, accessed 29 March 2013.

26. The Jumeaux Damara were in fact later among a small group of artists who received cars from Alpha Condé in June 2017 in thanks for their support for his regime. Condé had earlier made similar gifts to imams in the country.

27. Djanii Alfa, whose real name is Alpha Midaou Bah, is of Fulbe ethnicity, and the song is in the Fulbe language.

Chapter Six

1. The newspaper *Le Lynx* even featured a cartoon of President Condé on its cover with the caption "Sékou Tyran is back!"—playing on Condé's phrase in 2010 that "Guinea is back!" *Le Lynx*, 4 December 2017.

2. This statement was made by Aly Nabé, deputy of the RPG, in the National Assembly on 4 December 2017. Quoted in Boubacar Diallo. "Deputy déclare qu'il faut massacrer pour l'autorité de l'État," *Les échos de Guinée*, 5 December 2017, 1.

3. The World Health Organization documented more than 28,000 reported cases in the subregion, with more than 11,000 confirmed deaths.

4. "Africa Stop Ebola" was also the name of a song contest held in 2015 in which aspiring musicians competed to write and perform a song about the disease. The five finalists performed at a concert at the Palais du Peuple in July 2015, sponsored by the French management company 3D Family.

5. As Fribault (2015) notes, Ebola has created such deep social discord that silence and a refusal to speak about it are often the easiest way to address it. "Ebola means nothing and every-thing to many Guineans," he told me in 2016.

6. The World Health Organization declared Guinea free of transmission of the Ebola virus on 29 December 2016, but nine new cases emerged in March and April 2016. Following a further waiting period after the last case, the WHO again declared the end of Ebola-virus transmission in Guinea on 1 June 2016.

7. Condé's ties to Bolloré date from their time together in Paris in the 1970s. Condé featured prominently at the press conference in Conakry at which Vivendi announced the September concert.

8. The company also announced that they would begin construction on a new concert hall in Conakry. These initiatives were announced as part of a larger "Living Together" initiative, coinciding with the end of Ebola and indicating Vivendi's plans to invest in Guinean arts and culture.

9. Plans also call for the Blue Zones eventually to be connected by a railroad, all sponsored and built by the Bolloré Group. The company is planning similar projects in Niger, Togo, and Benin.

10. The French newspaper *Le Monde* published an investigative piece on the port deal in September 2016 in which it noted the long-standing friendship between Condé and Bolloré, as well as the fact that the concession had previously been granted to another company before Condé rescinded the offer and awarded the contract to the Bolloré Group. Simon Piel and Joan Tilouine, "Bolloré: La saga du port maudit de Conakry," *Le Monde*, 16 September 2016. The company is currently under investigation by French authorities for corruption.

11. Quoted in Alpha Ousmane Ba, "Guinée: Bolloré/Vivendi lancent la construction d'une

grande salle de spectacle à Conakry . . . ," Africaguinee.com, 28 September 2015, http://www
.africaguinee.com/articles/2015/09/28/guinee-bollorevivendi-lancent-la-construction-d-une
-grande-salle-de-spectacle, accessed 22 February 2019.

12. "Are the Authoritarians Winning?" *New York Review of Books*, 10 July 2014, 53–55.

13. Takana recently launched a collective of artists under the name of Wonkhai 2020 (Let's
Go 2020, referencing presidential elections to be held that year) that includes Djanii Alfa, Single-
ton, and Steeve One Lockfs. The collective's relationship with the government has been somewhat unstable. Takana was arrested in July 2017 in an antigovernment protest shortly after the
collective was formed. A few months later, in October 2017, the group performed in the Upper
Coast towns of Kamsar and Boké in concerts calling on young people not to protest illegally or
engage in violent demonstrations in the wake of unemployment following a factory closure.
Rumors circulated that Wonkhai 2020 were paid by the Ministry of Culture to appease the local population, but the group itself strongly denied them. Djanii Alfa has since left the group
because of internal disputes.

Bibliography

Abu-Lughod, Lila. 1990. "The Romance of Resistance: Tracing Transformations of Power through Bedouin Women." *American Ethnologist* 17(1): 41–55.

———. 2005. *Dramas of Nationhood: The Politics of Television in Egypt.* Chicago: University of Chicago Press.

Adorno, Theodor, Walter Benjamin, Ernst Bloch, Bertolt Brecht, and Georg Lukács. 2007. *Aesthetics and Politics.* With an afterword by Fredric Jameson. London and New York: Verso.

Allman, Jean. 2004. "Fashioning Africa: Power and the Politics of Dress." In *Fashioning Africa: Power and the Politics of Dress*, edited by Jean Allman, 1–10. Bloomington: Indiana University Press.

Appadurai, Arjun. 1981. "The Past as a Scarce Resource." *Man* 16(2): 201–19.

Appiah, Kwame Anthony. 1992. *In My Father's House: Africa in the Philosophy of Culture.* New York: Oxford University Press.

Apter, Andrew. 2005. *The Pan-African Nation: Oil and the Spectacle of Culture in Nigeria.* Chicago: University of Chicago Press.

Ardener, Edwin. 1975a. "Belief and the Problem of Women." In *Perceiving Women*, edited by Shirley Ardener. London: Malaby Press.

———. 1975b. "The 'Problem' Revisited." In *Perceiving Women*, edited by Shirley Ardener. London: Malaby Press.

Arendt, Hannah. 1951. *The Origins of Totalitarianism.* New York: Schocken Books.

Arnott, D. W. 2001. "FulBe Music." *Grove Music Online.* 2nd ed. Edited by Deane L. Root. https://doi.org/10.1093/gmo/9781561592630.article.10365.

Askew, Kelly. 2002. *Performing the Nation: Swahili Music and Cultural Politics in Tanzania.* Chicago: University of Chicago Press.

Ba, Ousmane Ardo. 1986. Camp Boiro: *Sinistre geôle de Sékou Touré.* Paris: L'Harmattan.

Baker, Geoffrey. 2014. *El Sistema: Orchestrating Venezuela's Youth.* Oxford and New York: Oxford University Press.

Barber, Karin. 1987. "Popular Arts in Africa." *African Studies Review* 30(3): 1–78.

Barry, Ismael. 2010. "Réflexions sur le NON de la Guinée, cinquante ans après." In *Le NON de la Guinée (1958): Entre mythe, relecture historique et résonances contemporaines*, edited by Odile Goerg, Céline Pauthier, and Abdoulaye Diallo, 29–42. Paris: L'Harmattan.

Basso, Keith. 1970. "'To Give up on Words': Silence in Western Apache Culture." *Southwestern Journal of Anthropology* 26(3): 213–30.

Belafonte, Harry. 2012. *My Song: A Memoir of Art, Race and Defiance.* With Michael Schnayerson. Edinburgh: Canongate.

Bird, Charles S., and Martha B. Kendall. 1980. "The Mande Hero." In *Explorations in African Systems of Thought,* edited by Ivan Karp and Charles S. Bird, 13–26. Bloomington: Indiana University Press.

Bloch, Maurice. 1974. "Symbols, Song, Dance and Features of Articulation: Is Religion an Extreme Form of Traditional Authority?" *European Journal of Sociology* 15: 55–81.

Boym, Svetlana. 2001. *The Future of Nostalgia.* New York: Basic Books.

Brown, Wendy. 2005. *Edgework: Critical Essays on Knowledge and Politics.* Princeton, NJ: Princeton University Press.

Buchanan, Donna A. 2006. *Performing Democracy: Bulgarian Music and Musicians in Transition.* Chicago: University of Chicago Press.

Camara, Laye. 1976. *Le maître de la parole: Kouma Lafôlô Kouma.* Paris: Plon.

Camara, Mohamed Saliou. 2005. *His Master's Voice: Mass Communication and Single-Party Politics in Guinea under Sékou Touré.* Trenton, NJ: Africa World Press.

Camara, Mohamed Saliou, Thomas O'Toole, and Janice E. Baker. 2014. *Historical Dictionary of Guinea.* 4th ed. Plymouth: Scarecrow Press.

Camara, Sory. 1992. *Gens de la parole: Essai sur la condition et le rôle des griots dans la société malinké.* Paris: Karthala.

Carrithers, Michael. 2005. "Anthropology as a Moral Science of Possibilities." *Current Anthropology* 46(3): 433–56.

Chari, Sharad, and Katherine Verdery. 2009. "Thinking between the Posts: Postsocialism, Postcolonialism, and Ethnography after the Cold War." *Comparative Studies in Society and History* 51(1): 6–34.

Charry, Eric. 2000. *Mande Music: Traditional and Modern Music of the Maninka and Mandinka of Western Africa.* Chicago: University of Chicago Press.

Cheeseman, Nic. 2015. *Democracy in Africa: Successes, Failures, and the Struggle for Political Reform.* New York: Cambridge University Press.

Cherif, Alhassane. 2005. *L'importance de la parole chez les Manding de Guinée: Paroles de vie, paroles de mort et rituels funéraires.* Paris: L'Harmattan.

Cohen, Adrienne. 2016. "Inalienable Performances, Mutable Heirlooms: Dance, Cultural Inheritance, and Political Transformation in the Republic of Guinea." *American Ethnologist* 43(4): 650–62.

———. 2018. "Occult Return, Divine Grace, and Saabui: Practising Transnational Kinship in Postcolonial Guinea." *Journal of the Royal Anthropological Institute* 24(2): 275–92.

Counsel, Graeme. 2006. "Mande Popular Music and Cultural Policies in West Africa." Ph.D. diss., University of Melbourne.

———. 2010. "Music for a Coup: 'Armée guinéenne'; An Overview of Guinea's Recent Political Turmoil." *Australasian Review of African Studies* 31(2): 94–112.

———. 2015. "Music for a Revolution: The Sound Archives of Radio Télévision Guinée." In *From Dust to Digital: Ten Years of the Endangered Archives Programme,* edited by Maja Kominko, 547–86. Cambridge: Open Book.

Danto, Arthur C. 2013. *What Art Is.* New Haven, CT: Yale University Press.

Daughtry, Martin. 2015. *Listening to War: Sound, Music, Trauma, and Survival in Wartime Iraq.* Oxford and New York: Oxford University Press.

Dave, Nomi. 2009. "Une nouvelle révolution permanente: The Making of African Modernity in Sékou Touré's Guinea." *Forum for Modern Language Studies* 45(4): 455–71.

———. 2014. "The Politics of Silence: Music, Violence and Protest in Guinea." *Ethnomusicology* 58(1): 1–29.

———. 2015. "Music and the Myth of Universality: Sounding Human Rights and Capabilities." *Journal of Human Rights Practice* 7(1): 1–17.

———. 2017. "Sifting through Truths in Guinean Music." In *Researching Music Censorship*, edited by Annemette Kirkegaard, Helmi Järviluoma, Jan Sverre Knudsen, and Jonas Otterbeck, 122–37. Newcastle-upon-Tyne: Cambridge Scholars.

———. 2019. "Sexual Violence and the Politics of Forgiveness in Guinea: Musical Interventions." In *The Art of Emergency: Aesthetics and Aid in African Crises*, edited by Chérie Rivers Ndaliko and Samuel M. Anderson. New York: Oxford University Press.

Dean, Tim. 2012. "The Biopolitics of Pleasure." *South Atlantic Quarterly* 111(3): 477–96.

Derman, William. 1973. *Serfs, Peasants, and Socialists: A Former Serf Village in the Republic of Guinea*. Berkeley and Los Angeles: University of California Press.

Diakité, Mamadou. 2009. "Analyse du discours, tradition orale et histoire: Et si la *Charte de Kurakan Fuga* ne datait que de 1998?" *Revue electronique internationale de sciences du langage* 11: 107–30.

Diallo, Alpha Abdoulaye. 1985. *La Vérité du Ministre: Dix ans dans les geôles de Sákou Touré*. Paris: Calmann-Lévy.

Diallo, Amadou. 1983. *La mort de Diallo Telli: 1er Secrétaire-général de l'O.U.A.* Paris: Karthala.

Diawara, Manthia. 1998. *In Search of Africa*. Cambridge, MA: Harvard University Press.

DjeDje, Jacqueline Cogdell. 2008. *Fiddling in West Africa: Touching the Spirit in Fulbe, Hausa, and Dagbamba Cultures*. Bloomington: Indiana University Press.

Durán, Lucy. 2000. "Women, Music and the 'Mystique' of Hunters in Mali." In *The African Diaspora: A Musical Perspective*, edited by Ingrid Monson, 136–86. New York: Garland.

———. 2007. "Ngaraya: Women and Musical Mastery in Mali." *Bulletin of SOAS* 70(3): 569–602.

———. 2015. "'Soliyo' (Calling the Horses): Song and Memory in Mande Music." In *Pieces of the Musical World: The Study of Music in Culture*, edited by Rowan Pease and Rachel Harris, 27–44. Abingdon: Taylor & Francis.

Eagleton, Terry. 1991. *Ideology: An Introduction*. London: Verso.

Ebron, Paula A. 2002. *Performing Africa*. Princeton, NJ: Princeton University Press.

Emvana, Michel Roger. 2005. *Paul Biya: Les secrets de pouvoir*. Paris: Karthala.

Eyre, Banning. 2000. *In Griot Time: An American Guitarist in Mali*. Philadelphia: Temple University Press.

Fair, Laura. 2001. *Pastimes and Politics: Culture, Community, and Identity in Post-Abolition Urban Zanzibar, 1890–1945*. Athens: Ohio University Press.

Fanon, Frantz. 1952. *Black Skin, White Masks*. Translated by Charles Lam Markmann. London: Pluto Press.

———. 1965. *A Dying Colonialism*. Translated by Haakon Chevalier. New York: Grove Press.

Feld, Steven. 1996. "Pygmy POP: A Genealogy of Schizophonic Mimesis." *Yearbook for Traditional Music* 28: 1–35.

———. 2005. "Communication, Music, and Speech about Music." In Charles Keil and Steven Feld, *Music Grooves*. 2nd ed. Tucson: Fenestra Books.

Feld, Steven, Aaron A. Fox, Thomas Porcello, and David Samuels. 2004. "Vocal Anthropology: From the Music of Language to the Language of Song." In *A Companion to Linguistic Anthropology*, edited by Alessandro Duranti. Malden, MA: Blackwell.

Ferme, Mariane C. 2001. *The Underneath of Things: Violence, History, and the Everyday in Sierra Leone*. Berkeley and Los Angeles: University of California Press.

Fédération Internationale des Droits de l'Homme [FIDH]. 2018. *Mémoire collective: Une Histoire plurielle des violences politiques en Guinée*.

Fischlin, Daniel. 2003. "Take One/Rebel Musics: Human Rights, Resistant Sounds, and the Politics of Music Making." In *Rebel Musicians: Human Rights, Resistant Sounds, and the Politics of Music Making*, edited by Daniel Fischlin and Ajay Heble, 10–43. Montreal and New York: Black Rose Books.

Fraser, Nancy. 1995. "From Recognition to Redistribution? Dilemmas of Justice in a 'Post-Socialist' Age." *New Left Review* 212: 68–93.

Freud, Sigmund. 1920. *Beyond the Pleasure Principle*. Translated by C. J. M. Hubback. London: International Pscyho-Analytical Press.

Fribault, Mathieu. 2015. "Ebola en Guinée: violences historiques et régimes de doute." *Anthropologie et Santé* 11. https://journals.openedition.org/anthropologiesante/1761#quotation.

Foucault, Michel. 1976. *The History of Sexuality*. Volume 1. Translated by Robert Hurley. London: Penguin Books.

Fox, Aaron. 2004. *Real Country: Music and Language in Working-Class Culture*. Durham, NC: Duke University Press.

Gaut, Berys. 2002. "Art and Ethics." In *The Routledge Companion to Aesthetics*, edited by Berys Gaut and Dominic McIvers Lopes, 341–52. London and New York: Routledge.

Gilman, Lisa. 2009. *The Dance of Politics: Gender, Performance, and Democratization in Malawi*. Philadelphia: Temple University Press.

Goerg, Odile. 2011. "Couper la Guinée en quatre ou comment la colonisation a imaginé l'Afrique." *Vingtième siècle: Revue d'histoire* 3(111): 73–88.

Goerg, Odile, Céline Pauthier, and Abdoulaye Diallo. 2010. *Le NON de la Guinée (1958): Entre mythe, relecture historique et résonances contemporaines*. Paris: L'Harmattan.

Groys, Boris. 1992. *The Total Art of Stalinism: Avant-Garde, Aesthetic Dictatorship, and Beyond*. Translated by Charles Rougle. Princeton, NJ: Princeton University Press.

Guilbault, Jocelyne. 2007. *Governing Sound: The Cultural Politics of Trinidad's Carnival Musics*. Chicago: University of Chicago Press.

Hale, Thomas A. 1998. *Griots and Griottes: Masters of Words and Music*. Bloomington: Indiana University Press.

Harney, Elizabeth. 2004. *In Senghor's Shadow: Art, Politics, and the Avant-Garde in Senegal, 1960–1995*. Durham, NC: Duke University Press.

Herzfeld, Michael. 1991. "Silence, Submission, and Subversion: Towards a Poetics of Womanhood." In *Contested Identities: Gender and Kinship in Modern Greece*, edited by Peter Loizos and Evthymios Papataxiarchis. Princeton, NJ: Princeton University Press.

———. 1997. *Cultural Intimacy: Social Poetics in a Nation-State*. New York: Routledge.

Hoffman, Barbara G. 1995. "Power, Structure, and Mande Jeliw." In *Status and Identity in West Africa: Nyamakalaw of Mande*, edited by David C. Conrad and Barbara E. Frank, 36–45. Bloomington: Indiana University Press.

———. 2000. *Griots at War: Conflict, Conciliation, and Caste in Mande*. Bloomington: Indiana University Press.

Hopkins, Nicholas. 1997. "Memories of Griots." *Alif: Journal of Comparative Poetics* 17: 43–72.

Horkheimer, Max, and Theodor W. Adorno. 1969. *Dialectic of Enlightenment* Translated by John Cumming. New York: Continuum.

Huizinga, Johan. 1949. *Homo Ludens: A Study of the Play-Element in Culture.* London and Boston: Routledge & Kegan Paul.

Irele, Abiola. 1965. "Négritude or Black Cultural Nationalism." *Journal of Modern African Studies* 3(3): 321–48.

James, Wendy. 2003. *The Ceremonial Animal: A New Portrait of Anthropology.* Oxford and New York: Oxford University Press.

Johnson, John William. 1999. "The Dichotomy of Power and Authority in Mande Society and in the Epic of Sunjata." In *In Search of Sunjata: The Mande Oral Epic as History, Literature, and Performance,* edited by Ralph A. Austen, 9–22. Bloomington: Indiana University Press.

Joseph, Richard. 2014. "Growth, Security, and Democracy in Africa." *Journal of Democracy* 25(4): 61–75.

Kaba, Lansiné. 1976. "The Cultural Revolution, Artistic Creativity, and Freedom of Expression in Guinea." *Journal of Modern African Studies* 14(2): 201–18.

Kaké, Ibrahima Baba. 1987. *Sékou Touré: Le héros et le tyran.* Paris: Collection Jeune Afrique Livres.

Keita, Cheick Mahamadou Chérif. 1995. "Jaliya in the Modern World: A Tribute to Banzumana Sissoko and Massa Makan Diabaté." In *Status and Identity in West Africa: Nyamakalaw of Mande,* edited by David C. Conrad and Barbara E. Frank, 182–96. Bloomington: Indiana University Press.

———. 2011. *Outcast to Ambassador: The Musical Odyssey of Salif Keita.* St. Paul, MN: Mogoya Books.

Keita, Fodéba. 1957. "La danse africain et la scène." *Présence africaine* 14–15: 202–9.

Kelley, Robin D. G. 1997. *Yo' Mama's Disfunktional! Fighting the Culture Wars in Urban America.* Boston: Beacon Press

Kouyaté, Mamadou. 2012. *Sory Kandia Kouyaté: Chantre immortel d'une Afrique eternelle.* Paris: L'Harmattan.

Lamp, Frederick. 1996. *Art of the Baga: A Drama of Cultural Reinvention.* New York: Museum for African Art and Munich: Prestal Verlag.

Larkin, Brian. 2008. *Signal and Noise: Media, Infrastructure, and Urban Culture in Nigeria.* Durham, NC: Duke University Press.

Lee, Hélène. 1988. *Rockers d'Afrique: Stars et légendes du rock mandingue.* Paris: Albin Michel.

Lewin, André. 1990. *Diallo Telli: Le tragique destin d'un grand Africain.* Paris: Jeune Afrique Livres.

———. 2009. *Ahmed Sékou Touré (1922–1984), président de la Guinée.* Vol. 1, *1922–février 1955.* Paris: L'Harmattan.

———. 2011. "Préface." In Justin Morel Junior and Souleymane Keita, *Bembeya Jazz National: Cinquante ans après, la légende continue. . . .* Paris: L'Harmattan.

Lindfors, Bernth. 1970. "Anti-Negritude in Algiers." *Africa Today* 17(1): 5–7.

Lobeck, Katarina. 2003. "Fallen Saints and Pardoned Sinners: Music, Status and Identity of the Fulbe Nyamakala." Ph.D. diss., University of London.

McDonald, David A. 2013. *My Voice Is My Weapon: Music, Nationalism, and the Poetics of Palestinian Resistance.* Durham, NC: Duke University Press.

McClary, Susan. 2012. *Desire and Pleasure in Seventeenth-Century Music.* Berkeley and Los Angeles: University of California Press.

Makeba, Miriam, with James Hall. 1987. *My Story.* New York: Plume.

Makhulu, Anne-Maria, Beth A. Buggenhagen, and Stephen Jackson. 2010. "Introduction." In

Hard Work, Hard Times: Global Volatility and African Subjectivities, edited by Anne-Maria Makhulu, Beth A. Buggenhagen, and Stephen Jackson, 1–27. Berkeley and Los Angeles: University of California Press.

Manabe, Noriko. 2016. *The Revolution Will Not Be Televised: Protest Music after Fukushima.* Oxford and New York: Oxford University Press.

Masekela, Hugh, and D. Michael Cheers. 2004. *Still Grazing: The Musical Journey of Hugh Masekela.* New York: Crown.

Mbembe, Achille. 2001. *On the Postcolony.* Berkeley and Los Angeles: University of California Press.

———. 2006. "Variations on the Beautiful in Congolese Worlds of Sound." In *Beautiful/Ugly: African and Diaspora Aesthetics*, edited by Sarah Nuttall, 60–93. Durham, NC: Duke University Press.

McGovern, Mike. 2010. "The Refusal to Celebrate the Fiftieth Anniversary of the 1958 NO." In *Le NON de la Guinée (1958): Entre mythe, relecture historique et résonances contemporaines*, edited by Odile Goerg, Céline Pauthier, and Abdoulaye Diallo, 17–27. Paris: L'Harmattan.

———. 2013. *Unmasking the State: Making Guinea Modern.* Chicago: University of Chicago Press.

———. 2017. *A Socialist Peace? Explaining the Absence of War in an African Country.* Chicago: University of Chicago Press.

McNaughton, Patrick. 1988. *The Mande Blacksmiths: Knowledge, Power, and Art in West Africa.* Bloomington: Indiana University Press.

Meintjes, Louise. 2003. *Sound of Africa! Making Music Zulu in a South African Studio.* Durham, NC: Duke University Press.

———. 2017. *Dust of the Zulu: Ngoma Aesthetics after Apartheid.* With photographs by T. J. Lemon. Durham, NC: Duke University Press.

Meserve, Walter J., and Ruth I. Meserve. 1992. "Revolutionary Realism: China's Path to the Future." *Journal of South Asian Literature* 27(2): 29–39.

Moorman, Marissa J. 2008. *Intonations: A Social History of Music and Nation in Luanda, Angola from 1945 to Recent Times.* Athens: Ohio University Press.

Monson, Sarah. 2017. "Ebola as African: American Media Discourses of Panic and Otherization." *Africa Today* 63(3): 2–27.

Morel, Justin, Jr., and Souleymane Keita. 2011. *Bembeya Jazz National: Cinquante ans après, la légende continue. . . .* Paris: L'Harmattan.

Morford, James. B. 2017. "Beyond Ebola: Fundraising and the Impact of Ebola on Music and Dance Tourism in Guinea." *Africa Today* 63(3): 44–60.

Mulvey, Laura. 1975. "Visual Pleasure and Narrative Cinema." *Screen* 16(3): 6–18.

Navaro-Yashin, Yael. 2002. *Faces of the State: Secularism and Public Life in Turkey.* Princeton, NJ: Princeton University Press.

Ndaliko, Chérie Rivers. 2016. *Necessary Noise: Music, Film, and Charitable Imperialism in the East of Congo.* New York: Oxford University Press.

Neveu Kringelbach, Hélène. 2007. "Cool Play: Emotionality in Dance as a Resource in Senegalese Urban Women's Associations." In *The Emotions: A Cultural Reader*, edited by Helena Wulff. Oxford: Berg.

———. 2013. *Dance Circles: Movement, Morality and Self-Fashioning in Urban Senegal.* New York: Berghahn.

Newell, Sasha. 2012. *The Modernity Bluff: Crime, Consumption, and Citizenship in Côte d'Ivoire.* Chicago: University of Chicago Press.

Niane, D. T. 1995. *Sundiata: An Epic of Old Mali.* Portsmouth, NH: Heineman.

Novak, David. 2017. "Project Fukushima! Performativity and the Politics of Festival in post-3/11 Japan." *Anthropological Quarterly* 90(1): 226–53.

Nussbaum, Martha C. 2013. *Political Emotions: Why Love Matters to Justice.* Cambridge, MA: Harvard University Press.

Nuttall, Sarah. 2006. "Rethinking Beauty." In *Beautiful/Ugly: African and Diaspora Aesthetics,* edited by Sarah Nuttall, 6–29. Durham, NC: Duke University Press.

O'Toole, Thomas, with Ibrahima Bah-Lalya. 1995. *The Historical Dictionary of Guinea.* 3rd ed. African Historical Dictionaries 16. Lanham, MD: Scarecrow Press.

Olaniyan, Tejumola. 2004. *Arrest the Music! Fela and His Rebel Art and Politics.* Bloomington: Indiana University Press.

Ortner, Sherry B. 2006. *Anthropology and Social Theory: Culture, Power, and the Acting Subject.* Durham, NC: Duke University Press.

Osborn, Emily Lynn. 2011. *Our New Husbands Are Here: Households, Gender, and Politics in a West African State from the Slave Trade to Colonial Rule.* Athens: Ohio University Press.

Pauthier, Céline. 2010. "Le NON de la Guinée: Un lieu de mémoire national." In *Le NON de la Guinée (1958): Entre mythe, relecture historique et résonances contemporaines,* edited by Odile Goerg, Céline Pauthier, and Abdoulaye Diallo, 59–79. Paris: L'Harmattan.

Pitcher, M. Anne, and Kelly M. Askew. 2006. "African Socialisms and Postsocialisms." *Africa* 76(1): 1–14.

Piot, Charles. 2010. *Nostalgia for the Future: West Africa after the Cold War.* Chicago: University of Chicago Press.

Povey, John. 1966. "Dakar: An African Rendez-vous." *Africa Today* 13(5): 4–6.

Rancière, Jacques. 2004. *The Politics of Aesthetics.* Translated by Gabriel Rockhill. London and New York: Continuum.

Samuels, David W., Louise Meintjes, Ana Maria Ochoa, and Thomas Porcello. 2010. "Soundscapes: Toward a Sounded Anthropology." *Annual Review of Anthropology* 39: 329–45.

Sarró, Ramon. 2009. *The Politics of Religious Change on the Upper Guinea Coast: Iconoclasm Done and Undone.* Edinburgh: Edinburgh University Press for the International African Institute, London.

Scott, James C. 1990. *Domination and the Arts of Resistance: Hidden Transcripts.* New Haven, CT: Yale University Press.

Schmidt, Elizabeth. 2005a. *Mobilizing the Masses: Gender, Ethnicity, and Class in the Nationalist Movement in Guinea, 1939–1958.* Portsmouth, NH: Heinemann.

———. 2005b. "Top Down or Bottom Up? Nationalist Mobilization Reconsidered, with Special Reference to Guinea (French West Africa)." *American Historical Review* 110(4): 975–1014.

Schulz, Dorothea E. 2001. *Perpetuating the Politics of Praise: Jeli Singers, Radios, and Political Mediation in Mali.* Cologne: Rüdiger Köppe Verlag.

Shain, Richard, M. 2002. "Roots in Reverse: Cubanismo in Twentieth-Century Senegalese Music." *International Journal of African Historical Studies* 35(1): 83–101.

Shelemay, Kay Kaufman. 2009. "The Power of Silent Voices: Women in the Syrian Jewish Musical Tradition." In *Music and the Play of Power in the Middle East, North Africa, and Central Asia,* edited by Laudan Nooshin, 269–88. Farnham, UK, and Burlington, VT: Ashgate.

Shipley, Jesse Weaver. 2013. *Living the Hiplife: Celebrity and Entrepreneurship in Ghanaian Popular Music.* Durham, NC: Duke University Press.

Skinner, Ryan Thomas. 2012. "Cultural Politics in the Post-Colony: Music, Nationalism, and Statism in Mali, 1964–75." *Africa* 82(4): 511–34.

———. 2015. *Bamako Sounds: The Afropolitan Ethics of Malian Music.* Minneapolis: University of Minnesota Press.

Slaughter, Joseph. 1997. "A Question of Narration: The Voice in International Human Rights Law." *Human Rights Quarterly* 19(2): 406–30.

Sontag, Susan. 1961. *Against Interpretation and Other Essays.* New York: Farrar, Straus & Giroux.

Sorce Keller, Marcello. 2007. "Why Is Music So Ideological, and Why Do Totalitarian States Take It So Seriously? A Personal View from History and the Social Sciences." *Journal of Musicological Studies* 26(2–3): 91–122.

Spivak, Gayatri Chakravorty. 1988. "Can the Subaltern Speak?" In *Marxism and the Interpretation of Culture,* edited by Cary Nelson and Lawrence Grossberg. London: Macmillan.

Steiner, Wendy. 1995. *The Scandal of Pleasure: Art in an Age of Fundamentalism.* Chicago: University of Chicago Press.

Stewart, Kathleen. 1988. "Nostalgia: A Polemic." *Cultural Anthropology* 3(3): 227–41.

Stirr, Anna Marie. 2017. *Singing across Divides: Music and Intimate Politics in Nepal.* Oxford and New York: Oxford University Press.

Stone, Ruth M. 2005. *Music in West Africa: Experiencing Music, Expressing Culture.* Oxford and New York: Oxford University Press.

Stokes, Martin. 2004. "Music and the Global Order." *Annual Review of Anthropology* 33: 47–72.

———. 2010. *The Republic of Love: Cultural Intimacy in Turkish Popular Music.* Chicago: University of Chicago Press.

———. 2015. "The Politics of Aesthetics in the Muslim Middle East." In *The Wiley-Blackwell Companion to the Anthropology of the Middle East,* edited by Soraya Altorki, 91–106. Hoboken, NJ: Wiley-Blackwell.

Straker, Jay. 2009. *Youth, Nationalism, and the Guinean Revolution.* Bloomington: Indiana University Press.

Taylor, Charles. 1994. *Multiculturalism: Examining the Politics of Recognition.* Edited and introduced by Amy Guttman. Princeton, NJ: Princeton University Press.

Thayer, James Steel. 1983. "Nature, Culture and the Supernatural among the Susu." *American Ethnologist* 10(1): 116–32.

Thomas, Dominic. 2002. *Nation-Building, Propaganda, and Literature in Francophone Africa.* Bloomington: Indiana University Press.

Todorova, Maria. 2010. "From Utopia to Propaganda and Back." In *Post-Communist Nostalgia,* edited by Maria Todorova and Zsuzsa Gille, 1–13. Oxford and New York: Berghahn Books.

Touré, Sékou. 1961. *Expérience guinéenne et unité africaine.* Paris: Présence Africaine.

———. 1967. *L'Afrique en marche.* Vol. 10. 4th ed. Geneva: Kundig.

———. 1972. *La révolution culturelle.* Vol. 17. 4th ed. Geneva: Kundig.

———. 1977. *L'Islam au service du people.* 3rd ed. Conakry: Bureau de Presse de la Présidence de la République.

Treitler, Leo. 1989. *Music and the Historical Imagination.* Cambridge, MA: Harvard University Press.

Turino, Thomas. 2000. *Nationalists, Cosmopolitans and Popular Music in Zimbabwe.* Chicago: University of Chicago Press.

Vail, Leroy, and Landeg White. 1997. "Plantation Protest: The History of a Mozambican Song." In *Readings in African Popular Culture,* edited by Karin Barber, 54–62. Bloomington: Indiana University Press and Oxford: James Currey.

Veal, Michael E. 2000. *Fela: The Life and Times of an African Musical Icon.* Philadelphia: Temple University Press.

Verdery, Katherine. 2018. *My Life as a Spy: Investigations in a Secret Police File.* Durham, NC: Duke University Press.

Wedeen, Lisa. 1999. *Ambiguities of Domination: Politics, Rhetoric, and Symbols in Contemporary Syria.* Chicago: University of Chicago Press.

Weidman, Amanda. 2006. *Singing the Classical, Voicing the Modern: The Postcolonial Politics of Music in South India.* Durham, NC: Duke University Press.

———. 2014. "Anthropology and Voice." *Annual Review of Anthropology* 43: 37–51.

White, Bob. 2008. *Rumba Rules: The Politics of Dance Music in Mobutu's Zaire.* Durham, NC: Duke University Press.

Yurchak, Alexei. 2005. *Everything Was Forever Until It Was No More: The Last Soviet Generation.* Princeton, NJ: Princeton University Press.

Index